*The Black Hills Journals
of
Colonel Richard Irving Dodge*

The American Exploration and Travel Series

Colonel Richard Irving Dodge, c. 1875 (*Newberry Library, Chicago*)

The Black Hills Journals of Colonel Richard Irving Dodge

Edited by Wayne R. Kime

University of Oklahoma Press : Norman

Other Works Written or Edited by Wayne R. Kime

Pierre M. Irving and Washington Irving: A Collaboration in Life and Letters (Waterloo, Canada, 1978)

(ed.) *Raising the Wind: The Legend of Lapland and Finland Wizards in Literature* (Newark, Del., 1981)

(ed.) *Miscellaneous Writings, 1803-1859*, by Washington Irving (Boston, 1981)

(ed.) with Andrew G. Myers) *Journals and Notebooks, Volume IV, 1826-1829*, by Washington Irving (Boston, 1984)

Donald G. Mitchell (Boston, 1985)

(ed.) *The Plains of North America and Their Inhabitants: A Critical Edition*, by Richard Irving Dodge (Newark, Del., and London, 1989)

The Black Hills Journals of Colonel Richard Irving Dodge is Volume 74 in The American Exploration and Travel Series.

This book is published with the generous assistance of A. Earl Ziegler and Frances E. Ziegler.

Library of Congress Cataloging-in-Publication Data

Dodge, Richard Irving, 1827–1895.
    The Black Hills journals of Colonel Richard Irving Dodge / edited by Wayne R. Kime.
       p. cm. — (The American exploration and travel series ; v. 74)
    ISBN 978-0-8061-5982-9 (paper)
    Includes bibliographical references and index.
    1. Black Hills (S.D. and Wyo.)—Discovery and exploration. 2. Black Hills (S.D. and Wyo.)—Description and travel. I. Kime, Wayne R. II. Title. III. Series.
F657.B6D63 1996
917.83'9042—dc20   95-41149
                                                                                   CIP

The paper in this book meets the guidelines for permanence and durability of the Committee on Production Guidelines for Book Longevity of the Council on Library Resources, Inc. ∞

Copyright © 1996 by the University of Oklahoma Press, Norman, Publishing Division of the University. All rights reserved. Paperback published 2017. Manufactured in the U.S.A.

For the late Ernest J. Moyne,
my academic mentor

Contents

List of Illustrations	ix
Preface	xi
Introduction	3
Note on Editorial Policy	27
Journal One: May 6–June 6, 1875	37
Journal Two: June 7–28, 1875	66
Journal Three: June 29–July 20, 1875	111
Journal Four: July 21–August 13, 1875	143
Journal Five: August 14–September 10, 1875	177
Journal Six: September 11–October 19, 1875	211
Bibliography	253
Index	263

Illustrations

Richard Irving Dodge, c. 1875	*Frontispiece*
Dodge's itinerary, Fort Laramie–Camp Jenney, May 25–June 8	47
Itinerary, Camp Jenney–Camp Harney, June 9–28	74
"Saw teeth" of granite, near Harney Peak	94
Granite forms near Harney Peak	125
Itinerary, Camp Harney–Camp Crook, June 29–August 13	133
Itinerary, Camp Crook–Camp Bradley, August 13–September 10	178
Itinerary, September 11–October 13	212
Itinerary, October 6–13	237
Itinerary, the Black Hills Expedition, 1875	242–43

Preface

FOR ME THIS BOOK IS A MILESTONE, MARKING three decades of engagement with the history and literature of the American West. The name Richard Irving Dodge first caught my attention in the mid-1960s, while I was at work on a doctoral dissertation in English on Washington Irving, Dodge's great-uncle. My early studies of *Astoria* (1836), Irving's masterly and still authoritative history of an effort to establish an American fur-trading empire in the far Northwest, fixed in me an affinity for nonfictional prose writings that exhibit both historical significance and literary merit. Eventually that inclination led me back to Dodge, who, though all but forgotten in this century, was among the ablest of the American soldier-authors in his time and enjoyed the respect of his contemporaries as an authority on the plains and the Indians. A few years ago I had the pleasure of preparing, under almost ideal circumstances for research, a critical edition of Dodge's finest book, *The Plains of North America and Their Inhabitants* (1876). While engaged on that project I visited the Everett D. Graff Collection of Western Americana at the Newberry Library, Chicago, and there I encountered Dodge's unpublished journals, one group of which forms the basis of the present volume.

Colonel Dodge's private record of his involvement in the Black Hills Expedition of 1875 seemed to me then a remarkable document. Almost incidentally, yet more effectively than any other primary documents I knew, the six journals captured for me the tense and confused tone of activities, official and unofficial, that had centered on the Black Hills just before the Great Sioux War of 1876. And even as they detailed the progress of an enterprise that had clear historical importance, they made lively reading. I hope that, in their edited form, Dodge's Black Hills journals may confirm in others my own initial impression and so make a useful contribution to the documentary record of a critical period in American history.

For courtesies and assistance extended to me as I prepared this book I am indebted to many persons and organizations, not all of whom are mentioned here. Financial support, sine qua non, came from Fairmont State College, the West Virginia Humanities Council, the National Endowment for the Humanities, and the Newberry Library, to all of which I express sincere thanks. For their support of my applications for research aid I am grateful to Professors Ralph M. Aderman and Richard D. Rust and to Robert G. Masters, library director, Fairmont State College. Eleanore Hofstetter, Wallace and Susannah Jungers, Kathleen Moyne, and Jude Olsen were gracious hosts during my expeditions in search of information. Robert Heffner Jr. provided expert assistance with the maps, John Piscitelli with photography, and Professor Charles H. McCormick with his counsel. I am happy to thank Dr. Lys Ann Shore for her perspicuity and perseverance as a copyeditor. I also owe thanks to Jerome A. Greene and Paul L. Hedren for their readings of the completed manuscript and especially for their suggestions of ways to improve it. Hedren's *Fort Laramie in 1876* has been a vade mecum, deftly guiding me on many occasions as I sought to run down facts and set matters straight. And from first to last, as usual, I have incurred obligations of all kinds to my wife, Dr. Alicia M. Kime.

Institutions whose facilities and personnel have assisted me in my research include the Newberry Library, Chicago; the National Archives, Washington, D.C.; U.S. Army Military History Institute, Carlisle Barracks, Pa.; U.S. Military Academy, West Point, N.Y.; Beinecke Library, Yale University, New Haven, Conn.; New York Public Library, New York City; New-York Historical Society,

New York City; Columbia University Library, New York City; Rutgers University Library, New Brunswick, N.J.; University of Pennsylvania Library, Philadelphia; University of Delaware Library, Newark; Enoch Pratt Free Library, Baltimore; History Library, Museum of New Mexico, Santa Fe; Northwestern University Library, Evanston, Ill.; West Virginia University Library, Morgantown; Vermont Historical Society, Montpelier; and Fairmont State College Library, Fairmont W.V. I am especially grateful to the interlibrary loan staff of the Fairmont State College Library for their helpful services.

For permission to quote from unpublished or copyrighted material I thank the following: Newberry Library, Chicago; Ross and Haines Old Books, Inc., Hudson, Wis.; Special Collections Division, U.S. Military Academy Library, West Point, N.Y.; Stanford University Press, Stanford, Calif.

Finally, I extend grateful thanks to Sarah Iselin, who deftly supervised the editing and production of this volume, and to her colleagues at the University of Oklahoma Press.

WAYNE R. KIME

Fairmont, West Virginia

Introduction

Introduction

A REPORT BY LIEUTENANT COLONEL GEORGE A. Custer, Seventh Cavalry, that men of his command had discovered gold in the Black Hills of Dakota Territory captured national attention during the summer of 1874. Miners engaged to accompany Custer's military reconnaissance of the region had panned gold along several mountain streams, and on August 2 he dispatched a messenger to Fort Laramie with news of the find. In his account he praised the Black Hills generally as the site of prosperous future settlements, but his main theme, as he expressed it in a second report a few days later, was gold "among the roots of the grass."[1] Custer's dispatches soon resulted in an influx of miners, suppliers, and speculators at frontier towns like Sioux City and Cheyenne that offered access to what might prove a northern El Dorado. Newspaper stories fanned the enthusiasm, and by the end of the year groups of men willing to brave the harsh winter conditions had already reached the diggings.

The presence of U.S. citizens in the Black Hills was an embarrassment to the federal government, for the greater part of the region lay within a territory which, by the Fort Laramie Treaty of 1868, was reserved for permanent occupation by the Sioux

---

1. Custer's dispatches of August 2 and 15, 1874, are included in his report to the U.S. Senate, *Report of the Expedition to the Black Hills*, pp. 1–9; the quotation is from p. 8. A general account of the 1874 expedition in the Black Hills is given by Jackson, *Custer's Gold*; the published reports of correspondents who accompanied Custer have been gathered and reprinted by Krause and Olson in *Prelude to Glory*. See also Parker, *Gold in the Black Hills*.

Indians alone. The miners were trespassing on Sioux lands, and to honor its treaty obligation the government had to expel them. Thus the army, which for years had served in a police capacity to help control the Indians, was now called upon to operate against delinquent American citizens. On December 26, 1874, a detachment of the Third Cavalry under Captain Guy V. Henry marched north into the Black Hills from Camp Robinson, adjacent to Red Cloud Agency, in search of miners. Two weeks later the soldiers returned, having suffered terribly from the wind and cold but without finding even one of the interlopers.[2]

A second command, sent from Fort Laramie in late March 1875 under Captain John Mix, Second Cavalry, was more successful. Entering the Black Hills from the west, along French Creek the force came upon the settlement and defensive stockade of a group of twenty-eight persons, who became known as the Gordon party. Remaining a few days to enable these enterprising persons to gather their effects, Mix then escorted them back to the fort, where they were released.[3] Despite the official efforts at deterrence, defiant miners vowed that they would return to the Black Hills as often as they should be expelled. But the federal government made known its own resolve. In March the secretary of war confirmed to General William T. Sherman, in command of the army, that as long as the treaty of 1868 remained in force all new expeditions must be turned back. Efforts to extinguish the Indian title had begun, but should these fail such unauthorized citizens as were already present within the Black Hills would have to be removed.[4]

---

2. For Henry's report of this almost disastrous errand, see *Army and Navy Journal* (hereafter cited as *ANJ*), January 30, 1875, p. 387. Years later, in 1895, Henry published a popular account of the mission, "A Winter March to the Black Hills."

3. Mix to Post Adjutant, Fort Laramie, in Military Division of the Missouri Papers, U.S. Army Military History Institute (hereafter cited as USAMHI), pp. 244–51. Mix's report was published in *ANJ*, May 8, 1875, p. 613; see also Parker, "The Report of Captain John Mix of a Scout to the Black Hills, March–April 1875."

4. Secretary of War to Secretary of the Interior, Washington, D.C., March 10, 1875, Letters Sent, 2465/WD 1875.

Meanwhile, an acrimonious debate grew up over the accuracy of Custer's dispatches. Reverend Samuel D. Hinman, a missionary to the Sioux and an advocate of their cause, passed through the Black Hills within three weeks after Custer and reported finding no gold whatever. The testimony of Hinman was ascribed by some to a wish to protect the Indians from victimization by opportunistic contractors, prospectors, and others.[5] But disagreement also arose from within Custer's own party. Newton H. Winchell, the official geologist to the army reconnaissance, reported before the Minnesota Academy of Sciences that he had seen no evidence of gold in the Black Hills and indeed rather doubted its existence there. Widely reported, this professional opinion aroused suspicion that Custer might for some reason have lied, or perhaps "salted" the diggings. In December Custer spoke out in a spirited public letter, declaring that if Professor Winchell failed to see gold the reason was simply "that he neglected to look for it."[6] For his part, Custer suggested collusion between Winchell and the Office of Indian Affairs. Nefarious motives continued to be ascribed to those on both sides of the gold question, while on the Sioux reservation the anger of the Indians festered. Already aggrieved by what they considered systematic mistreatment at their agencies, they now suspected that American citizens might be permitted to appropriate the lands set aside for their exclusive use. Even though the Custer expedition of 1874 did not clearly contravene the terms of the Fort Laramie treaty, the Indians viewed it as a hostile intrusion. One of their leaders spoke of the trail left by the army as "that thieves' road."[7]

5. The activities of this controversial figure (1839–90) have been detailed by Anderson, "Samuel D. Hinman and the Opening of the Black Hills"; and by Parker, "Report of the Reverend Samuel D. Hinman of an Expedition to the Black Hills during August, 1874."

6. Custer's letter to the editor of the *New York World*, dated December 13, 1874, was reprinted in *ANJ*, January 9, 1875, pp. 341–42; the quotation is from p. 341.

7. "Report of the Commission Appointed to Treat with the Sioux Indians for the Relinquishment of the Black Hills," in *Report of the Secretary of the Interior* (1875), p. 691. The speaker was Fast (or Quick) Bear, of Red Cloud Agency.

Against this background of conflicting interests, disputed facts, and mutual suspicion, early in 1875 the federal government authorized a scientific study of the Black Hills, especially with regard to their reputed mineral wealth. The results of the examination would provide a useful basis, it was thought, for evaluating the potential of the region and its fair value in trade to the Indians. Organized under the auspices of the Office of Indian Affairs, the Black Hills surveying party was placed under the direction of Professor Walter P. Jenney of the Columbia School of Mines, New York.[8] When complete, the scientific mission included seventeen persons: geologist-in-charge, assistant geologist, topographer, astronomer, naturalist, photographer, head miner, and ten laborers. Although the Office of Indian Affairs and the Department of War were often bitterly at odds during this period, in the present instance they managed to cooperate. The army was to provide a sizable escort that would ensure the scientists' ability to complete their mission in security and without haste. Accordingly, shortly after he had assumed command of the Department of the Platte, on May 1, 1875, Brigadier General George Crook ordered six companies of cavalry and two of infantry, with a proportionate complement of supply wagons and pack animals under civilian care, to convene at Fort Laramie.[9] The expedition would march north from that point as soon as arrangements were complete and the advancing season ensured an adequate supply of forage.

For a time a rumor circulated that Lieutenant Colonel Custer would command the military escort. However, in the event another

---

8. A protégé of the geologist J. S. Newberry, who nominated him for the position, Jenney (1849–1921) had only a limited amount of field experience. He had spent fourteen months in western Texas and New Mexico, participating in explorations and surveys for the projected Texas and Southwest Railroad. Later in his career Jenney served with the U.S. Geological Survey, in charge of the Division of Zinc.

9. Crook assumed command of the military Department of the Platte on April 27, 1875, replacing Brigadier General E.O.C. Ord, who had served in the position since 1871 and was being transferred to the Department of Texas.

officer was detailed, one less likely to further antagonize the Sioux and also more recognizably impartial on the question of gold. This was Lieutenant Colonel Richard I. Dodge, Twenty-third Infantry, who was then on garrison duty at his regimental headquarters, Omaha Barracks, Nebraska.[10] A seasoned soldier with a reputation for discreet good judgment, administrative competence, and ability in conducting military forces through difficult territory, Dodge was a solid choice.[11] The Black Hills expedition would be the most visible and politically sensitive assignment he had received in twenty-seven years of army service. Perhaps anticipating that the summer ahead would be one worthy of his remembrance, on May 6 he began compiling a record of his daily activities and observations. By his return to Omaha Barracks on October 19 he had filled six notebooks with this private account, which forms the basis of the present volume.[12]

Accompanied by his sixteen-year-old son Fred, who was to be an unofficial member of the expedition, Dodge journeyed on the Union Pacific Railroad to Cheyenne, Wyoming Territory, where

---

10. S.O. (Special Order) 59, D.P. (Department of the Platte), dated May 1, directed Dodge to "proceed at once to Fort Laramie and report, in person, to the commander District of the Black Hills." The military district of the Black Hills was under the administration of Lieutenant Colonel Luther P. Bradley, Ninth Infantry, the commanding officer at Fort Laramie.

11. A West Point graduate (1848), Dodge (1827–95) had passed almost his entire career, except the Civil War years, as an infantry officer in the western states and territories. Since the war he had commanded at forts in Arizona, Colorado, Kansas, and Wyoming. Upon the reorganization of the army in 1869 he was transferred from the Thirtieth to the Third Regiment of Infantry, and on October 23, 1873, he was promoted to the lieutenant colonelcy of the Twenty-third Infantry.

12. The manuscript journals describing the Black Hills Expedition are among the Dodge papers in the Everett D. Graff Collection of Western Americana, Newberry Library, Chicago. All six are copies of "The Office Scratch Book" produced by H. M. Hinsdill, Wholesale Stationer, Grand Rapids, Mich. Sturdy and versatile, these inexpensive notebooks consisted of a stiff cardboard pad at bottom, folded upward and forward at its top edge and pressed so as to clasp tightly the sheets for writing. The top fold formed a lip that left a writing space on each page of 3 3/16 by 4 5/8 inches or larger, the pads being offered in various sizes. The notebook was designed to permit easy ripping away of its individual sheets, which were of cheap unlined paper.

a swirl of activity now centered on the Black Hills. The town bustled with outfitters and would-be miners, and sentiment was strong there in favor of the government's annexing the Black Hills by whatever means might be necessary. On the ninety-four-mile stage ride to Fort Laramie, he met a delegation of Indians from Red Cloud and Spotted Tail Agencies, bound for Washington, D.C. They intended to continue discussing with federal officials the future of their treaty land, along with other matters, but they were bitterly resentful. Through their interpreters they assured Dodge that his new incursion into the sacred places of the Sioux would meet with resistance. Meanwhile, the Jenney-Dodge expedition was making front-page news. When the command set out from Fort Laramie, on May 25, 1875, no fewer than five persons with it were correspondents for major newspapers.[13] Of course, their readers were interested less in abstruse geological researches than in the latest developments in the search for gold.

As weeks passed and the surveying, mapping, and prospecting parties settled into their work, issues and personages not directly connected with the Black Hills expedition often claimed the attention of Dodge. Despite the recent precedent of citizen miners being expelled by the army, he did not intend to attempt performing a similar function. Should he arrest these persons, he lacked sufficient personnel and facilities to maintain and transport them while at the same time carrying out his orders. He knew that miners were in the vicinity—in fact, taking advantage of the security afforded by proximity to his command, they had followed him at a wary distance—but for the sake of appearances he preferred to have no contact with them. Practical considerations aside, he sympathized with their effort to seek wealth in this

---

13. These were Second Lieutenant John G. Bourke, Third Cavalry, for the *San Francisco Alta California* and *Cincinnati Gazette*; Captain Andrew S. Burt, Ninth Infantry, for the *New York Tribune*; Reuben B. Davenport for the *New York Herald*; Acting Assistant Surgeon J. R. Lane for the *Chicago Tribune*; and Thomas C. MacMillan for the *Chicago Inter-Ocean*.

magnificent land which, so far as he could tell, the Indians almost never entered and had no real use for.

On June 14, chancing to encounter a group of miners hard at work, Dodge let them know his disposition not to interfere. He maintained this policy until the arrival on July 28 of General Crook, who had himself received new orders to expel unauthorized persons. In an unpublished autobiography Crook recalled that the "sovereign citizens" he talked with on his visit to the Black Hills were at first incredulous that anyone in "'these here United States,'" even a general, would interfere with their right to go where they pleased and do what they chose.[14] However, explaining that he had come merely to perform an unpleasant duty, Crook advised them to depart the Black Hills peaceably for the time being. He and Dodge drafted together a formal proclamation ordering them to leave the country but also inviting them to convene a meeting not later than August 10, before their departure. At that meeting, he suggested, they could adopt measures to secure rights to their several claims, subject to the eventual opening up of the territory. Crook's firm but considerate treatment won the gratitude of the miners and helped him avoid a resort to force. He left camp on August 1, designating Dodge to

---

14. George Crook Papers, USAMHI. The coverage in another narrative by Crook, edited by Martin Schmitt and published as *General George Crook: His Autobiography*, breaks off before this date. In his annual report, dated September 15, 1875, Crook further described the circumstances surrounding his talk with the miners. In recent months approximately four hundred horses had been stolen from settlers along the Union Pacific Railroad, and although all the stock had been traced to the Sioux reservation, it had not been recovered. This state of affairs was "well known," Crook wrote, "not only to the parties who lost [the horses] but to people generally throughout the country." When he pointed out to the Black Hills miners that they were violating a treaty, they responded that "the Indians themselves violated the treaty hundreds of times every summer by predatory incursions, whereby settlers were utterly ruined . . . and this by Indians who are fed, clothed, and maintained in utter idleness by the government they, themselves, help to support." Crook urged that the miners' side of the story be heard, predicting that unless an arrangement were made speedily by which the Indians would cede the mining region, "serious trouble will ensue" (*Report of the Secretary of War* [1875], pp. 69–70).

represent the army at the miners' meeting. Among other business transacted on that occasion, resolutions of gratitude to both officers were passed, followed in each instance by three rousing cheers.[15] The miners then departed, or most did. To deal with any who remained, a temporary post, Camp Collins, was established near the meeting place under command of Captain Edwin Pollock, Ninth Infantry. Recognizing that the blustering and officious Pollock utterly lacked ability to control the miners without antagonizing them, Crook had directed that he remain subject to the authority of Dodge for as long as the latter should remain in the vicinity.

Thanks perhaps to the elaborate security procedures adopted by the Black Hills command, it was never attacked or beset in any way by Indian marauders. Dodge once remarked that he feared attempts at theft by renegade whites more than by Indians.[16] But the military escort did encounter groups of Sioux and others who were involved in the effort to renegotiate the legal status of the Black Hills. The discussions at Washington, D.C., in May and June had been unsuccessful, but officials still hoped to effect an arrangement whereby, in return for cash payment and other considerations, the Sioux would cede the Black Hills or at least consent to the presence of American citizens on their lands. Preparations were afoot for a grand council between a government commission, under Senator William B. Allison of Ohio, and representatives of all the affected bands. Deputations of Indians, commissioners, and other interested persons journeyed to and through the Black Hills, either to witness the activity there or else to seek out various groups of Sioux so as to ensure their attendance. On one occasion before the arrival of General Crook, Dodge was called upon to hold council with a group of Indian representatives. At this meeting a chief named Red Dog, of Spotted

---

15. According to the *Chicago Tribune* of August 21, 1875, p. 2, Dodge was given "three hearty cheers" and Crook "three cheers and a tiger."
16. Journal, June 30, 1875.

Tail Agency, demanded that he justify the friendly relations that obviously prevailed between his soldiers and the miners. Why did he not arrest those men? Dodge explained the specific, limited reason for the presence of his command in the Black Hills. The miners, he informed the disgusted Red Dog, were not his responsibility; they were "a matter for the chiefs above me" to deal with.[17]

The supply trains that passed back and forth between Dodge's party and Fort Laramie brought with them a selection of sometimes weeks-old newspapers, and by this means it was possible to estimate the impact of news from the Black Hills on popular sentiment. On June 11 and 17, respectively, Jenney and Dodge had written official dispatches reporting the rediscovery of gold. Jenney expressed doubt of its presence in quantities sufficient "to warrant extended explorations in mining," but Dodge was more sanguine. Gold had been found "in paying quantities," he wrote, and the original dispatch from Custer was "confirmed in every particular."[18] Upon taking up newspapers that reported these developments, Dodge saw with dismay how quick they were to impugn the character and competence of those—including himself—whose statements failed to confirm their editorial biases. For example, the *Chicago Tribune* attacked the more encouraging accounts of gold as exaggerated if not fraudulent—certain to disappoint credulous citizens and likely even to precipitate war. On the other hand, its rival the *Chicago Inter-Ocean* dismissed less favorable dispatches as attempts to conceal the true wealth of the Black Hills, discourage further investigation, and preserve the cozy status quo. For newspapers like these, the latest accounts from the mining region were occasions for continued debate over federal policy in regard to territorial expansion and the admin-

17. Journal, July 22, 1875.
18. The text of Jenney's telegram to Edward P. Smith, the commissioner of Indian affairs, was printed in the *New York Tribune*, June 24, 1875, p. 2. Dodge's dispatch appeared in the *Chicago Inter-Ocean*, June 23, 1875, p. 1; *New York Tribune*, June 23, 1875, p. 1.

istration of Indian affairs. The newspapers seemed no more willing to modify their positions than either the Sioux or the miners were disposed to vacate the Black Hills. In all, the information that reached Dodge offered little hope of an early or amicable resolution to the conflicts of interest and opinion that centered on the region.

Notwithstanding occasional distractions, during the greater part of the summer Dodge was able to focus his attention on guiding the cooperative effort of the geological surveying party and its outsized escort. The logistical challenges that confronted him as he began the march in May were substantial. Considering the relative proximity of the Black Hills to Fort Laramie, that tract of country, with an area approximately equal to that of Connecticut, was then remarkably little known. Dodge carried with him maps that incorporated observations made on prior military expeditions, but these had tended to skirt the Black Hills, leaving unrecorded the topography of the interior sections. The map prepared by the engineer officer on the Custer expedition, Captain William Ludlow, was the most potentially useful one he had,[19] though Custer had entered the area from the east and north rather than from the south and west as Dodge did.

A professional guide, Joe Merivale, was attached to the command. Merivale was a longtime resident of the Fort Laramie vicinity and had served the army on several previous occasions. Despite his known aversion to danger and undue effort, he was said to be the equal of anyone in his knowledge of the Black Hills and the routes thereto. But after a few days on the march Dodge concluded that Joe was virtually worthless as a guide.[20]

---

19. The map had accompanied Ludlow's thorough report on the expedition, which was forwarded to the Military Division of the Missouri on May 10, 1875. The Ludlow account was incorporated in the *Report of the Secretary of War* (1875), Appendix PP, pp. 1113–1230; it was also published independently in 1875 as *Report of a Reconnaissance of the Black Hills of Dakota*.

20. Merivale's moment of truth as a guide is recounted through Dr. Valentine T. McGillycuddy, the topographer on Jenney's staff. According to this source, Shortly after crossing the Cheyenne River, the old plainsman assured Dodge

INTRODUCTION   13

Thereafter he kept the genial old campaigner on the payroll but used him only as a messenger and interpreter in case Indians should be met with. The problem of seeking out a route across a tract of increasingly rugged terrain became in effect his own. Old-timers had agreed that the country ahead was, as he put it, "exceedingly difficult if not impassible [*sic*] for wagons," and the military force carried with it a cumbrous assortment of impedimenta. A supply train of 71 wagons, a herd of 134 beeves, a contingent of 452 men and 376 horses, with a proportionate number of civilian employees—not to mention the scientists with their gear—were to be moved together over yawning divides, across treacherous streams carrying unhealthy alkaline water, through thickets, up steep banks, and by some means over a more than 2000-foot rise in elevation into the central hills.[21] On June 3, 9 days and 138 miles out from the fort, the command went into its first permanent camp, Camp Jenney. It remained there until the morning of June 9 while, among other employments, parties searched without success for a practicable wagon route ahead. Late the next day, having left supplies behind and marched due north, Dodge and the three companies with him crossed a high divide and descended into a pleasant upland valley. Presently they recognized their location as the head of what Custer had named "Floral Valley," and that night they camped at a position that they identified from the Ludlow map as Custer's

---

that, once having passed through a long gulch directly ahead, the command would reach an easy slope that led to the foothills of the Black Hills. Many miles later, at the end of the slope, they stood together at the foot of a 500-foot precipice that blocked their further progress. For a moment Merivale looked up at this obstruction in silence. Then he burst out, "Jese Christ, how this damn country he change since I was here last!" (McGillycuddy, *McGillycuddy, Agent*, p. 32).

21. Dodge to Assistant Adjutant General, Department of the Platte, Omaha Barracks, December 22, 1875, Record Group 393, Letters Received, D.P. (1955/D.P. 1875), National Archives. The text of this document, Dodge's official report, forms part of Turchen and McLaird, *The Black Hills Expedition of 1875*, pp. 30–93; the quotation and statistics are on p. 31.

campsite of July 25 the year before. A wagon route into the hills had been found, and the most critical pioneering effort was now behind them.

As his command pushed ahead, Dodge kept in mind the need to ensure timely access to supplies at Fort Laramie. At the outset he had prevailed upon General Crook to authorize ten extra wagons, which, he argued, would lessen the strain on pack animals during the first leg of the journey and would enable him, if necessary, to carry provisions on a long march. On June 5 he dispatched a wagon train, with an infantry escort, from Camp Jenney to the fort for resupply. Leaving camp four days later to search out a wagon trail, he ordered three companies to remain there on guard. Once he had penetrated the Black Hills and located a suitable area of activity for the scientists, he planned to send back for the returning supply train and the men and materiel still at Camp Jenney. This scheme was a makeshift, but with a few minor adjustments it succeeded admirably. On June 23 the supply wagons made their welcome appearance at the second permanent camp, Camp Harney, concluding the first of several long errands to and from Fort Laramie. Simplified variations of the same arrangement—parties temporarily dispersing under orders to rendezvous at some predetermined point and time—became standard procedure. The scientists, or "bug-stuffers," divided themselves into two subgroups, one for mapping and exploration, the other for geology and practical mining, each with a small detachment of cavalry as escort. The army forces broke into their own units assigned to mapmaking, roadmaking, guard duty, resupply, messenger duty, and other functions. On occasion a party would fail to appear at camp as appointed, and a search would be instituted, but the lost ones were invariably found, usually having suffered nothing worse than a day without food and a night without shelter. Considering the manifold possibilities for accident and miscalculation, operations went forward with notable efficiency. In a letter of July 2 to General Crook, Dodge actually characterized the expedition as "a delightful pic nic

INTRODUCTION   15

(without the ladies)."²² In this sally of wit he ignored the difficulties, uncertainties, and dangers his command had faced thus far, but in view of the steady progress and many satisfactions of the undertaking his metaphor was apt enough. Members of the expedition agreed that the country they were passing through was as beautiful as almost any other they had seen.

So far as possible Dodge was expected to shape his course to accommodate the needs and wishes of the geologist-in-charge, Walter P. Jenney. In fact, adapting to the whims and eccentricities of Jenney was the sternest trial he faced. Another officer described the chief of the scientific party as "a very inexperienced young man, who has not apparently succeeded in making a striking impression on any who have been thrown in contact with him."²³ Other persons, especially the correspondents, were harsher in their judgments.²⁴ Jenney undermined the effort to make plans because he refused to divulge his own intentions. He made cooperation difficult because he sought to pursue his researches in secret, away from soldiers or other persons whom he thought might be spies.²⁵ While at work in the field he repeatedly got

---

22. See Journal Three.
23. John G. Bourke Diary, June 3, 1875, U.S. Military Academy, West Point, N.Y. (hereafter cited as USMA).
24. Examples: "The Chief [of the scientific corps] is Prof. Walter P. Jenny [*sic*], geologist and mining engineer (but Professor of what I am not able to say).... What he knows of mining remains to be seen" (*Chicago Tribune*, June 19, 1875, p. 9); "Like all great minds, Mr. Jenney glibly lays bare his intentions, conclusions, and the contents of the text books which he committed to memory as an undergraduate on the slightest provocation" (*New York Herald*, July 8, 1875, p. 4). As the summer continued, Jenney received even rougher treatment, especially from Reuben B. Davenport of the *Herald*.
25. On May 2 Jenney wrote from Cheyenne to the commissioner of Indian affairs that Reuben B. Davenport was in town with a letter from Lieutenant General Philip H. Sheridan, commander of the Military Division of the Missouri, to "the Commander of my Escort." This letter, he said, left it to the discretion of that commander whether Davenport would be permitted to accompany the expedition. Jenney was not pleased, and he expressed his intention "to hold no communication with newspapers, correspondents or other unauthorized persons, or permit any of the party to do so" unless the commissioner so directed (Turchen and McLaird, *The Black Hills Expedition of 1875*, p. 11). A

his party into difficulty and had to be rescued from the consequences of his ineptitude and want of foresight. Whatever his good intentions—and much of his odd behavior may be ascribed to an anxious wish to perform his official duties well—Jenney soon alienated the other members of the scientific party.

Working with, or around, this callow representative of the Office of Indian Affairs demanded all Dodge's diplomatic skill. He took an active interest in the work of the scientists, most of whom were able professionals, and he was glad to assist them however he could; but he found that to do so he must sometimes refuse to comply with the wishes of Jenney. And since that meant incurring the risk of official repercussions, he preempted the authority of the geologist-in-charge as seldom and as quietly as he could. When possible he let him have his way and guided him, if asked, with informal advice. Early in the expedition it became clear that Jenney would prefer to direct the entire operation. For example, even though his instructions included no reference to the line of 104° longitude which separated Indian treaty land from Wyoming Territory to the west, for some reason he determined to follow this line as he entered the Black Hills. His subordinates lacked the instruments and manpower even confidently to locate the as yet unsurveyed line, and thus the entire party watched bemused as he sought to carry out his plan. When this quixotic aim began to interfere seriously with the stated purpose of the expedition, Dodge stepped in. Moving the unwieldy command over forbidding terrain was sufficient trouble without the complication of marches and countermarches in search of some

---

few days later Jenney wrote again, objecting to a "*mining speculator*," William Ashton, who was to accompany the party as employee of an unspecified newspaper reporter (ibid., p. 13). Ashton appears to have been kept from joining the expedition. A dispatch from Washington, D.C., published in the *Chicago Tribune* for June 11, 1875, reported (p. 4) that Jenney had been instructed to send away from the party all persons not duly authorized by the Department of the Interior or himself. See also Secretary of War to Secretary of the Interior, Washington, D.C., June 8, 1875 (4875/WD 1875), in Letters Sent.

particular line of longitude. Always the gentleman except when strongly provoked, Dodge laid the problem before Jenney, explaining why they must choose between searching for the Wyoming boundary and taking up the work they had been assigned. Fortunately the younger man acceded to his point of view, and the march resumed with new efficiency.

Weeks later, Jenney again caused confusion—and this time needless suffering as well—by his failure to provide adequate supplies and rations for the men under his direct supervision. Previously Dodge had watched misadventures of this sort without comment, but he was now moved to effect a quiet coup d'état, summarily assuming control of the pack trains that served the scientists. And near the end of the expedition, faced with Jenney's determination to explore the "bone fields" near Red Cloud Agency in quest of new fossil discoveries, Dodge reluctantly decided once more to risk tainting the atmosphere of cooperation that had been preserved thus far. Shortage of provisions necessitated that he separate from Jenney, leaving him and a small detachment of escort troops to look after themselves while the main force moved ahead toward Fort Laramie. This move was a gamble, but it proved a wise one. Four days later Jenney rejoined the command, and the military and scientific parties arrived at the fort together.

During the summer Dodge became known among the younger officers as "Richard the First," a playful sobriquet derived from his first name and middle initial and perhaps also from his authoritative bearing.[26] Yet if at times he did play the tyrant—as when he summarily ordered Captain Andrew S. Burt, Ninth Infantry, to cease and desist from his disruptive mining operations—he was liberal in praise of those who performed their duties well. He enjoyed the respect of his subordinates, and sessions of sociable "gassing" around his campfire occurred often. His deft handling of Professor Jenney confirmed the estimate of him by one junior

26. McGillycuddy, *McGillycuddy, Agent*, p. 34.

officer as a man "of great natural sagacity in matters military and otherwise."[27] Even so, Jenney remained for him something of a riddle. The young scientist always wanted his own way, yet on those occasions when Dodge overruled him, he acquiesced and seemed positively grateful for the intervention. At such times this troublesome colleague seemed ingenuous and immensely likeable. Speculations about the character and motives of Jenney are a recurrent feature in Dodge's 1875 journals.

The Black Hills command moved through the region for study in stages, its headquarters ordinarily remaining at one location for several days while parties worked in that vicinity. During the stationary interludes Dodge pursued interests of his own. He was an avid sportsman, rather vain of his skill as a fisherman and hunter, and he delighted to spend a day away from camp in search of game, accompanied by an orderly and a fellow officer or two. During the visit of General Crook he organized a two-day hunt on Box Elder Creek that yielded excellent results for the general and his several civilian guests. A snarl of duties in camp kept him from fully enjoying that excursion, but in the weeks that followed he made up splendidly for the missed opportunity. While the command passed through the geologically less interesting north and northwest sections of the Black Hills he had good luck in pursuit of elk, black-tailed deer, red (or white-tailed) deer, and other species. On some days, accompanied by his son Fred and a small additional party, he would explore the surrounding country on horseback or attempt to scale prominent peaks. The names of Dodge's and Fred's Peaks in the central Black Hills bear continuing witness to these ascents.

In mid-June Dodge resumed work on a private project that had engaged his intense interest in recent months. He was writing an as yet untitled book that would explore three general topics related to the great American plains: the Indians, especially their beliefs and customs; the plains environment and the best ways

---

27. Bourke Diary, May 16, 1875, USMA.

of adapting to its rigors; and the indigenous game animals. Although he had no experience as a professional author, he was a lifelong reader, was not without strongly held opinions, and enjoyed expressing himself.[28] He possessed a plentiful supply of frontier tales and plains lore, and for some time past his friend, the English land speculator William Blackmore, had urged upon him the idea of gathering some of this colorful material into a book. Blackmore was insistent, and being himself a published author he had volunteered to edit the work and even help arrange for its publication. After some hesitation Dodge came to believe that the public might indeed welcome the variety of firsthand information he had to offer. In the winter of 1874–75 he began work in earnest, and the manuscript rapidly took shape. By May 1 two sections, on the Indians and the plains, were virtually complete in draft form.[29]

After a few false starts Dodge resumed progress on his book on June 25, and the Black Hills journals trace his steady progress thereafter as he wrote out the chapters dealing with game animals. Each of these was devoted to the behavior, habitat, and best methods for bagging a particular species or a group of related species. Thus he completed a lengthy discussion of the buffalo on July 3, of wild cattle on July 8, of elk on July 13, and so on.

---

28. Dodge's powers as a conversationalist are emphasized in a vivid verbal portrait of him in the *Chicago Tribune*, August 21, 1875, p. 2: "The commanding officer of the Black Hills expedition, Col. R. I. Dodge, was born in North Carolina, of a good old stock, that bequeathed to him a powerful physique, a large brain, and an active mind. Standing full six feet in his stockings, his powerful frame surmounted by a fine Grecian profile, graced by a pair of intensely human blue eyes, and bearded like a pard, with the heavy growth slightly streaked with gray, he is a fine type of the rapidly-passing-away Southern gentleman and soldier. He is a close student, a keen observer, and a fine conversationalist, and of course loves to talk; but, when a man can talk well, he is pardonable in any little display of vanity. Col. Dodge's greatest weakness is map-making and shooting, and he excels in these two accomplishments to a wonderful degree."

29. For a fuller account of the genesis of this book, see the introduction by Wayne R. Kime to Dodge's *Plains of North America and Their Inhabitants* (hereafter cited as *PNA*), pp. 16–18, 382–85.

His exploits of hunting and fishing in the Black Hills evidently stimulated his creative powers, for anecdotes of this summer's experience found their way into the swelling manuscript.[30] By the end of September the section on game, 340 manuscript pages in length, was all but complete. In the coming months he planned to revise the entire work and then, with the assistance of Blackmore, to negotiate for its publication both in England and in the United States. In his journal entry for October 14 he remarked with satisfaction that his army colleagues would likely be "surprised" when they saw the final product.

In the published book, *The Plains of North America and Their Inhabitants*, Dodge drew upon his Black Hills journals at only one point.[31] But these rich compilations served him more extensively as he prepared his official report of the expedition and drafted a second book, a slim volume issued in April 1876. The latter work was entitled *The Black Hills. A Minute Description of the Routes, Scenery, Soil, Climate, Timber, Gold, Geology, Zoölogy, etc. With an Accurate Map, Four Sectional Drawings, and Ten Plates from Photographs, Taken on the Spot* (New York: James Miller). In his preface Dodge described the book as "asserting no claim to literary merit"; he emphasized instead that it was a "reliable and authentic statement," written without bias and in "strict and impartial accordance with facts."[32] The work was a potboiler, though the parallels between what he had written in the 1875 journals and what he selected for this popular account

---

30. See *PNA*, pp. 171–72, 180, 187.
31. Compare the fanciful description of the badlands in Journal Six, entry for October 4, 1875 ("Imagine... sees it."), with the corresponding passage in *PNA*, p. 65. Although *The Plains of North America and Their Inhabitants* was the author's final choice of title for his book, owing to the editorial intervention of William Blackmore the work was issued in England as *The Hunting Grounds of the Great West* (London: Chatto and Windus, 1876). To signify that the American edition was in fact the same work, it was given a compromise title, *The Plains of the Great West and Their Inhabitants* (New York: G. P. Putnam's Sons, 1877).
32. *The Black Hills*, p. [3]. A facsimile edition of this work was issued in 1965 (Minneapolis: Ross and Haines).

do reveal that he intended faithfully to convey the facts as he knew them.

Dodge used only a small fraction of the Black Hills journals in his later official communications and published works. His motives in writing the daily entries had been more varied than simply to accumulate data for future reference and reshaping. At some points—as when he set down alternative solutions to problems he faced, in order to weigh their respective merits—the journals served him as means for thinking matters through. Elsewhere, as in his detailed and sometimes pungent estimates of his colleagues, he seems to have expressed himself for the mere satisfaction of doing so, as a kind of private conversation. The journals were the privileged repository of his own views, and there is little likelihood that he intended them to be read by anyone else. His distaste for the Office of Indian Affairs and suspicion of anyone connected with it; his pride in army service, especially the infantry; his hopeful attention as he watched young Fred grow accustomed to camp life and seem to develop a taste for the outdoors; his distress at the crippling injury suffered by his able quartermaster, Lieutenant John F. Trout, Twenty-third Infantry; his impatience with Jenney; his eager anticipation of letters, especially from his wife; his respect for Custer as a pathfinder; his troubles with dysentery; his curiosity about new species of birds: these diverse topics indicate the predominantly private character of Dodge's Black Hills journals. In their variety, discursiveness, and detail they convey clearly the pleasure he took in writing them.

The journals of Lieutenant Colonel Dodge are easily the fullest and most evocative account of the Black Hills expedition we have, but they include no reference to one participant who has since become legendary. This was Jane Dalton, alias Jane or Martha Canary, better known as Calamity Jane, who rode with a cavalry company during the first few days' march, disguised as an army private. The presence of "Calam" was known to many but was not officially acknowledged until, sixty miles out from Fort

Laramie, she was discovered and reported to the commanding officer by an irate sergeant. According to an observer, Dodge "tried to look impressive" as he complied with regulations and ordered the unauthorized woman from camp, but "a smile hovered about his lips" as he did so.[33] Having pronounced sentence, he let the matter rest. The next morning Calamity Jane surreptitiously hitched a ride with the wagon train and continued on the journey. For the rest of the summer she was permitted to remain, helping about camp and proving a valuable member of the party. According to a newspaper correspondent, she enjoyed a reputation as "a better horseback rider, mule and bull whacker (driver) and a more unctious [sic] coiner of English, and not the Queen's-pure, either, than any (other) man in the command."[34]

Of several colorful characters who formed part of the Black Hills party, perhaps the next best remembered was "California Joe."[35] This eccentric veteran mountain man and backwoods philosopher favored the newspapermen with a steady stream of stories and droll observations, and he is mentioned often by Dodge. Joe had wished to see the gold diggings in the Black Hills—one of the few territories, he said, that he had not yet explored—and was hired at Fort Laramie as a packer. However, while yet at the fort he got riotously drunk and was dismissed. Dodge was familiar with Custer's *My Life on the Plains* (1874) and knew of the generous praise given California Joe in that work,[36] but at this point he judged the famous scout a "worthless vagabond." Contrite, and determined to see the Black Hills in any event, Joe followed the command at a few miles' distance, keeping in contact with the rear guard and gradually insinuating

---

33. McGillycuddy, *McGillycuddy, Agent*, p. 34.
34. *Chicago Inter-Ocean*, July 3, 1875, p. 9. See also the *Chicago Tribune*, June 19, 1875, p. 8; and Young, *Hard Knocks*, pp. 169–72.
35. The fullest account of this legendary figure is Milner, *California Joe*; Joe's activities on the Black Hills Expedition are described on pp. 222–35. See also Collins, *My Experiences in the West*, pp. 131–37.
36. See Custer, *My Life on the Plains* (1874), pp. 134–35 and passim.

himself. And once Joe Merivale had been discredited as a guide, California Joe began to seem of potential use. Even though he was ignorant of the Black Hills, his educated instinct for the lay of the land revealed him so valuable a resource that at last, on July 27, Dodge rehired him, now as a guide. Harry Young, who drove the headquarters wagon and was privy to some of the commander's private conversations, claimed to have overheard an interchange late in the expedition between Dodge and California Joe. "Joe," declared the commander at the beginning of a day's march into new country, "I would follow you through the wilds of Africa." With a shrug the scout allowed in reply, "Well, I could take you and the outfit through there."[37]

The Black Hills command returned to Fort Laramie on October 13, having been absent almost five months. During the summer the headquarters wagon had passed over 795 miles, the military had opened up more than 1,500 miles of wagon road, and the scientists and surveying parties had established more than 6,000 miles of horse trail.[38] As a result of this exhaustive study, the information was at hand to produce a map that Dodge believed would rival any other that purported to describe so rugged and extensive a country.[39] The steady, deliberate manner in which the geological survey party had performed its duties contrasted strikingly with the hectic pace and poor coordination of related events elsewhere. The public's hunger for a definitive statement about whether gold existed in the Black Hills had been satisfied in June and July by the telegraph dispatches of Jenney and Dodge and the reports of newspaper correspondents. Once the presence of gold was confirmed, attention shifted to new topics. After

37. Young, *Hard Knocks*, pp. 167–68.
38. Turchen and McLaird, *The Black Hills Expedition of 1875*, p. 92.
39. The completed map, showing the routes traveled by the main party, was published as a foldout in the endpapers of *The Black Hills*. A military map that incorporates the information provided by Dodge, showing his itinerary, is Sheet No. 3, Western Territories Map, by Major G. L. Gillespie, U. S. Army Corps of Engineers (1876).

mid-July the correspondents who accompanied Dodge filed stories less often, and one by one they either left the expedition or, if they were members of the army contingent, simply stopped writing.

The grand council that convened near Red Cloud Agency on September 20, 1875, to discuss the possible cession of the Black Hills was a failure, for the Sioux were unwilling to negotiate.[40] Given this impasse, the forthcoming published assessment by Professor Jenney and his men on the probable value in trade of the Black Hills hardly seemed crucial or even relevant.[41] Events were verging toward armed conflict. In late fall Camp Collins, the army post Dodge had helped establish in order to arrest miners who defied the proclamation of General Crook, was abandoned. The government would continue forbidding citizens to enter the Black Hills, but it would no longer attempt to enforce the policy. Early in December the Office of Indian Affairs ordered all Indians within the treaty territory to report to their respective agencies by January 31, 1876, and when many refused, the matter was turned over to the army. The bloody Sioux War of 1876 was at hand.

This dire result of the effort to solve the problem of the Black Hills through police action, diplomatic negotiation, and scientific study had not been difficult for some to foresee. Dodge's engineer officer through the end of June, Second Lieutenant John G. Bourke, Third Cavalry, was junior aide-de-camp to General Crook, and naturally he regarded the situation from the point of view

---

40. A full account of the council, which lasted through September 29, is found in *Report of the Secretary of the Interior* (1875), pp. 688–96.

41. On April 25, 1876, a portion of Jenney's interim assessment was ordered by the Senate to be printed; it was entitled *Report on the Mineral Wealth, Climate, and Rain-Fall, and Natural Resources of the Black Hills of Dakota*. The final document, *Report on the Geology and Resources of the Black Hills of Dakota. With Atlas*, by Henry Newton and Walter P. Jenney, remained unpublished until 1880. The latter work formed part of the Department of the Interior's geological and geographical survey of the Rocky Mountain region, under the direction of J. W. Powell.

of his department commander. On June 1, just having arrived within sight of the Black Hills, this young officer wondered in his diary "what good does the present expedition do except to witness that our Government is not desirous of depriving the Sioux of any treaty rights until after careful consideration of the subject involved, and maybe a feeble scientific light thrown upon the topography of the country and the true astronomical position of a few insignificant peaks and streams?" Bourke suspected thus early that the Jenney-Dodge expedition would not exert a decisive influence on contemporary affairs. Eventually, he thought, the army would face a war with the Sioux and Cheyenne Indians "in which those tribes will be doomed to receive the castigation so long merited."[42]

Officially at least, Dodge witnessed the current troubles from a somewhat less encompassing viewpoint. He had long been a sharp critic of the government's ineffective policy toward the Indians, but when ordered to do so he duly played his part in the army's effort to enforce the proscription against miners. As the months passed he must have anticipated the limited impact the explorations of his party were likely to exert on the threatened crisis. After all, by the time his command returned to Fort Laramie, the negotiations to cede the Black Hills had already broken off. But as he had told Red Dog at the impromptu council in July, all these were matters "for the chiefs above" him to address. He had performed with credit the duties assigned him, winning the praise of General Crook and forming a smooth working relationship with that redoubtable Indian fighter.[43] From a personal point

---

42. Bourke Diary, June 1, 1875, USMA. Bourke concluded his entry with the confident observation that "under General Crook, the subjection of all hostile Indians within the limits of this department may be accepted as a foregone conclusion." The career of this talented officer and student of Indian culture has been described by Porter, *Paper Medicine Man: John Gregory Bourke and His American West.*

43. Dodge again took the field under General Crook in November 1876, when he commanded the infantry and artillery battalions in the Powder River campaign. In December of that year, however, his regiment was transferred to

of view as well, the summer had been a success. He had hunted amid glorious scenery, made good progress on his book, and cemented an outdoors relationship with his son that gave promise of happy summer comradeship in years to come. Now, upon his return to Omaha Barracks, he would set about writing an official report in which, frankly mixing the professional with the personal, he characterized the Black Hills expedition as comprising "the most delightful summer of my life."[44]

---

the military Department of the Missouri. Upon his return from the winter campaign under Crook, Dodge took post as commander of Fort Riley, Kansas.

44. Turchen and McLaird, *The Black Hills Expedition of 1875*, p. 92.

Note on Editorial Policy

THE AIM IN PRESENTING THIS EDITED TEXT OF Dodge's journals is in general to coordinate realization of two not always compatible goals: first, fidelity to what the author actually wrote and second, utility for the reader. Dodge compiled his manuscript journals under a variety of circumstances—indoors and outdoors, at leisure and in haste, in comfortable conditions and in awkward or trying ones. Not surprisingly, the character of his journal entries varies widely, from considered, relatively finished discourses to disjointed "telegraphic" notes. Yet despite the variations in their style, the manuscript texts all exhibit Dodge's tendency as a journalist to take liberties with the standard practices of written expression. For example, he abbreviated words and names with unusual freedom, and at some points he almost dispensed with punctuation. At the ends of lines in the manuscripts he seems to have regarded the pause to shift his pen to the line below as serving adequately—for himself at least—as a substitute for whatever punctuation the context might require. Dodge felt free to adopt practices like these, in part because he was writing for his own eyes alone. Knowing as he did what his abbreviations signified and how his ideas fit together, he could fashion a shorthand style that suited his private purposes, however ragged or cryptic it might seem to others. Of course, the particular journals he wrote in imposed a constraint that to some degree obliged him to adopt the compressed style he did. Small enough to be carried in a shirt pocket or other convenient place, even the largest of the notebooks afforded him a maximum of

3 9/16 inches per writing line, enough for only four or five words in compressed script. Ordinarily Dodge wrote in a freer, more expansive hand, but to economize the space taken up by his entries he adopted a relatively cramped handwriting style.

Presenting the texts of Dodge's manuscript journals in printed form clearly necessitates certain adjustments in order to render them accessible to a modern reader. The procedures I have followed in editing these texts are summarized below.

When Dodge wrote out words and names in full he ordinarily spelled with a reasonable degree of accuracy, or at least consistency. He did habitually misspell some words, as *vecinity* for *vicinity*, and he often failed to include the apostrophe in contractions (*dont, isnt*); but errors like these pose no difficulties of comprehension. Certain other words and names he spelled in more than one way, as *tomorw, tomorro*, and *tomorrow* or *Sand Hill, sand-hill*, and *Sand hill* cranes; but the reader quickly grows accustomed to these variations. Thus, except to correct errors so serious as potentially to baffle or so odd as likely to distract, I have allowed Dodge's variant spellings and even misspellings to stand. If confusion seems possible, it is obviated either by an editorial interpolation within square brackets or by a footnote. For proper names that Dodge spells in more than one way, the correct spelling is indicated in an identifying note at the point where that name is first mentioned.

Abbreviations employed by Dodge appear here, with few exceptions, just as he wrote them. Many of these pertain to military matters—*Qr Mr* for *Quarter Master, Co* or *Compy* for *Company*—and quickly become familiar. Others often relate to aspects of the weather or else to Dodge's itinerary and location—*ther* or *therm* for *thermometer*, or *m, mi,* or *ms* for *miles*—and seem natural enough in their contexts. Abbreviations that may be problematical are filled out within square brackets or explained in notes at the points where they appear. Superscript letters written in connection with abbreviations are brought down to the line except in datelines, for which a standard format is used.

When Dodge underscored or otherwise punctuated superscripts, as D^r, D^r, D^r, or D^r, the abbreviation is followed here by a period (e.g., *Dr.*). When an abbreviation goes unpunctuated, as *Dr*, it is given as written. Ampersands and *&c* (for *et cetera*) are allowed to stand.

Dodge's habits of capitalization, generally conventional though far from consistent, are respected. He did adopt quite often the traditional practice of capitalizing for emphasis, but his intention in doing so is clear and presents no difficulty. Transcribing his entries does involve some uncertainty in distinguishing between capital and lower-case letters. In particular, the letters *c*, *m*, and *p* create problems of interpretation when they appear at the beginnings of words and especially at the beginnings of lines, for they often rise above the lower-case letters that surround them. In deciding whether to transcribe a letter as capital or lower case, I have taken into consideration both Dodge's habitual practices and also those observable in the immediate context. No effort is made to regularize his capitalization, except that the first letters in proper names and in daily entries are always capitalized.

The inconsistent punctuation and formatting of Dodge's journal entries requires some editorial regularization, for to present it unchanged would result in pervasive distraction and frequent ambiguity. Thus, for example, the sometimes irregular spacing between his paragraphs and entries is regularized unless it seems to carry a special significance, such as to mark a place for information he expected to receive in the future, or to signify text written at a new sitting. Within paragraphs, lines left unfilled toward the right margin are ignored when the spaces have no apparent significance. Similarly, wider than usual spaces between words and between statements are regularized unless a reason for the practice is discernible.

Dodge habitually observed only slight indentations for the first lines of paragraphs, and in these journals, with their limited writing space, he indented hardly at all. The problem of deciding with confidence whether a small indentation at the left margin was intended to signal a paragraph break or was merely a chance occurrence is often unsolvable. Thus, paragraph breaks appear in this edited text only when physical evidence, or a combination of physical and contextual evidence, in the manuscript warrants them. When Dodge significantly indents any statement that begins a new line, the line is represented here as the beginning of a paragraph, irrespective of whether its content represents a break in subject matter from the material that has gone before. But when the indentation is even smaller than normal, the new line is considered to begin a paragraph only if the context justifies it. The sole exception to this rule is that throughout the edited journals each entry that follows a dateline is indented on a new line.

Dodge's terminal punctuation, when he supplied it, took a wide range of forms, from a neat period to a dot extended slightly to the right and perhaps marking a moment of thought, to a yet longer hyphen, and finally to dashes of varying length. The spaces intervening between the final words of statements and these marks of punctuation also varied. To reproduce all the conformations in print is manifestly impossible. Instead, a few rules of thumb have been adopted to govern the representation of Dodge's terminal punctuation. If a sentence at the end of a paragraph or a day's entry concludes without punctuation, none is supplied. If, within paragraphs, a sentence concludes without punctuation and the one that follows it begins with a capital letter, no punctuation is supplied. If a sentence concludes with a period or an "extended period," both of which Dodge often (though not always) placed along the line and immediately following the final letter, a period is shown here. If a sentence concludes with some longer mark—a hyphen, a dash, or an extended dash—Dodge ordinarily (though not always) placed the punctuation above or else below the line and separated it from the preceding letter by a blank space. Marks like these are shown with one space intervening after the final letter; they appear as en dashes, em dashes, or something longer that approximates what Dodge wrote. If, as occasionally occurs, a sentence concludes with a comma, semicolon, or colon, the error is corrected and the change is noted. Question marks and exclamation points are supplied as called for when Dodge concluded sentences without punctuation, but otherwise his terminal pointing is left as he wrote it.

Dodge liked to record colorful and characteristic dialogue, but in doing so he often failed to complete pairs of quotation marks or to insert them at all. Thus, when necessary, omitted quotation marks are supplied within brackets. Parentheses and dashes, whether single or in pairs, are treated similarly.

Within sentences, distinguishing between what Dodge may have regarded as commas, hyphens, or something else can be fully as difficult as determining with confidence what marks would accurately represent his terminal punctuation. He did write real commas, but these stand at the extreme end of a spectrum of usage. At the other end is a characteristic hyphen or "extended dot," marking both conclusion of a phrase and also, apparently, a moment of thought about what should come next. This latter mark may be arced or slanted upward or downward and may appear above, at, or below the line; but ordinarily a space intervenes between it and whatever precedes it. The variations between these two extremes of internal punctuation are myriad. Although at some points a down-slanted extended dot seems clearly intended by Dodge as a comma, at others the configuration is different enough that such an identification cannot be made with confidence. Fortunately, once one recognizes the effective interchangeability within sentences of Dodge's commas and extended dots— or whatever we may call them—problems of interpreting his meaning are rare. In transcribing the journals I have recorded as hyphens only those marks that clearly justify the identification; they appear in the edited text with a space intervening between them and what precedes them. In more doubtful situations I have interpreted the marks as commas and have placed them immediately after what precedes them.

Cancellations are relatively infrequent in Dodge's journals, and on the whole they are not especially significant. Most often he deleted matter not to censor himself but to correct errors, insert afterthoughts, and revise for style. However, in the interest of completeness all canceled matter is included here, except that deleted words and phrases that were immediately rewritten are ignored. Mere slips of the pencil and canceled fragments of illegible letters are also ignored.

Dodge often, though not always, employed the caret (∧) to indicate placement of inserted matter. Here the caret is used to denote all interlineated material, which is shown in a free space above the printed line; see the list of editorial symbols and abbreviations below. In the few instances where he inserted an asterisk or other mark to show the proper placement of material located elsewhere, the situation is explained in a note.

Dodge assigned no page numbers in any of his journals. Ordinarily he wrote his entries straightforwardly, more or less filling each page, writing first on the front and then on the back of each leaf, and passing from front to back in a journal. A few journals are double-enders: that is, they are written from front to back and meanwhile, often for some special purpose, written also from back to front until the two series of pages meet or almost meet. Arrangements of this sort are noted where they occur. No systematic numbering of journal pages is supplied, but to facilitate the location of drawings, blank pages, reversed text, and other variations from the norm, journal page numbers are supplied within square brackets at the points where that information is called for. The page numbers given include a designation of either *R* for recto, the first or front side of a sheet on which Dodge ordinarily wrote before turning it over, or else *V* for verso, the reverse side. Page numbers given without *R* or *V* denote both sides of a sheet.

Dodge's drawings in the journals are all sketches of terrain or draft maps of the country he was then traversing. Although they are not reproduced here, their presence is noted at the points where they appear and their subjects and chief features are identified.

Dodge began almost all his entries with a dateline, but in doing so he adopted several formats, providing varying amounts of information. On some occasions he recorded the day of the week, the date, the month, the year, and the location; at other times he set down something much briefer. Often he drew a line or a series of hatchmarks across the page to separate the dateline from the entry that followed; at other times he began the entry immediately to the right of the date. When he added a place name or a camp number, as he often did while compiling an itinerary to be reported later or else to be incorporated on a map, he might write it at the beginning or the end of his dateline, or else above or below it.

Some consistency is imposed here on these diverse practices. Making use of all the information Dodge included in any particular dateline, but presenting at a minimum the month and date, the information is given in the following format: *Day of the week, Month, Date, Year. Place, Camp Number.* Abbreviations in the manuscript dateline, as in *March 23rd*, are deleted, so that in this case the date would appear as *March 23*.

Editorial Symbols and Abbreviations

[roman]	Editorial additions
[*italic*]	Editorial explanations
< >	Restorations of canceled matter. Cancellations immediately written over are shown next to the letters or numerals written over them, without intervening space.
? ? or [?]	Doubtful readings. The former are used within square or angle brackets. The latter are used for a single doubtful word and follow it without an intervening space.

unrecovered	Unrecovered word. When more than one word is involved, the fact is indicated (e.g., *three words unrecovered*).
∧	Interlinear insertions.

Editorial situations not covered by these symbols are explained in the notes.

*The Black Hills Journals
of
Colonel Richard Irving Dodge*

Journal One:
May 6–June 6, 1875

May 6[1]

[...][2] of passengers. Saw Wheaton's Company going west to Pawnee Res -[3] Mrs. Egan on board.[4] Got sleeping <car> ∧ by berths ruse de guerre - got Mama to buy them The Co[mpany']s people were saving some for Ladies - Mr. Hurd on board used to know him at Sanders.[5] Introduced me to Mr. Clark, Supdt.[6] Spent an hour or so very pleasantly in Supdts car. Dinner at Fremont pretty good. <Picked up my negro at the train in Omaha ->[7]

---

1. This manuscript journal consists of seventy-two pages. On the bottom side of its cardboard pad, Dodge has written in ink "Black Hills [/] 1875," and three inches below, in pencil, an encircled "1." Except as noted, entries in the journal are in pencil. Entries begin on p. [1R].

2. The text on p. [1R] is almost entirely rubbed away. The page was once filled with handwriting, but except for the dateline only the words "Up early," "Tooty," and "Got all arrgd" remain legible. The text that follows begins at top of p. [1V]. "Tooty" was Dodge's nickname for his wife, Julia Rhinelander Paulding Dodge (b. 1837).

3. Captain Charles Wheaton's Company G, Twenty-third Infantry, was assigned to a subpost of Omaha Barracks on the Pawnee reservation at Genoa, Nebraska.

4. The wife of Captain James Egan, Company K, Second Cavalry, who at this time was stationed at Fort Sanders, Wyoming Territory. Egan had recently been attached to Omaha Barracks in charge of the Department of the Platte's preparations for mounted service.

5. Fort Sanders, established in 1866 to protect the stage line between Denver and Salt Lake City and the crews at work on the Union Pacific Railroad, was three miles south of Laramie, Wyoming Territory. Dodge had been stationed there in 1868.

6. S.H.H. Clark was assistant general superintendent of the Union Pacific Railroad.

7. This was James, a servant hired for the duration of the expedition.

Wheaton left us at Fremont - Supper 9 1/2 p.m. at Grand Island. Exps. today - $8 for berths, 50¢ for lock - $3 dinner, $3 Sup, Book 2.00 - Total 16.50.

Saw new moon all night - lost my pipe & a bot of whisky leaked out - also left my big knife - Extremely hot day.

May 7

Passed a poor night from heat - Luckily a norther sprung up & about 3 oclk I crept under a blanket - Breakfast at Sidney - Met Egan - & other off[icer]s - 3 hours late - Cold and blustery - Arrived Cheyenne 3 p.m. Met Reynolds, Bradley and other Offs at Depot -[8] After dinner called on Genl Reynolds Dallas & the other offs of 23d - Also on Woolley -[9] After went to town & called on Genl Bradley & Mr Jenney the Geologist - pleasant call - went to bed about 12

May 8

Went down to see Moore,[10] & got my horses tents &c all right. Moore very accommodating - Long talk on hunting. Wrote to Father Ma P.[11] and to Tooty - Went to Town and saw Mr Jenney - also the Herald reporter Mr. Davenport -[12] Telegraphed to Genl Crook about guide and packers. Mr. Jenney seems very good man. Apparently rather timid and fearful of his knowledge of

---

8. Colonel Joseph J. Reynolds, whom Dodge refers to below by his brevet rank, was at this time in command of the Third Cavalry; the headquarters of that regiment were at Fort D. A. Russell near Cheyenne. Lieutenant Colonel Luther P. Bradley, Ninth Infantry, was the commanding officer at Fort Laramie.

9. Major Alexander J. Dallas, Twenty-third Infantry, was the commanding officer at Fort D. A. Russell. Companies F and H of the Twenty-third Infantry were stationed at that post; Company E was at Cheyenne Depot, three miles away. J. D. Wooley was the post trader at Fort D. A. Russell.

10. Major James M. Moore was quartermaster at Cheyenne Depot.

11. Dodge's father, James R. Dodge (1795–1880), lived with his wife Susan Williams Dodge on a farm along the Yadkin River in rural North Carolina. "Ma P." was Dodge's mother-in-law, Maria Paulding (d. 1876).

12. Reuben B. Davenport, the enterprising young correspondent of the *New York Herald*.

things. Hope he has plenty of Vanity on Geology. Long[13] & wife[,] Moore & Mother-in-law (I suspect) came in to call on me at night - Sat up till late, with Brady[14] and Madam & had pleasant evening - Gave James $5, pipe $1. Recd cases of Corned Beef from Chicago - also box of instruments from Stanton[15]

May 9

Bade good by to our kind entertainers at 8.30 am Took Genl Bradleys spring wagon - Mules look badly but travel wonderfully or the distances are greatly overrated - Arrived Horse Creek 25 miles 12.15, or 3 3/4 hours - Left H Creek at 1.45 & reached Phillips ranche[16] on Chug at 5.15 - 25 miles - Total distance said to be 50 miles Made it in 7.15 - dont believe the distance - Road is generally very good [-] very broken, up and down but no <t> bad places - Passed Pole Ck 15 m - No other permanent water besides the three places mentioned - At Horse Ck met Red Cloud Spotted Tail & other Chiefs going to Washington in charge of the Agent -[17] They say I will have trouble, possibly a fight with northern Sioux who are now in Black Hills. They have gone to destroy what was left in Harney City -[18] Must have a guide, &

---

13. Captain Andrew Kennedy Long was commissary of subsistence at Cheyenne Depot.

14. Captain George K. Brady commanded Company E, Twenty-third Infantry, then stationed at Cheyenne Depot.

15. Captain W. S. Stanton, at Omaha, was chief of engineers for the Department of the Platte.

16. John "Portugee" Philips, an old settler remembered for his exploit in December 1866 when he brought to Fort Laramie the news of the Fetterman Massacre at Fort Phil Kearny, was now an innkeeper whose ranch was a landmark on the Laramie road.

17. The Ogallalas under Red Cloud were accompanied by J. J. Saville, their agent, and William Garnett, an interpreter. The Brulés under Spotted Tail were with their agent, E. O. Howard; their interpreter was Louis Bordeaux. The party included twenty-one Indian representatives in all.

18. This was the name given to the settlement and stockade on French Creek whose inhabitants had been escorted from the Black Hills a few weeks before by a force under Captain John Mix, Second Cavalry. The prediction that Harney City would soon be destroyed proved inaccurate.

if possible one or two Indians. Must *not* go by the Afrucus - Informed persons all tell me it is far out of the way - Bed at 10 pm Slept well - Phillips is a Portugese from the Azores -

May 10

Started 7.35. Thirty one miles at 10.20 - Arrived at Fort Laramie, 1.45 p.m. Road bad along the Chug, but good over the hills. Disappointed in appearance of Post. Went to Genl Bradleys reported - stop with Spaulding - met many officers & old Col Bullock, a 47th Cos. of mine from Virginia. Suttler here from time immemorial to the advent of Belknap.[19] Called on Genl Bradley at night - Met his two sisters in law, Misses Dewey -[20] nice girls - Went over to see Mix. Little lady as charming as ever - Met lots of Officers - Dont even know their names yet.

May 11

Slept well - up at 8 a.m. Paid official call on Comdg Off. He has no orders for me - Telegraphed to Ruggles[21] about guides and packers - Recd answer that Genl C[rook]. would attend to all when he arrived - Saw all the Offs - played Billiards - Had talk with Collins, Post Trader -[22] <Dined post> Breakfasted with Mix -

19. Captain Edward J. Spaulding commanded Company C, Second Cavalry, one of the units that made up the Black Hills Expedition. "Colonel" William B. Bullock, a veteran of service with the Missouri Volunteers in the 1840s, had been a fixture at Fort Laramie since 1858, when he formed a partnership with Seth E. Ward to run the post sutler's (or trader's) store there. Visitors to the fort during the 1860s described Bullock as a courteous and hospitable Virginia gentleman. In 1875 Bullock owned a nearby ranch and was engaged in the cattle business. See Mattes, "The Sutler's Store at Fort Laramie," pp. 102-11 and passim. William North Belknap became secretary of war, with the privilege of assigning potentially lucrative post traderships, in 1869. In May 1876 he resigned, having been impeached for malfeasance in selling various traderships.

20. Lieutenant Colonel Bradley had married Ione Dewey in Chicago in 1868. In May 1875 her two sisters Grace and Louise were staying at Fort Laramie while she and the Bradleys' five-year-old son Willie visited in Chicago (Bradley Papers, USAMHI).

21. Major George D. Ruggles, at Omaha, was assistant adjutant general, D.P.

22. John S. Collins had been appointed post trader at Fort Laramie in 1872. In the decade that followed he and his brother Gilbert H. Collins held the

May 12

Telegrams from all parts - One from John Adair, wanting to go with me -[23] answered by tel - also by letter - Tel. from Secy of War about Collins, & his spirituous outfit.[24] Yesterday recd tel from Tooty & answered it - Telegraphed to Jenney about horses - Tomorw is mail day. Wrote letters to Tooty, Father, & others - Dined with General Bradley - today - but did not stop long after dinner. Played billiards & went to bed late.

Went after the Q[uarte]r M[aste]r.[25] about my outfit - Rode up to the Cavalry camp, a mile up the Platte - Capt Hawley & 4 Cos ordered on scout -[26] Ferry very bad - all day getting over.[27] Telegram from Trout saying he can be here by 20th -[28] Answered by telegram.

Am doing nothing here - can do nothing until Trout and Genl C arrive -

May 13

Did a large amt of nothing today. Visited Mrs. Mix in evening Met many offs - Played billiards - gassed - & went to bed late -

---

commission in alternate years. A friend of Presidents Grant and Hayes and other prominent persons, Collins lived at the fort in princely style.

23. John G. Adair, an Irishman who owned a vast livestock ranch in northern Texas, had accompanied Dodge and their mutual friend William Blackmore on a ten-day hunt along the South Platte River in October 1874.

24. This telegram, dated May 13, informed Dodge that "J. S. Collins has been authorized to take with him a limited amount of spirituous liquors subject to your approval" (Secretary of War, Letters Sent, 4203/WD 1875).

25. Lieutenant Alfred Morton, Ninth Infantry, was at this time acting assistant quartermaster at Fort Laramie.

26. On May 12 Captain William Hawley, Third Cavalry, with Companies A, F, H, and K of his regiment marched from Fort Laramie to locate and intercept a band of hostile Southern Cheyennes thought to be bound northward into the Powder River country. Hawley was unsuccessful in his search and returned to the post on May 19, having marched 229 miles.

27. In *The Black Hills* Dodge observed that a sturdy iron bridge was under construction at this time but that his command had been obliged to use "a very shaky ferry-boat, which, however, I ought not to abuse, as it carried us all over safely" (p. 12).

28. On May 14 Lieutenant John F. Trout, Twenty-third Infantry, was ordered to proceed from his post at Omaha Barracks and report to Dodge at Fort Laramie (S.O. 68, D.P.).

May 14

Moved my horses to Spauldings stable - Got my things together - Qr Mr has only 50 wagons for me - very scant supply for such a trip - Saw Genl B. about ammunition. Spaulding and Col Bullock went to ranch of latter.

May 15

Same routine Genl Crook to arrive tomorw -

May 16

About 2 pm the Genl, Nickerson and Burke arrived -[29] Went over to see Genl in afternoon. Had a very satisfactory interview - & got pretty nearly all I wanted from him - Called on him at night -

May 17

Saw Genl again - got a few more things Genl left for [Camp] Robinson about 12 m. Burke goes with me as topographical Officer - Took a bad cold somehow - Nothing new - A good deal of excitement about Exp[edition] of course - Got 10 wagons more out of the Qr. Mr. Am pretty well fixed now -

May 18

Trout arrived - Too sick with cold to do much today, tho I went to <the> Genl Bradley & got my ordnance - 12 lb Howitzer and gatling gun. Got my mess chest started, but a tortoise is rapid to that workman. Tel. from Jenney - His party will be here on Thursday - or Friday - Am to get my Comd tomorw - Commenced work in earnest on by birth day[30] & hope to be ready to get away before 25th.

---

29. General George Crook was accompanied by his two aides-de-camp, Captain Azor H. Nickerson, Twenty-third Infantry, and Second Lieutenant John G. Bourke, Third Cavalry. Having recently consulted at Chicago with Lieutenant General Philip H. Sheridan, Crook was on a tour to inspect facilities and conditions in his new command, the Department of the Platte.

30. Dodge was born May 19, 1827.

May 19

Woke up with the terrible cold still hanging on - Order was issued designating the Cos to go with me.[31] Spaulding packing up. Trout at work like a man. Visited Mrs. M. at night - also called on General Bradley - Passed a rather stupid birth-day. Mail arrived bringing several letters. One from Tooty, another from Father and Mother. Wrote letters in evening to <e>both these & several friends. Wrote to Adair telling him not to come & one to Blackmore telling him to come *sure* -[32]

May 20

Still suffering from an awful cold - Janney[33] & party arrived quite early - put them in Camp above Post. Trout at work - All the forage loaded & put across river - Gave my attention to the men working at my boxes &c - very slow. Chairs nearly done - Hop at night -[34] did not go. Spent evening writing letter to Tooty, then went to Collins to get him to take it - He promised to call on her at Omaha B[arrac]ks. He is en route to Washington on the Indian question.[35]

---

31. The military escort consisted of Companies C and I, Second Cavalry; A, H, I, and K, Third Cavalry; and C and H, Ninth Infantry.

32. Dodge had met Adair only the year before, but he and his English friend Blackmore (1827–78) had known each other since 1868. They had enjoyed hunts together on several occasions during the lawyer-speculator's visits to the United States; see *PNA*, pp. 15–16. Dodge and Blackmore had made tentative plans for a grand hunt during the summer or fall of 1875.

33. Although this misspelling of *Jenney* soon disappears from Dodge's journals, it persisted in the newspaper coverage, in which the entire party was often designated as the "Janney" or "Jenny" expedition.

34. A "hop" was a formal dance, often followed by refreshments, much favored by officers and citizen gentry at army posts. A correspondent of *ANJ* described a hop held at Fort Laramie on February 18, 1875: "When one heard the soft and sweet strains of the music of a fine band, and saw the handsome toilettes of the ladies and the gorgeous uniforms of the officers, and joined in the prevailing mirth and happiness, he could scarcely realize that civilization was so far away" (March 6, p. 468).

35. According to the *Omaha Herald* for May 25, 1875, both Red Cloud and Spotted Tail trusted John S. Collins and wished him to accompany them to Washington, D.C. At first he declined, explaining that the issues to be discussed

May 21

Terribly racked with cough during night & in morning - Genl B issued orders relieving all my Cos from duty at Post - Trout loaded and got all the Com[missar]y stores over river. Issued orders assuming Comd. Cattle over river - Bad job - hard work - but finally all swum but two (2) which had to be killed. Packed up my things and can start in an hour No news of guide - Hired "California Joe" as packer. Staff of Expedition

Lieut Foote	9th Inf Adj[utan]t[36]
Lt Trout	23d " AQM AC[37]
Lt B[o]urke	3 Cavy Engr.

May 22

Slept better but cold still very bad racking me with cough. Loaded up my ordnance & got the guns in order, also got my sub[sisten]ce. stores. Called on all the Ladies in evening - Maj Staunton, Pay[maste]r - and Sutorious 3 Cavy arrived -[38] Drew $10.50 for Exp[ense]s from Omaha to Ft Laramie - Got all my ambulances - Every thing ready except Guide. My potatoes, Trouts clothing, & some am[munitio]n for one compy. Burke paid $30 towards Comy Bill - Wrote to Tooty at night. A mail goes off tomorw.

---

there were not his business. But later the Indians petitioned the Department of the Interior that Collins be officially requested to assist in the negotiations, and upon being telegraphed by the department, he agreed to make the journey (clipping in Bourke Diary, USMA).

36. Lieutenant Morris Cooper Foote, Company B, Ninth Infantry; his company was stationed at Fort Laramie.

37. Lieutenant John F. Trout was acting assistant quartermaster and acting commissary of subsistence on the expedition.

38. Escorted by a detachment under command of Captain Alexander Sutorius, Third Cavalry, Major Thaddeus H. Stanton was on a bimonthly journey to pay the troops. His next destinations were Camps Robinson and Sheridan.

May 23

Sent off letters early Cold bad, but better - Paymaster & all visitors went east. Orders for the Cos to move in the morning, across river - Guide to be here tonight Can't hear of potatoes &c. Geologist Janney will be ready to start Tuesday 25th - Visited Genl Bradley & all the ladies at night -

May 24

Up pretty early and got all packed. Infantry Cos got over river quite early. I went down with Spaulding's Co. Mix['s] wife and sister came to see us off - also Genl B. & many of the Officers.[39] Guide arrived yesterday. Discharged "California Joe" for drunkenness. - Hired a man named Duffell. Camped on bank of Platte 1/2 mile above ferry - very good camp - Got everything over. Issued my marching and camp order.[40] Had a pleasant evening & went to bed early - Janney & scientists got over about 5 p.m. - all ready for start in the morning - except that the Photographer

---

39. Lieutenant John G. Bourke evocatively described Dodge's camp just before departure: "Those officers of the post who were not to form part of the expedition, now presented themselves to say goodbye to their comrades and receive parting messages of the description usual upon such occasions. Old and almost forgotten war times were vividly recalled by the long streets of white canvass sheltering officers and soldiers, by the long train of 75 wagons laden with a three months supply of provisions, by the thousands of rounds of extra ammunition supplied in case of need against hostile Sioux. In the cavalry companies and in the Quartermaster train, long lines of animals were groomed and rubbed preparatory to the long march of the morrow; our efficient Quartermaster, Trout, ran from point to point, inspecting and examining to see that every essential had been supplied and jotting down at intervals memoranda of mistakes to be rectified and omissions to be made good. The infantry companies were drilled in the school of the skirmisher and exercised in the evolutions of the company formation; bustle prevailed on all sides, indicative of the earnestness with which all concerned regarded the duty to which they were assigned" (Diary, May 24, 1875, USMA).

40. Black Hills Expedition (hereafter cited as BHE), General Order (hereafter cited as G.O.), No. 2. The full text of Dodge's order designating the arrangement of columns on the march, times for trumpet calls, revolving daily assignments as picket guard and camp guard, and other details, was printed in the *New York Tribune*, June 7, 1875, p. 3.

has not arrived neither have Trouts baggage or my potatoes and onions - Left Corp[ora]l 6 men and wagon to bring up Phot[ographe]r and mail

May 25

Up at 4 a.m. Fred's first night in tent - got scared during sleep and accused his Dad of snoring.[51] Broke camp 6 a.m. Cavy (3d) wagons heavily loaded, & took a long time to get started - good march over an undulating country. High second plain - plenty of sand - & some mud from rain on 23d. Heavy hauling for animals. Most delightful day for marching. Camped on Rawhide at 1.30 p.m. 17 miles from last Camp. Everything travelled well - Caught some chubs, & late in evening went out & shot some doves - Officers very agreeable and efficient. Had nice evening - several officers visiting me. Good camp - water grass & wood.

May 26

Broke camp 6 am - Adv. guard left 5.45 & I went with it. Merivale left road, & passed to the west over a sandy cactus prairie - and had to come back to road again to cross Creek. Crossed with little work. At 8.20 crossed a tributary from North. Part of wagons crossed on natural bottom, which cut deep, and we had to build a bridge. Followed up Rawhide by a Trail hugging the hills - a good deal of work necessary on road - At crossing of the other stream Joe Merivale told me that it was the main Rawhide, that the stream we followed was a dry fork, that the main stream made a great bend & we would save some miles by the cut off, & camp on main Rawhide. Left trail & struck up a dry fork from the north - sand deep and travelling abominable. 2 1/2 miles up Jo came to me and said he was mistaken & that we had passed the water on which we ought to camp, & that the

41. Frederick Paulding Dodge (1859–1937), Dodge's only child, had been raised primarily in New York by his mother. Of a delicate constitution, he was unused to his father's active mode of life. Bourke described him as "a young boy of (14)" (Diary, May 16, 1875, USMA).

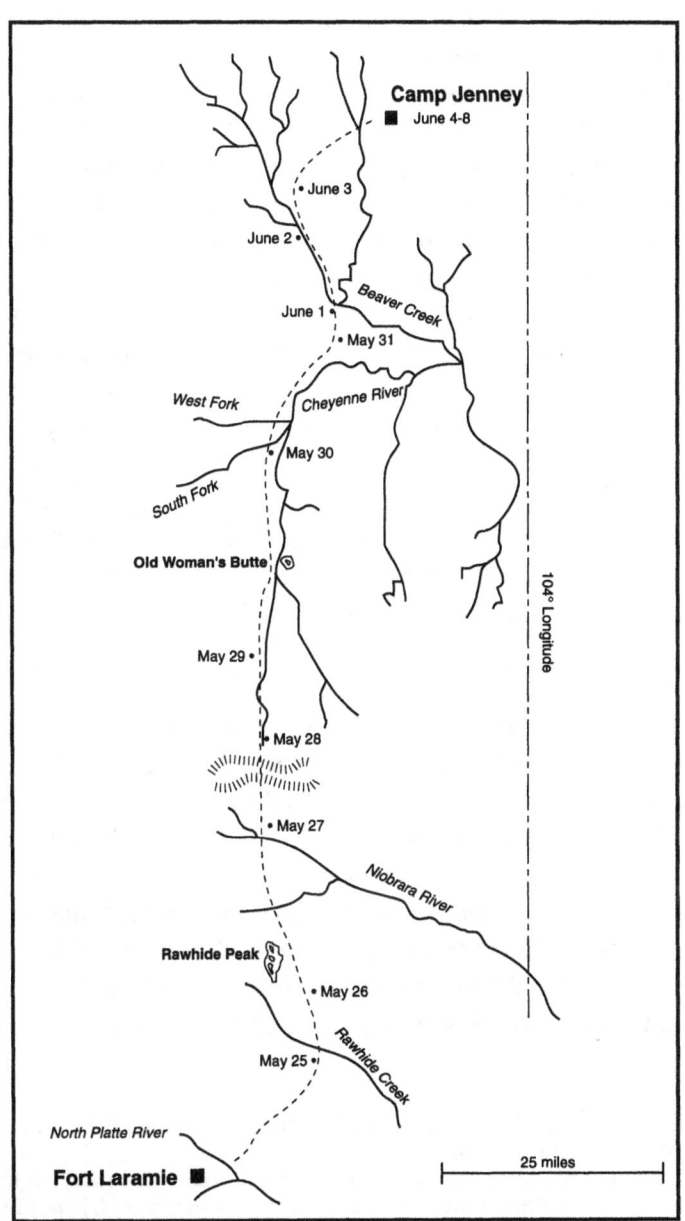

Dodge's itinerary, Fort Laramie–Camp Jenney, May 25–June 8

nearest water north was the Niobrara 15 miles at least I turned back at once, sent courier to stop wagons - and sending the Adjt Lieut Foote 9th Infy, to make Camp on Rawhide, I took a couple of orderlies & went on the divide to look for a proper crossing. My faith in Merivale is gone, & I must myself play guide. Followed divide to Rawhide Butte   Struck Mix' trail[42] & followed it back to Camp. Saw the lay of the land & shall have no difficulty tomorw except in crossing ravines. Joe feels very badly so I did not blow him up. Nice camp at junction of Dry fork with main Rawhide. Good wood water & grass. Distance made 7 1/2 miles[,] distance lost, 5 miles - Total march only 12 1/2 m. & very trying on the mules. Men arrived with the wagon I left behind for photographer, potatoes & onions & Trouts cloths.[43] Brought mail. Letter fr Tooty - very comforting - Wrote to her, to Father & Mother - private reports to Genls Crook & Bradley. Burts hunter[44] killed antelope and sent me the saddle. Rain in evening. Having a nice time every way. My Comd very fine -

May 27

Started with adv. guard 5.30 am - Camp broke at 5.45. Followed Mix' trail to the great disgust of Joe Merivale, who wanted to experiment with me and Comd on divide. I knew both & took trail. Excellent route to Rawhide Butte. Then some pretty tough ravines were crossed. As soon as I had fairly turned the Butte, I struck north by Compas. Merivale said I could not get through. Found a splendid route except a few bad ravines which had to be worked. The Rawhide range of hills is very fine, & we passed through a lovely & most picturesque country   None of the maps

---

42. The trail made by Mix in March when bound into the Black Hills to expel unauthorized persons there.

43. The photographer had still not arrived; he joined the party on June 23.

44. Captain Andrew S. Burt, who commanded Company H, Ninth Infantry, had been posted at Fort Laramie since August 1874. A brief account of his experiences in the Black Hills Expedition is found in Mattes, *Indians, Infants, and Infantry*, pp. 200–205.

even indicate the characteristics of the range & the water shed.
11

About ∧ <unrecovered> we struck an old trail supposed to be Reynolds of Engrs.[45] If so it is exactly what I want. Reached the Niobrara by a most excellent route at 12.40. Every one is delighted with the route & I have had many congratulations on my performance as guide. Distance 20 miles. Excellent camp fine water & grass but wood very scarce nothing but brush. The day has been very cold - wore my Canada over coat all day with comfort. Country passed through today very attractive - Sent off mail by Baptiste, the Ft. Laramie guide,[46] who was sent out to me for that purpose by Genl Bradley, who has done all that could be done in kindness & consideration for our comfort & to make my expedition a success. Everything is going on admirably & my officers seem to vie with each other in doing all I desire. Niobrara belies its name, "running water," where I struck it, but soon begins to run and is a nice little stream. It has been very cold all day & towards evening it became so much worse that I went to bed at 8.30 to keep warm.

May 28. Camp 5

Slept well. Very cold during night. Heavy frost and ice formed in tents. Adv. guard and I started at 5.30 am, Comd 6 - followed old Indian trail which led in direction wanted. The wagon trail followed yesterday gave out. Discovered that Reynolds

45. In 1859 Captain William F. Raynolds of the U.S. Army Topographical Engineers had led an expedition from Fort Pierre, on the Missouri River, to explore the Yellowstone region. But as Dodge was soon to discover, the Raynolds party did not pass anywhere near Rawhide Butte. The old trail struck by Dodge was likely made in 1856 by a pack train under another engineer, Lieutenant Gouverneur K. Warren. According to Henry Newton, assistant geologist of the Black Hills Expedition of 1875, Warren's route north from Fort Laramie in 1856 was much the same as that followed by Dodge and his command, and Warren's camp of September 12, 1856, was "almost the same as our first [permanent] camp in the Hills, known as Camp Jenney" (Newton and Jenney, *Report*, p. 11). See Dodge's journal entries for June 9 and 10.

46. Baptiste Poirrier or Pourier, a Fort Laramie veteran.

(Engrs) was never in this country but marked the route on this map, from description of a guide at Ft Laramie. No wagons have ever been here except small light affairs trading with Indians. For 9 miles this a.m. the road was very fine passing over long divides seperating waters of the Niobrara. The ground got very high at last, when we suddenly came to a steep pitch, from the top of which is one of the most splendid views I have seen. The whole valley of "Old Woman" Creek spread out at our feet bounded by steep crags, high rounded hills covered with pine, & in the distance the haven of our hopes "The Black Hills" The country is most lovely, & I don't blame the Indians for wishing to hold on to it -

The route was most difficult and it required no little Engineering skill to get down. My pioneering and Trout's wagon management finally got us down without accident or delay - Once in the bottom however, our troubles began. A few days ago, there was a very severe rain storm here & the overflowed valley is now in most places a bog, while the little creek which one can step across, looms into formidable proportions for a wagon train, requiring to be bridged every little way. Our work was slow & tedious in the extreme. Going down in this way for about four miles we were finally stuck the bog of the valley becoming impassible - & the steep hills on each [side] being broken into bad ravines - almost impossible to cross or turn. After a deal of work, & travelling myself over every route which gave hope of practicability, I at last determined at 1.20 to stop & go into camp - on a beautiful spot, with good wood and water and splendid grass. Unusually careful about Stock today. We are in the home of the Red Man, & just where we came into the valley passed the camp of a war party of about 100 strong bound west, probably for Fetterman and the R.R.[47] The camp was about three

---

47. Ninety miles due north from Medicine Bow Station on the Union Pacific Railroad, Fort Fetterman was approximately sixty-five miles west from Dodge's present position.

days old. Distance today 14 miles. Total 58 1/2 m. My Cavalry is very finely mounted, & my transportation as good as I have ever seen -

May 29. Camp 6

Out early 5.15, looking for route. Pioneer Co. out on foot. Had d——l of a time. Ravines had to be headed by going into the hills, or turned by crossing main stream. Sometimes one, other times the other was resorted to. Crossed river three times & made two long stretches into the hills. Crossings abominable - no bottom - bog everywhere. Made two corduroy,[48] & one brush bridge, besides a good log bridge over a side stream. The Comd did not get out of camp until after 7 am & has had a series of long rests, so that men & animals have had an easy day Except the Pioneer Co. and the wagon mules. On these it has been tough enough. About 2 1/2 a shower came up while I was building the last bridge on the branch of Old Woman we have been following down. As it was a very bad crossing I did not expect the wagons to get over for two hours, so I sent the Adjt to pick out a camp below the junction of the two branches of the stream This had so stimulating an effect on all concerned that the whole Comd was safely over & in camp by 3 1/2 pm Country not so beautiful as yesterday. Tertiary deposit entirely.[49] Very little timber on stream which is a broad shallow bed 75 ft wide filled with mud or quick sands.

---

48. In his diary entry for May 31, Bourke described a corduroy bridge built across a stream. Beginning the process, "men move out with axes, fell suitable cottonwood trees, which another party strip of their branches and cut into lengths suitable for stretchers and cross-pieces. Stretchers are disposed across the stream, two feet apart, while the cross pieces cover these closely at right angles. Smaller branches fill in any gaps that may occur while a uniform hand-packed covering of earth makes the road-bed. The bluffs, edging the stream are now cut down to make a convenient ramp and wagons and horse are crossing almost before the written description is completed" (USMA).

49. In his geological speculations Dodge distinguishes between primary (or primitive or paleozoic) rocks, the earliest in origin; secondary rocks, which bear marks of mechanical origin, such as scraping, and contain organic remains; and tertiary formations, which occur in strata and represent more recent activity.

No Indians, or signs of any except the war party which went west spoken of yesterday. They came up this creek and left plenty of sign. Very warm today, until shower. Nice camp water & wood plenty. grass excellent. Distance 15 miles. Total 73 1/2 m.

May 30. Camp 7

Got out early 5.20 with Pioneer Compy, everything following soon after. Had a splendid march over long rolling slopes, having only to bridge an occasional ravine, or cut a bank. At 10 1/2 arrived at a crossing of the "Old Woman" which bothered us dreadfully. Had to build a corduroy & bridge over 200 feet long. It took three solid hours of hard work. At about 2 p.m. we were ready to cross, & got over safely, bidding good by to the "Old Womans Fork" of which we have not many pleasant reminiscences so far as route is concerned

By a good trail & with only one cutting we came to the South Cheyenne which I immediately crossed. It is a nasty stream of thirty feet in width - bottom sandy - banks mud - Had to corduroy both banks for fifty feet from water Got over safely without accident, & all in camp on North bank by 4 1/2 - p.m. Excellent camp Wood & grass abundant & fine. Water muddy & very thick. Cleared with cactus it is very palateable, so we have nothing to complain of. It has been a hard day, <the> all hands having been over eleven hours at work or marching - & the animals in harness or under the saddle - but it has been really tiresome only to the Pioneer Co., Trout and myself. I am greatly disappointed in the Cheyenne River. It is a miserable insignificant dirty stream affording however evidence of sometimes getting on the rampage. We are camped in a lovely grassy lawn surrounded on all sides by woods of Cotton wood - Country not beautiful,
very <interesting> ∧ but interesting - plenty of fossils bones &c. Fred went wild over the lovely flowers, & today saw his first rattlesnake, which was to his delight, dead. We have been following since yesterday noon, the trail of a party of emigrants,

who in 1865 under the Comd of a man named Sawyer, made a route from Sioux City to Montana.[50] The trail is very plain to be ten years old, & is remarkably good, considering the country I prefer it greatly to the guidance of Joe Merivale, who knows nothing of this country, nothing of distance, nothing of road hunting for wagons. Saw fine Black tail Deer No chance for shot - Game very scarce but deer tracks more plenty today than heretofore. Distance today 18 miles Total 91 1/2 miles. Total distance travelled on the Old Woman's Fork 31. miles.

May 31. Camp 8

Slept splendidly, though the camp was aroused partially by a shot about midnight. Trout came to my tent somewhat excited. I told him not to stampede anybody, & he went off after his herd, in the darkness. It appears that one shot is the signal he has established to indicate trouble in the Beef herd, for which he is responsible. There was nothing the matter a *"Doboy"* recruit having got scared at a loose horse, & fired to give the alarm. Up at reveille, out rather earlier than usual 5:15. Went but a short distance before the trail struck the river again This time the crossing was good, & no work was needed. In half a mile had to cross again, this time at a very bad place, which we had to bridge & corduroy for 50 yds Merivale the guide soon after this wanted me to cross again, but my mad was up & I told him I would not do so. I therefore struck for the hills and made a good trail - He is no sort of a guide. He insisted that the great West fork of the Cheyenne emptied still east of us - that the large stream passed was the "Dry Fork." Acting on this I kept down the river, making several bridges over ravines until we arrived at the stream which he was sure ought to be West Fork, & which turned out

---

50. For an account of the wagon road established by Colonel James A. Sawyer, see Hafen and Hafen, *Powder River Campaigns and Sawyer's Expedition of 1865*. According to the *New York Tribune* (June 21, p. 2), the identification of this road was made by James Sanders, an old plainsman who was employed with the wagon train.

to be a very small arroyo. The map showing that we are as far East as we ought to be, and not knowing the distance to Beaver I determined to camp, & at 12 m. went into a fine lovely camp on Cheyenne. Splendid wood & grass & good water by digging - River very muddy.

It has been a lovely day for marching - no sun - yet not rainy - The Indians have just found us out. Two Smokes were sent up today on edge of Black Hills. I hope some of them will come in tomorw. My course tomorw is due north. Distance 13 - Total Dis 104 1/2 m Several deer & antelope killed today. Spaulding sent me a nice ham of Antelope off which we dined sumptuously - Had camp fire at my tent, & nearly all the offs & scientifics came around, & we had a very pleasant evening - telling stories &c ———— ————

Killed a rattlesnake today - the first one Fred ever saw alive - He - Master Fred - is extracting a deal of pleasure out of this trip - rides all the time and behaves very well generally. Is getting over his disposition to tantrums.

There is likely to be some trouble between the Herald reporter Davenport and the scientific party. In the Herald of 17th appears a letter of Davenport giving a history of the Expedition in advance, the letter being written from Cheyenne.[51] Some of the remarks about the escort attributed to the Scientific people - being rather crude -[52] I laughingly attacked Jenney on them - He expressed a great contempt for the reporter - & said that no one had ever made any such statements - <In the> A short time after Davenport came in, and I rallied him on his Military knowledge. He

---

51. "The Sioux Paradise," *New York Herald*, May 17, 1875, p. 4. The dispatch is dated May 8 at Cheyenne.

52. By "crude" Dodge means naive in regard to military matters. The remarks in question were: "The troops composing the escort are now camped at Fort Laramie, ready for moving northward at any time. They number about 600, comprising six companies of cavalry and two of infantry. The proportion of cavalry and infantry may be changed, as Mr. Jenney is understood to prefer that the majority of the body should not move rapidly, in order that a compact form may be presented in marching."

colored up & said he was told so & so by a member of the scientific party. No answer was made to this by Jenney who however seemed uncomfortable. This morning Davenport came to me & said that what he stated in that letter was almost word for word what was told him by Jenney, himself - & that he did not say so at the time because he wanted to have no trouble. I think Jenney is an aspiring man - ready to do any thing for his own advancement. I doubt very much whether he makes a fair & candid statement of the facts in regard to the Blk Hills. He is a very Young man - very boyish in manner, & that he has been put in charge of such an expedition indicates a job of some kind. My opinion is that the report to be made in regard to Gold has been decided upon already at Washington, & that the sending him out is the merest blind -

He is undoubtedly a man of some ability, but very weak, very jealous, and very much disappointed that he has not Military Comd of the Expedition. I think he is a small man & that he will not only try to arrogate to himself every particle of the credit of the Expedition, but will cast slurs on every other member of it who he thinks can in any way come in competition with him. I treat him with the greatest kindness, & do everything for him, but I feel that I get no thanks & that he will eventually show hostility - not while we are together,, but after he leaves me, & comes to make out his report.[53] His Astronomer Asst Captain Tuttle[54] is a Gentleman of culture refinement & sense, & it would

---

53. Jenney's final report, dated November 8, 1875, included gracious thanks to Dodge for the "uniform kindness and aid in many forms, which have contributed very largely to the success of the expedition" ("Report of Geological Survey of the Black Hills," in *Report of the Secretary of the Interior* [1875], p. 685). In his official summaries preceding this one, Jenney was similarly appreciative.

54. Horace P. Tuttle, formerly of the Cambridge Observatory, Massachusetts. His detailed account of "Astronomy and Barometric Hypsometry" readings in the Black Hills formed part of Newton and Jenney's *Report* (pp. 543–55). In 1877 Tuttle was a member of the party that mapped the boundary between Wyoming and Dakota Territories.

be far better for the Expedition if he were the leader of it. He is modest, unassuming, quiet devoted to his work & a most agreeable gentleman.

Dr. MacGilli<g>cuddy, the Topographer[55] is the next in rank & merit. He is smart and bright, well up in his business as a professional map maker, but runs too much to fancy, & pretty. He sticks not at outside work for the sake of embellishment, & I think fails, either in experience or in that knowledge of country which is indispensable to a map maker - I think Burke's map will be better than his - that is as a military Chart. His will be far more fancy - but very much of it will be green work.

Davenport the Herald man writes well, & has the regular reporter knack of pumping people - but he is as green as a gourd, as credulous as a ninny. The young officers have been stuffing him with the most incredible stories - and lately the men have got at it. He is not blessed with a vast amount of courage, & the boys keep him in hot water all the time Last night they persuaded him that the hooting of an owl was the songs of Indian women over an approaching fight, & scared him almost to death by predicting a hard fight today.

Jenney tells a story on him - that Davenport told him that he did not know when we might be attacked, that he intended to put his "Herald Flag" over his tent so that the Indians would know he was a non-combatant ———

I told him yesterday that he was being imposed on by these youngsters & to beware of publishing any stories or rumors coming from them.

---

55. The versatile Dr. Valentine T. McGillycuddy (1849-1937), who had taken part in the Northern Boundary Survey exploration of 1873-74, had been recruited for the Black Hills Expedition by his chief at the survey office, J. W. Powell. McGillycuddy's striking relief map of the Black Hills country was included in the atlas that accompanied Newton and Jenney's *Report*. In 1876-77 he served as a surgeon at Camp Robinson, and in 1879 he began his many years of service as Indian agent at the Pine Ridge reservation.

MacMillan the man of the Inter Ocean[56] is of entirely different stamp - very gentlemanly, hard to stuff, & with excellent good sense, & tho this is the first time he has been on the plains he takes to it so kindly & well, as to win the liking and respect of everyone.

June 1, 1875. Camp 9

Broke camp 5.20 and marched directly north Crossed divide with little trouble - only two bridges - one 30 feet over tributary of Beaver - Struck the latter stream below forks at 9.30 and went into camp to enable the Astronomer Captain Tuttle to get the Longitude. Fortunately the day gave him opportunity to see the sun at the proper times tho it was cloudy and showery all day & rained quite hard in afternoon. The water of Beaver Ck is wretched - alkali & full of all abominable tastes - I am grievously disappointed. From the reports of the guide I expected a lovely stream of pure water filled with fine fish. On the contrary tho a fine full running stream, it is about as nasty as Bitter Creek itself & has no fish except a small shiner - that is after several patient hours, I was able to develop only about a dozen of these small fry -

I had a talk with Mr Jenney this afternoon & told him we must move camp - the water here would make my men sick very soon. So we go on north tomorw, hoping to find a pure mountain stream - We are just at the door of the great unknown - the Black Hills. To the North East of us they tower in majesty covered with a fine growth of pine.

Our first day in the Black Hills will I hope be an earnest of our success in hunting. There were killed after getting into this camp 4 elk 3 deer and 1 Brown Bear about 250 to 300 pounds -

---

56. A slender, twenty-four-year-old Scotsman, Thomas C. MacMillan had been a reporter for the *Chicago Inter-Ocean* since 1873. On the Black Hills Expedition he acquired the nickname "Little Mac." His activities during the Sioux campaigns of 1876 have been described by Knight in *Following the Indian Wars*.

So the camp is full of meat, & we rejoice in fatness, but mourn over the bad water which requires to be mixed -

The country passed today is of "bad-land" formation that is the ravines have a tendency to cut down very deep, with abrupt banks. This is only near the hills. The valleys are broad & covered with excellent grass. It will be some day the grazing ground of miriads of cattle.

Had quite a talk with the Herald man today. He is intelligent but ignorant of life, of human nature and a mere child in his contact with the wild Lieutenant[57] of the plains. Jenney is more sociable today - No Indians yet. They know we are here & their failing to come in is a rather bad sign. They will get our stock if possible - but I will keep it if I can. Our camp [is] in a thin grove of very old & large cottonwood trees the tops of which have been cut off year after year by the squaws, to feed ponies in the winter. In one was an Indian grave which I am sorry to say, was rifled by the Doctors of the Expedition (there are two (2) military and several civil Doctors)[58] & the head & all curious articles carried off. Dr. MacGillicuddy of the scientific got the lower jaw, which he proposes to take home as a present for a dear friend to be used as a pen holder. "To what base uses may we come at last."[59] The jawbone of a Native Chief to assist in the midnight oil business - Cold & blustery in afternoon & evening. Had fine campfire - most everybody around it - Distance today 9 2/3 Total 114 1/6 miles from Ft. Laramie -

June 2. Camp 10

Broke Camp 5.20 a.m. Had to bridge Beaver Ck which occupied about an hour, & then to cut down the banks of a large

---

57. "Lieutenant" is what Dodge wrote, probably (though not certainly) owing to a mental lapse. If indeed he was not poking fun at his junior officers, he may have intended something like "element."

58. The two military physicians were Assistant Surgeon George P. Jaquette and Acting Assistant Surgeon J. R. Lane. The civilians included V. T. McGillycuddy and perhaps others.

59. An approximation of *Hamlet* V.i.222.

tributary from the <East> North which joins main stream less than a mile from camp. Soon after struck the great North and South Indian Trail - from the White River Country to the Powder River Country. It is as large & well worn as a country road - From astronomical observations it was found yesterday that we were 4 1/2 miles too far east - that is we were in Dacotah. Mr Jenney wanted therefore to make that much westing today. In doing this we followed up a middle branch of Beaver, which resulted in taking us away from the Mountains, & by 11 a.m. we were at least 1 1/2 miles too far west. In a conversation at lunch with Prof. Tuttle and Dr. McGillicuddy they told me that they had no orders to run the west line of Dacotah, & had not the instruments to do it. "On this hint I spake"[60] to Jenney. I told him that there were too many points to his problem. We must for the health of the men have good water, for the strength of the animals, good grass, for the comfort of all plenty of wood. In addition he wanted to work in the mountains, & he wanted the camp on 104 Long[itude]. which would not go into the mountains He must either abandon good wood, water & grass, & mountain work for 104 - or abandon 104 for these. He is an indecisive man, and hemmed & hawed on the proposition. He is a mere boy in experience & has still the boyish hope of getting everything just as he desires. At last however he decided to give up 104, & as we had got a very considerable distance from the mountains, & as the train had got considerably behind in crossing the bad arroyos, I immediately moved to the creek and went into camp about 12 m.

The branch of Beaver we are on does not run here, but stands in long narrow water holes, in which there is no life. Not a fish to be caught though I tried faithfully It is not so alkaline as the main Beaver, but is not good water. Wood not abundant but enough for camp. Grass good. I am very glad that I finally settled with Mr J. We have been piddling along a few miles a

60. *Othello* I.iii.155.

day hoping to suit all his ideas. I told him I could do this no longer. I must send my train back, & promptly. My Comd is rationed to 28th, & it will take 20 days for the train to go & come, so I have only six days for accidents - He saw it all, & tomorw we strike straight for the mountains for what appears to be a pass, & is practicable for horsemen - I hope to find a decent place for my permanent camp. Spaulding went hunting today. Saw 5 Elk & a Mountain Lion, but got nothing. Burt killed an Elk,[61] & 1 antelope was brought in by one of the men. Game is only tolerably abundant. Some of the men claim to have seen Indians. All have orders to treat them kindly & bring them into Camp if possible. There are very few Indians in vicinity No recent trails have been seen on this creek. Distance today 10 1/2 miles - Total 124-4/6 - Day pleasant, camp fire & genial evening -

June 3. Camp 11

Broke Camp 5.20 am & struck at once for the mountains - as nearly as I could conjecture to a pass from which comes the large East fork which we forded yesterday - The march was an excellent one - nothing bad to cross - & only a couple of narrow arroyos to bridge with sage brush. Arrived at a gorge of the mountains at 10.10 & went into camp in a most beautiful spot on a lovely stream of water - pure for this part of the world - & as defensible as any position I have ever seen. If I had had the making the spot I could not have suited better all my ideas of what we want in our permanent camp -[62]

---

61. In the *New York Tribune*, June 21, p. 5, Captain Burt, writing anonymously as that newspaper's "special correspondent," summarized his exploits of June 2: "I killed an elk, climbed the first range of the hills, nearly fell into a deep cañon, skinned my hands and knees scaling a cliff after an eagle's nest, and ended the day's adventures by nearly drowning a horse—and that in a stream not three feet wide, one of those alkali ditches which have no bottom to speak of and water so brackish, though clear, that quinine or epsom salts is delicious in comparison."

62. Bourke noted that the little stream in front of the tents "rises in the hills north of us about five miles and about half-mile *below* camp receives the

Just as I arrived in camp I met with a disaster in the shape of a tumble from my horse, which "bucked" me off in a moment & finished the job by stepping on me with both fore feet. One gentle pressure on the arm, I will remember for a day or two.

I have given orders for the Infantry to go back on the day after tomorw for supplies. Burt called at night & is full of grievances. He is a turbulent, ill-contrived fellow, wise in his own conceit, and gives me great exercise in my virtue of patience. He is the only officer along who I have a contempt for. He is visionary & so full of vanity that it requires tact to manage him, & so disposed to say ill natured & impertinent things that I have hard work not to "go back on him" - I wish I could get rid of him - Made the details for work tomorw - must build my store house & also two redoubts -

The Geologist is delighted with the place I have put him in. He says his work is all around him & is more than delighted with the prospects before him for work. Some of them have already been to the highest points of the Mountains & put up stakes preparatory to triangulations. There has been a very high wind all afternoon, & I thought at one time my tent would come down - but its all right so far - & I hope we will get through the night safely. I must again express my delight at the efficiency of my command, & the interest all the officers take in my wishes. I am teaching them plains travel, & all appreciate my capacity in that particular. One elk killed today. I went out fishing but had no proper bait, and got nothing. There seems to be nothing but Rocky Mountain suckers, but they take Grasshoppers greedily even from the surface. A piece of petrified wood was given me today -

---

salty, disagreeable washings of a little brook running out from the breaks to the west of it." At this site, Camp Jenney, Dodge ordered construction of a commissary storehouse, a stockade, and what Bourke described as "a little palisade work on the crest of a little hill. . .from which our artillery [notably a Gatling gun] can be enabled to play with deadly force on any party of Indians that may have the temerity to attack us" (Diary, June 3, 1875, USMA).

part stone and part wood. The most unique specimen I have ever seen. Distance today 13 miles Total distance 138 miles. The return trip can I think be made in about 120 miles.

June 4. Camp 11

Had reveille an hour late this morning, & woke to find Master Fred reading in bed, the extra hour being too much for him.

After breakfast went to work on Storehouse. Made details last evening from the Cavy Cos & had fifty men at work today. Got walls of store house up & dug the trenches for the pickets of the redoubts. Men worked very well - Unloaded all the wagons that go back & issued orders for Burt and the Infy to start tomorw with the train for Laramie after supplies -

There was a vast amount of work done by all today that is all the working men. I wrote my reports to Genls Crook and Bradley - letter to Father and Mother then visited Burt and Munson,[63] & bade them good by. Came back and wrote a long letter to Tooty, a short one to Bradley enclosing telegrams, & a short one to Mix. Five Indians reported seen today & a trail of 15 passing north - in the M[oun]t[ain]s - Signed my field returns also all Trouts Papers Went to bed after 12 pm

June 5, 1875. Camp Jenney, Camp 11

Up pretty early, but not soon enough to see the train start - Mr Jenney asked for an escort to go into the hills exploring - gave him ten men. He came back this afternoon perfectly wild with delight at the beauties developed by his trip. The Black Hills, according to him is an Earthly Paradise, the most lovely streams the most beautiful timber, the finest game. He brought in an elk and three deer. Other parties brought in game (Spaulding's hunter three deer.) so that I do not know how much has been killed today - a[64] great deal however.

---

63. Captain Samuel Munson commanded Company C, Ninth Infantry.
64. Dodge wrote "I," an obvious error.

I moved Hd Qr tents this a.m. and have now got a beautiful position a tent each for Fred and myself floored with the bridge timber, & exceedingly comfortable. My camp now is a picture - green sward, graceful trees, the box elder, the most beautiful of the plains trees, as thick & green in foliage & as various in shape & grouping as can be imagined. I have got out of the draught of the canon & we have now but little wind. I am delighted with the change except that now lying in my bed, and listening to the murmuring of the stream, only fifty feet away, I cannot but remember the sudden rampages to which these Plains Streams are subject, & hope that no vagary may astonish us with a wall of water some night -[65]

I have finished the Com[missar]y storehouse & got all the stores in. The redoubts are in a fair way, but the men have been very slow in getting logs today. I will go for them tomorw but it will take me two days yet to finish them to my satisfaction

Show of gold said to have been found in this Creek below Camp today. Mr Jenney says there is no quartz above on the creek - I have not seen the show. Some of Jenneys party caught a beaver last night. He was not much hurt, and this am I took Fred over to see him. He was very quiet, and allowed himself to be handled & felt of by us all. I felt sorry for the poor beast, especially as his fur was of no account at this season and persuaded them to turn it loose. We then drove it quietly to the water and when he had got where it was deep enough he gave us a fine specimen of his skill in diving & soon disappeared -

Mr Jenney found where a dozen Indians had camped last night only eight miles above us on this Creek. One of the number had come down to where he could see the camp, & went back in a hurry. They were travelling south. Another trail of a party of 15 or 20 was found going north - but some miles to the east of us. Those evidently knew of our position, while the party

65. Not long before, in drafting his book-in-progress, Dodge had described the dangers posed by sudden floods to travelers encamped beside apparently innocuous streams; see *PNA*, pp. 114–18.

going south almost ran upon us before we were discovered. Mr. Jenney's party saw a great deal of game and one of his hunters told me that he had never seen so many deer in one day in his life -

Six or seven bear were also seen but none killed today -

Fred is delighted at <not> having a tent to himself, & is full of fixing it up. Spent a pleasant evening at Spauldings and Hall's tents,[66] & went to bed after a very satisfactory day -

Sunday, June 6, 1875. Camp Jenney, Camp 11

Slept rather late. After breakfast I went up to the redoubt, & got the walls well started. It is slow work however the logs being hard to get at. They grow well up on the sides of the Mountain & have to be snaked down by a team. Mr Jenney expects to <be back> start on his expedition on Wednesday 9th, to be gone ten to fourteen days. Trout is to go out with the log cutters tomorw & I hope to finish both redoubts in the two days. Quiet lovely day - several deer killed. In fact we are overloaded with meat Read & took a nap in afternoon. Joe Merivale the Guide returned about 3 1/2 p.m. Party of miners reported to be encamped about ten miles from us, on another creek, the Salt branch of this. Shall not interfere with them unless they force themselves on me. My force is too small for the subdivision which would be required to send all these parties in to Fort Laramie.

The weather has been unusually cold & disagreeable. The days are pleasant enough - but the nights are very cold and I have no stove. Have to go visiting or to bed to keep warm Mr Jenney came over this evening & we talked over the route of our scout. I am to go out with him tomorw on a flyer to see how the land lays, & whether we can get through the Hills into the Park Country with wagons. I am sure it can be done but it will take time & some skill in the selection of route -

---

66. Lieutenant Christopher T. Hall commanded Company I, Second Cavalry, in the absence of its regular commander, Captain Henry E. Noyes.

Camp Jenney
Long. 104° 19' 30"
Lat.   43° 50' 12"

Camp 11 - 1st Permanent

Black Twin
Little Big Man
Crazy Horse
Little Hawk[67]

67. The source and significance of this list of Indian leaders, apparently set down for reference, is doubtful.

Journal Two: June 7–28, 1875

June 7, 1875. Camp Jenney, Camp 11[68]

[...][69] third - &c. The second took us up about a thousand feet above the creek bottom. We then had to go down a steep grade before attacking the third which I judge was near 1500 feet above creek This was a terrible hill to climb, but perfectly level on top. The divide led us on to another rise. <As we> Before gaining the top of each we congratulated ourselves that this would bring us to the real top - but each top only showed us a still higher ridge in our front - This continued until we reached the top of the sixth ridge & an elevation I judge of near 2000 feet above the Creek, or about <7>8000 above sea level. This last sixth ridge seemed not to be overtopped by any in advance, but a mile ahead & on nearly the same level with us was a well defined ridge which shut us out from any view. So we went down a gentle slope & up a gentle slope, & got onto the next ridge, only to find another at our same level still in advance. After going on and on until we had thus passed four ridges, and seeing nothing but ridges still in advance the affair became seriously monotonous. There seemed no end to the ridges. We had fully demonstrated

---

68. This manuscript journal consists of eighty-five pages. On the bottom side of its cardboard pad, Dodge has written in ink "Black Hills," and 1 1/2 inches below it, "1875." Except as noted, entries are in pencil. The entries begin on p. [1R]. The dateline is supplied by the editor.

69. The ellipses within brackets indicate that at least one sheet containing part of this day's entry has been lost.

the impracticability of this route, for though it might be passed with wagons, it would be with extreme difficulty and by doubling teams. Besides no power could take wagons over those hills so far in a day as we went on horseback, & we found no water for camps. So about 2 p.m. we turned our course nearly north for a mile or two, & then to the west for "home again" - It is a monstrous easy and nice thing to go up a divide. It is a most difficult and nasty job to come down. Going up, every little divide leads to the main divide - Going down, every little divide branches off from the main divide, & looks so like it that no one can tell which is which ——[70] We found a promising looking divide & followed it for about a mile, when it suddenly sunk away between two immense cañons. We had either to go back and turn one of these cañons with the almost certainty of having a dozen more to turn before getting the right divide, or to take to the bottom of the cañon With all its difficulties we tried the latter. The slope down was an angle of about 45° but by zigzaging we managed to get down without dismounting. At the bottom I found a lovely spring of the best water I have tasted since I left Omaha. I drank about a gallon of it (for I was heated to red heat, it being terribly hot today -) Mixed a little[71] <for> to prevent its injuring me - took my lunch, & then set down the ravine. Spaulding is a great fellow for short cuts, & thinking I was wasting too much time in <short cut> zigzaging, he made a short cut for the bottom of the ravine. The result was that he not only missed the spring, the drink & the lunch, but was floundering about trying to get down a 30 foot precipice without breaking his neck. He at last accomplished the feat by turning the obstacle, & soon after I found him. We were now in a cañon, the North wall of which was almost an absolute precipice. The South wall was in some places almost a precipice - in other places it sloped

---

70. In drafting his book manuscript Dodge had discussed at length the problem of traveling among ravines and divides; see *PNA*, pp. 93-99.
71. With whisky.

away at an angle of from 60 to 75°. The canon was not less
than 1000 feet deep and in some places not a <1000> ∧ 500 feet
wide. The bottom was a narrow V averaging some 20 feet wide - in some places not six feet - filled with huge boulders, broken masses of stone, fallen trees white birch, quaking asp, plum & cherry bushes, & the sides a mass of strawberry vines in bloom. To get along was a work of constant difficulty. Sometimes we had to shin along the side of the cañon - to avoid boulders, or huge rafts of fallen timber - <& also> sometimes we went over logs, sometimes under, & I was constantly expecting to come on a sudden fall of 15 or 20 feet, which would force us to go back & look for another pass. Most fortunately none such occurred, and after an interminable time we got through all right -

We arrived in camp 5.30 pretty well used up, having ridden up & down at least 30 miles, & clambered and scrambled on foot 5 or 6. Spaulding got one shot & bagged a Black Tail very nicely. I got no shot. Game was very scarce though we saw plenty of fresh elk and deer tracks. We were surprised to find no bear. The walls of the canon are of mountain limestone & full of caves, & would appear to be the home of the bear tribe - but we saw no sign whatever in the canon.

Jenney returned soon after us. He went straight up the valley of this creek, & found a good road, onto what he thinks is a high plain, by which we can turn the Hills, & get inside. We will start the day after tomorw. The redoubts are nearly done. Tomorw will finish them & I can leave this camp safe if the captain will only keep on the watch. I was greatly disappointed in the timber of the mountains. In the foot hills & low valleys there are very fair pines, some 2 feet in diameter & probably 20 ft to the limbs. On the high hills it is very small, & is besides wind-shaken. Fires have made huge rifts through it - & we travelled for about 4 miles through a mass of blown down trees from 3 in[ches] to a foot in diameter - The pine is all Rocky Mountain pine, which is very poor timber at the best. No gold - all secondary rocks, & formation.

June 8, 1875. Camp Jenney, Camp 11

I was kept awake for a long time last night thinking of the problem of our advance. I finally decided to move with all the force I can transport, & after finding a new Camp to send back for the Co[mpanie]s left here. Early in the morning I met Mr Jenney. He opened the conversation by proposing to take a Command & go back down the Beaver to 104, & run out that line first. I explained to him that it would be only a loss of time, & finally convinced him that the best thing he could do would be to go on, & get another camp He is not a strong man, & I soon had him fixed. I at once gave orders for Hd Qrs & 3 Cos to move tomorw a.m, with necessary details.[72] Went up to the redoubts which are completed - all but the platform in one. Finished up all preliminary arrangements - played several games of cribbage & whist & beat all my opponents. The Herald Reporter, Davenport, asked to mess with me on this trip. I declined, telling him very frankly, that I could not have a man with me all the time, with whom I must be constantly on my guard in conversation - That my mess was composed of my staff off[icer]s, with whom I constantly conversed very freely, especially at meals, & that his presence would not be satisfactory to me. I believe he was satisfied with my reasons. Had a nice nap, very grateful after my fatigue of yesterday, & feel perfectly well and capable of going on another trip -

J<a>enney came over after dinner. He is morbidly anxious lest some one should be ahead of him in reporting Gold. Asked

---

72. BHE G.O. 3, dated June 8, designated Companies C and I, Second Cavalry, and Company H, Third Cavalry, to accompany headquarters on the march. Twelve days' rations were to be taken, with a minimum of other baggage. Assistant Surgeon Jaquette was to go with the companies leaving camp, while Acting Assistant Surgeon Lane would remain with the troops at Camp Jenney. The cattle herd was to go with the marching companies. Lieutenant Trout, the quartermaster, was ordered to accompany Dodge and later to return to Camp Jenney with the pack train. The three companies to remain in camp—A, K, and I, Third Cavalry, under Captain William Hawley—were supplied with twelve days' rations.

me if I would please prevent any "outsiders" from going along. Told him that there were but two outsiders in Camp - one of whom is conditionally employed by him, the other by me.[73] Every other person is a part of the expedition & must go along, even at the expense of the secrecy to which he aspires. He was but little satisfied, & said that it was very important that no one should discover gold before he did, & that he must make the first report — Soon after he left, Davenport came to me to ask me to recommend a man who could be relied on to take in to Ft Laramie a Herald despatch, announcing the first discovery of gold. I told him that he could not have a soldier, & that the only other man was "California Joe" (he of whom Custer speaks so highly, and who is a worthless vagabond)[74] Davenport said he was afraid to trust him, that he would take his money & then carry in despatches from other reporters. I told him I could not help him. He then told me that Jenney had a man, brought out here expressly to carry out despatches for him, & finally said, "I can afford to pay more than any body else, and I think I will go to Jenney's man and see if I can't get him to go back on Jenney, for money" - I told him they were all Kilkenney Cats & might use each other up, or "*beat*" & bribe as suited them. But I rejoice that I am a soldier, if success in civil life depends on such small dirty practices that Jenney & the Herald man, seem disposed to put in operation against each other. Nor do I want to be a reporter, if through it I fail to be a gentleman. One would suppose that a matter of life or death depended on which should be first to report gold, while I doubt if fifty men in the U. S. care one jot who reports it -

    73. Dodge here refers to civilian manservants.
    74. At this point Dodge wrote an asterisk corresponding to another in the right margin, which is followed by "Subsequently changed this opinion." California Joe had been permitted to rejoin the command, subject to the authority of Dodge. At this point he was officially the employee of Jenney in a general capacity. Joe's few days of limited contact with the command before rejoining it were described in the *Chicago Tribune*, June 19, 1875, p. 9; and the *New York Tribune*, June 21, 1875, p. 2.

Dr Lane & Morton came back this afternoon from a leave I gave them three days ago. They have been to Harney's peak, & made a wide circuit through the Hills.[75] Jenney is mad as a hornet that I let them go - though he has said nothing to me - They give no very satisfactory account of the Hills. The country is extremely broken, & very difficult every way - They think there is mineral on that side, & say that the other portion of the hills is worthless Hall and old man Bullock[76] tried to make Dr Macgillicuddy tight this afternoon & both fell in the experiment, while the Dr went off all right. Got off joke on King[77] who ran away from Spaulding & I yesterday, thinking we were Indians - Morton and Dr. got no game.

June 9, 1875. Spring, Camp 12

Got off at 6.45 which was doing remarkably, considering that we were breaking up a permanent camp. Took the 2 Cos 2d Cavy - Spauldings & Halls & Wessels[78] of 3d Cavy. This is much the largest & laziest Compy. As it was to have the lead today, I sent out an Officer and 20 men yesterday afternoon to fix the road near camp. It was done, but so badly that it took us nearly two hours to get it in condition for the wagons to pass. From then on we had nothing but trouble until 1 pm. Our route led up the creek, which being dammed by beavers to a bog, & having steep & deep banks is practically impassible except by bridging

---

75. Lane recounted this "daring scout" in the *Chicago Tribune*, June 30, 1875, p. 2. He and Second Lieutenant Charles Morton, Company A, Third Cavalry, were accompanied by California Joe, Sergeant J. H. Van Mall, and another enlisted man. According to Lane they had left camp "ostensibly on a hunt, but in reality to get through the barrier that had, up to this time, prevented any white man from gaining any information as to the character of this so called 'unexplored' country."

76. Colonel William G. Bullock, who accompanied the expedition as guest of Captain Spaulding. A lively sketch of him appeared in the *New York Herald*, August 19, 1875, p. 6.

77. Lieutenant Albert D. King, who commanded Company I, Third Cavalry, until the arrival of its proper commander, Captain William H. Andrews.

78. Captain Henry W. Wessells Jr. commanded Company H, Third Cavalry.

Wessels is a half hearted kind of a man with no snap to him, & the men take their tone from the Captain, & do as little work & as slowly as possible.

The eastern mountains pour numerous beautiful looking brooklets to the main creek. The water <ism> is filled with gypsum salt &c, & tho' cool and tolerably palatable is perfect poison to my stomach & keeps me sickish all the time. Besides this these streams run in ravines, which had to be cut down, or make bogs which have to be corduroyd. Trout worked like a beaver, & he is a most invaluable man not only possessing wonderful energy but great practical ability. By 1. pm we had passed the last bog, & entered on the hard level bottom land of the creek, following up the left bank. The road on is elegant, a great Indian trail as large as a wagon road. Warren passed over it many years ago, before the war, but his trail is entirely obliterated. The scenery today has been really very grand & beautiful. The valley owing to the number of streams is beautifully green with grass, & graceful with trees & shrubbery. On each side rise ranges of mountains 1000 to 1200 feet high, their tops covered with the thick growth of pine which gives the name of the "Black Hills" Below this, many of the hills show a face of several hundred feet of red sandstone, below this a belt of very uniform thickness - (<about> 20 to 40 feet) of limestone. Below this again several hundred feet of a red clay, filled with gypsum and salts of all kinds. Below all is the green valley and the combination & variety of colors, make as fine a picture as one may see in a long journey. About ten miles from Camp Jenney the stream gave out, that is, it has no water in it. Just before we came to the head springs, or rather the place where the water which has been for many miles running under the sand of the bed, makes its appearance I came suddenly on a mallard duck with a brood of nine little downy young ones. She was so fearful of her brood that she let us come quite close, & at last took refuge with the little ones in a thicket of bushes. I would not let anyone hurt her.

About 12 miles from last camp we crossed to the right bank of the ravine now dry - and rising rapidly on a series of long green treeless slopes, came at 4.30 to a beautiful spring with enough water for all the animals, & went into camp. Distance today 14 miles. Wood water & grass excellent & plenty. The water kept me sick today, & I had to "get out" several times - & have not felt well at all in the bowels, tho' first rate everywhere else. James, my no-account "Nig"[79] got to fooling with my gun today & broke the hair trigger, so that I shall not be able to use it until after I get to the next permanent camp

The sun set cloudy & with every appearance of a storm, & just after dark, a sharp storm with thunder & lightning came on, & now at 9. p.m. it is raining in heavy showers, with pretty sharp lightning. The cattle were stampeded by the thunder & Trout insisted on going out after them, though it rains hard and is as dark as Erebus. I gave him all the men he wanted, but I wouldn't go out tonight for all the Texas cattle in the country. No game today - I wanted to go about seven miles further, but we lost so much time this a.m. that I could not.

Overturned one wagon (one of the Hd Qr) & broke the tongue of the Drs ambulance. (Dr Jaquette). Very small casualties considering the circumstances, but as it happened both occurring on comparatively good ground from the carelessness of the drivers. All are in, repairs completed. Trout has just reported the herd all recovered, & the extra sentinels over them. He is just a little disposed to make the most of his work & I greatly disposed to give him full credit for all he does, but when he came after about 25 minutes absence and reported that he had followed the herd three (3) miles, I couldn't quite swallow it. He may have thought it full three miles and twould likely have been a dozen to me, but he could not have gone a mile. Still storming, & to bed.

---

79. Here and elsewhere, Dodge employs the terminology of racial stereotyping that, though considered offensive today, formed part of the vernacular of his era.

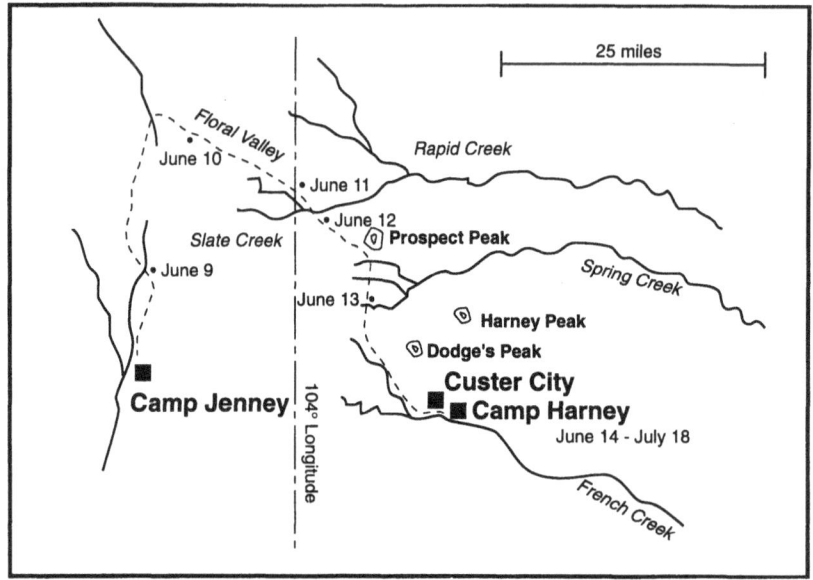

Itinerary, Camp Jenney–Camp Harney, June 9–28

June 10, 1875. Head of Branch of Red Water Creek, Camp 13

Rainy all night, but bright & clear in the morning. Broke camp 5.30 a.m. and travelled due North following an old Indian trail which led us thro' open pine woods covering long rounded slopes. On our right was the cañon of the Beaver (or Spauldings) Creek, here at least 500 feet deep, & inaccessible to any thing but bird or bear. Our route was not only excellent for travelling but was through a most beautiful country. About 3 miles from camp, <came into> crossed Warrens trail at a spring at which he camp[ed] (No 13). A mile further on we got onto a magnificent plain bare of timber, & extending to the North west as far as <the eye> we could see. It was about four miles across on the trail we came, almost perfectly level. The topographical features presented here are remarkable. Behind us the long slopes terminating in the valley of Spauldings creek, bounded on each side by mountains over 1000 feet. At our feet a vast plain, apparently limitless to West and N West. On the north some miles ahead a belt of timber. On our immediate right, or east, an impassible chasm of 500 feet, & on the other side of it, mountains rising 1000 feet yet higher & covered with a dense forest of pine. Seven miles from camp the trail led to the brink of the chasm, & we found all the sides not actually precipice, covered with quaking asp, sometimes called "bitter" & sometimes "white" cottonwood. Better still, from the steep sides of the cliff burst forth numerous streams of beautiful & perfectly pure water.[80] Here we stopped for half an hour to wait for the wagons. I picked a great variety of flowers, all very alpine in their characteristics There is a slight growth of dwarf juniper, & also of mountain ivy, both of which rarely get much below the limit of perpetual snow.

Leaving this wild & most interesting spot, we passed along the brink of the chasm & through a quaking asp thicket for about a mile when the trail suddenly dived down into its depths. I had sent Joe[81] forward a half hour before & when he met me he was in despair, recommended me to go into camp, & send out to find a way—as the route before us was impassible for wagons. Leaving the Comd I struck off on the trail, down into the depths. It was truly impassible, for we could with difficulty get down on horseback. Seeing that the fall in the bottom of the canon was very great, I had hopes of turning it, & at once struck up the bed. In less than an hour, I had found a route, & sent Spaulding back for the Comd The new route skirted the edge of the canon for about two miles, gradually turning towards the eastward, & then to my delight began to crawl up a backbone between the Spaulding's Ck Canons on our right, & an unknown set on our left. Where this backbone was narrowest, I spied symptoms of water on our

---

80. From evidence of Indian camps nearby, Dodge named this place Indian Springs.
81. Joe Merivale.

left, & crossing down to the valley we came to a lovely little stream, rushing out from a dense thicket of quaking asp. Here we regaled ourselves with the most delicious water, & took a drink of whiskey to our good success so far in route. From this point we made about a mile of climbing, still on the divide, & were soon rewarded by one of the most magnificent views I have had on the trip. The whole country to the North West and south was spread out at our feet. To the North West, the huge form of the Bear Lodge Butte[82] dwarfed every mountain in sight. Inyan Kara, of which Custer makes a good deal,[83] was 1600 feet below us, & scarcely distinguishable, except as a flat topped Mesa. The northern rim of the Blk Hills was plainly in view, but the north east and east views were cut off by dense clouds which hung over that section working, I am sorry to say around to our front. The elevation of the top of this divide is 7850 feet, above tide water or 3050 above our permanent camp. From this elevation I was enabled to study the water shed of the Blk Hills to the north and west. The streams break off to the south, north west, & north east, & I am satisfied that we were on the very back bone of this system of Hills & that with the exception of a few peaks, we were on the highest ground of the Hills. This supposition will have to be verified later. From this elevation we soon began to go down, & the trail (Indian) instead of following the divide, as I hoped, soon after passing the top, plunged down a series of steep hills, which would well try the temper & capacity of Teamsters & quarter master & finally came into a deep valley - almost a gorge - the sides of which are covered with quaking asp, & the tops occasionally with pine, tho the tops over which we came were nearly bare.

82. Above "Bear" Dodge wrote an "x" followed by "(all wrong—) as we afterwards found." Bear Lodge Butte, many miles to the north, was the unmistakable geological curiosity renamed by Dodge the Devil's Tower, a rough translation of its Indian name.
83. In his dispatch of August 2, 1874, Custer described his ascent of Inyan Kara (*Report of the Expedition to the Black Hills*, p. 2).

Our Indian trail had been going too much to the North and no sooner had we got down into the cañon, than Mr. Jenney insisted on turning sharp to the south west, following up another branch of the stream we are now on, & which proves to be a branch of Red Water Creek. I refused, telling him that it would only take us to the divide again not far from where we left the great Indian trail this a.m. He got angry & pouted like a schoolboy - but I went on my course. I tried to explain to him that the course we had would lead us in a short time to Custers trail, and that with our overloaded wagons, & scant provisions, we could not go rampaging around such a difficult country as this -

He didn't want to strike Custers trail. He was exploring and wanted to make trails of his own - but with my train I couldn't see the merit of experimenting, & kept on for Custer's trail - About 11 am. & less than two miles from where he got "mad" we struck Custer's trail, going South West in <the> a valley of which the one we came down is a tributary. Here I stopped again to wait for the wagons. Soon after we stopped a drizzle came on, which soon settled into showers. We donned our waterproofs, built fires, & tried to make ourselves comfortable with little success. It hailed & snowed, and at 12 when the wagons came up, it was snowing so hard that I determined to go into camp. Going down a short distance I found water & plenty of signs of a camp, and soon found that Custer had camped here. The weather was horrible - blowing snowing and raining. Nothing is more disagreeable than to go into camp in a rain storm, but it could not be helped. I found a sheltered nook, perpendicular to the main valley, & in which we are sheltered as much as we could hope. But it is a nasty storm, & we are having a by no means pleasant experience.

After dinner I got Custers map and Sandy Forsythes diary[84] and find we are at Custer's Camp of 25th July last year at the head

84. Major George Alexander Forsyth, Ninth Cavalry, formerly military secretary to Lieutenant General Sheridan, commanded one of the two battalions that made up the Custer expedition of 1874. His official report and diary were published in the *Chicago Tribune*, August 27, 1874; the diary is reprinted in Krause and Olson, *Prelude to Glory*, pp. 253-59.

of what he calls "Floral Valley." It is a very pretty little gorge even now, varying from one to two hundred yards in width, bounded by steep hills <on each side>, the sides of which are covered with quaking asp, pine & spruce. But alas for the "floral" part of it - It is very early Spring here. The trees are just budding. Only the hardiest flowers are in bloom. The grass is short. There are <tul> few birds, & they are not yet paired. On the ridge we fell in with a fine "pack" or covey of Spike Grouse, at least a dozen birds, apparently not yet thinking of the breeding season. The springs here are very fine - & perfectly pure water the timber rather poor. Grass very backward. The soil appears to be excellent in the valleys but from all indications the seasons must be so short as to prevent the raising of any grain or produce except grass. If the country is not mineral it is worth but little. Two months of summer & ten of winter is not a good climate for settlers.

Distance today 12 1/2 miles. Considering the country our road was excellent, & I have received congratulations from several of the Offs, on our success so far, especially in today's march. Geologically we are getting low, to the carboniferous formation - may get to bed-rock soon. The grass is just starting & our poor horses and mules suffer for food, while it is almost impossible to keep the cattle herd from wandering. The spring has really scarcely opened here, the buds barely having started, & even the strawberries not being yet in bloom. The Indians lied to Custer when they told him that the grass was good here in March, & his supposition that there was but little snow is also erroneous. The ground is yet wet from the melted snow and a deep bed of it was <yesterday> ∧today found on the side of the great canon of Spauldings Ck. Temperature of spring water 41° Fa[h]r[enheit]. Wood and water excellent - No grass.

June 11, 1875. Camp 14

Rain & sleet during night, with occasional high wind. Slept like a top, under a pile of covers. Ordered reveille an hour late.

Soon after Breakfast the sun came out - kept the tents standing to allow them to dry as much as possible - Wrote in journal and observations - Brok[e] camp 11.15 by which time the tents were pretty dry. Our route led up Custer's Floral Valley. Alas, for the floral. The trees were scarcely budded, indeed many of the smaller shrubs showed not even swollen buds. The grass was extremely poor, & the landscape though beautifully framed & set out was poor and bald. The lovely glades of which Forsythe speaks were yet glades, but the scant green of the valley or gorge, & the deeper green of the pine & spruce were the only variations of color. This "valley" soon came to a termination. By a very easy slope, and a succession of graceful curves, the route passed from the ascending to a descending grade, & almost imperceptibly we found ourselves going down. Only a few hundred yards from the divide we came to a splendid spring the true head of Custer's "Castle" Creek.[85] Shortly after we came to an old Indian Camp, where all the squaws seem to have devoted themselves to cutting & trimming Lodgepoles. There has been at some time a large camp of Indians here, & I could distinguish the remains of a Medicine Lodge, so I presume they had been making medicine. All along the route today were remains of Indian camps of last year. They are temporary, & all seem to have been devoted to Lodge pole making. This little valley affords an abundant growth of spruce on its sides. This timber being very straight, light and strong is particularly adapted for lodge poles, and Mr Lo[86] comes here to get it.

Just below this camp was one of the very longest and highest Beaver dams I have ever seen. It was irregular in shape but could

---

85. Custer wrote on August 2, 1874: "The creek which led us down into the interior of the Black Hills is bordered by high bluffs, on the crests of which are located prominent walls of solid rock, presenting here and there the appearance of castles constructed of masonry. From their marked resemblance, I named this stream Castle Creek" (*Report of the Expedition to the Black Hills*, p. 2).

86. After "Lo, the poor Indian!" in Alexander Pope's *Essay on Man*, Epistle I, line 99.

not have been less than 400 feet long. It was the beginning of a succession of dams, which cross the stream at short intervals for some miles. At this old camp was also the very coolest spring I have ever seen. I had no means of taking accurately the temperature but I am sure it was at least 5° colder than our spring of last night. The whole route today has been a succession of springs & the water is most delicious. Going down the valley gradually deepens. The hills on each side are topped by huge masses of Carboniferous limestone from which it takes its appropriate name of Castle Creek. The scenery is fine, but not to be compared with that of the Middle Park, or the western face of the Medicine Bow range. Great allowance must be made for difference in Season, & I can see that six weeks will make a very great change in the appearance of the Country, but I think Custer & his party, having come through the arid plains of the Little Missouri, & the horrible monotony of the Bad lands, were ready to believe almost any tolerably nice place a paradise.

We are now encamped at Custers camp of 26 July. It is very pretty, & since we have got down hill a little I have had to change my verdict on grass. For the last 5 miles the grass is superb, & we camp on a sward that cannot be beat. We are about 1000 feet below the summits of the bordering hills - & about 400 below our camp of last night. I saw some fish in a Beaver dam, & hoped they were trout. Sent back for my rod, & tried. They were chubs - dace - & I was greatly disappointed.

Wagons had a hard day - The snow & rain of yesterday made the creek bottom almost a bog, & the mules had a dead pull ever since we left camp. We have benefited somewhat by Custer's work, finding our bridge in tolerable repair, & several side cuttings which saved us work. Custer passed in dry weather, & crossed the creek when he pleased. Every crossing with us is a most serious matter.

Quartz has been found today in considerable quantities - some of it seems gold bearing. Jenney is going to stop & work part of tomorrow - The timber has been much burned. That on the mt tops is small - on the sides larger and better - Distance 12 1/2 miles. Wagons got into Camp 5.30 pm Only one or two deer today.

June 12, 1875. Woodchuck Creek, Camp 15

Broke Camp 5.30 a.m. Soon after leaving camp the road became a bottomless pit of bog. I got over tolerably well, with Trout, & we thought we had selected a fair route. Soon after Spaulding attempted to cross, & his horse went down to his <belly> sides & had to be pulled out with lariats. How Trout ever got the wagons over will be a constant wonder to me.

Custer's trail here led off from the Creek to make an aimless journey around a park and come back on the creek again 4 miles below. In spite of the bog I determined to make a route down the creek, & started at once. Finding it practicable I sent back an orderly, & brought the train through its most frightful and fatiguing day. Bog bog, all the time - 16 mules on a team, & as many men as could get hold prying & lifting the bed out of the mud. I reached this place, Custer's camp of July 28, at 7. am[.] Spaulding came in with his Co about 9. & Trout with the Wagons and Pioneers came in at 12 m. Before arriving however he sent me word that he had broken a wheel & <that> would have to abandon a wagon unless I could go into camp - so I went into camp. I tried fishing but could get nothing - If there are any fish they are surfeited with the millions of young grasshoppers that are drowned in the stream. It was a long "wait for the wagons" and I was tired of inaction, so as soon as I determined to camp here Spaulding Foote & myself rode to the front to see what was to be for tomorw. For four miles up this little creek, the road is bad - boggy - spoungy & requiring corduroy frequently. About 6 miles from camp we were attracted by a high bare hill, & going to the top were amply repaid for our trouble - The view is more than fine or grand or magnificent. We seemed to be fixed in the center of a circle formed of huge hills & mountains.[87] In

---

87. The party named this viewpoint Prospect Peak.

the North and East only a few prominent peaks broke the monotony of the general elevation of the "rim." A little to the south of East, a huge bare rock towering to an immense height was said to be Harneys peak.[88] It was not over ten miles away. The South and South West views were bounded by as ragged & jagged a mass of mountains as I have ever seen - and most of them must be very high. The interior of this basin was filled with a mass of hill and canon mixed together in the most indiscriminate manner & apparently without system or order. Generally such a view would give some idea of the water shed, the course of the streams &c - but very little can be gained from any study of this most disorderly mass of material. The more I see of the Black Hills & its travel, the more credit I am disposed to give to Custer for his exploration of last year - I find his map remarkably correct, & it is of the greatest use to me. Even with it, I find it no easy matter to go where I want - & to him who had no <guide> ˄thing but his compass & the capacity of his wagons for ups & downs to direct him, the finding of any route was a success. I am told he had several guides. They are generally a very worthless and unreliable set of men at best, but in a totally unknown country might possibly be made of use, by sending them forward to look out routes.[89] I have one so called Guide, Joe Merivale, who was in the Hills 30 years ago, & who knows no more about them than a New York Dandy. He has nothing to do as guide but I keep him as interpreter in case I should meet Indians.

The country passed today has been very beautiful. It is certainly remarkable for the fertility of the soil of the valleys, - for its picturesque beauty, & for its timber though in the latter I

---

88. This peak had been named by Lieutenant Warren after Brigadier General William S. Harney (1800–1889), who had won reputation for his services in the Platte country. Between 1858 and 1861 General Harney commanded the military Department of the West.

89. The limited value of guides in ordinary plains travel was a pet theme of Dodge; he discussed it in *PNA*, pp. 101–2.

confess I am disappointed. The grass is splendid here. As a grazing country it cannot be surpassed. The only doubt about its agricultural value is as to the length of the season. Today we struck for the first time - *Gold* - undeniable unmistakeable. It is only a little "show" - but it is *gold*.

In ten years the Black Hills will be the home of a numerous & thriving population, & all the Administrations & Interior Departments cant stop it. It is not an Indian Country. They can live in it for only a small portion of the year and being Plains Indians they do not like to go into a country where they cannot ride everywhere they wish to go. They use it as a nursery for game, & a fine one it is. There is too much water — Streams spring out from every hill, & the valleys or bottoms are all morasses - and when we remember that this spring water has a temperature from 36 to 42 degrees, it will readily be seen that the soil <tho> however rich will be kept too cold for agricultural purposes

We have seen today some of Custers Park Country, bare spots in the midst of the black mass of pines. The variety is very pleasing. Mr Jenney wishes to spend a few days here prospecting I leave Wessels' Co. with him, & go on to hunt a permanent camp with the other two.[90] 15 deer brought into camp today [-] several others killed but lost. Spaulding knocked one down which got away. Distance 4 1/2 miles. Wood water & grass excellent.

Sunday, June 13, 1875. Spring Creek,[91] Camp 16

Sent Spauldings Co out early this a.m. to make road. Went out myself 6:30, leaving orders for camp to break at 9 a.m. Leaving Wessels relieved us very much, giving us his & the "Bug-Stuffers" wagons. Our loads were so light that we could go almost any-

---

90. BHE S.O. 6, dated June 12, directed Captain Wessells to remain at this camp with Company H, Third Cavalry, until further orders. One each of the three wagons that had been assigned to that company was given to Companies C and I, Second Cavalry, and to headquarters.

91. Dodge first wrote "French" but later deleted it and supplied "Spring" above it.

where with little work. Had a D—l of a time working Custers trail out of a morass in which almost every wagon seems to have been stuck and to have each got out on its own hook. The first seven miles were easily made, & in good time. We crossed a divide & struck a stream which Joe says is the head of Spring Ck & which is the origin of the Morass spoken of - Once through that we had a good road, following Custer over the divide between Spring ∧ (Rapid and Spg) and French ∧ (wrong) Creeks.[92] The latter I followed closely. Custer's trail crosses it some eight or ten times, & not a good crossing of them all. The trail turned off from the creek, & I wishing to make my permanent camp on it, followed it down. It got worse & worse, & after several bad crossings, & a lot of bad road, I sent Spaulding down to look at the prospect. He returned after an hour & told me it was impossible to go down the Creek. Still hoping I left him to put the Comd in camp, and went down myself for about 4 miles. I can go down with wagons, though it will take a deal of work but could do nothing after I got there, the sides of the immense gorge being impassible even for pack mules. After a hard search for a better fate, I had to yield to imperative necessity & decide to go back tomorw to Custer's trail - after which I will be guided in my selection of permanent camp by circumstances.

The more I see of the Country the more disposed I am to give credit to Custer for his march through here. He must have had a corps of guides more reliable than usual - for they certainly have struck almost the only route at all practicable for wagons. As we go south the mountains grow higher, or what amounts to the same thing the canons are cut deeper. The valleys are bogs the hills crags, or covered with timber. He came in the dry season and had that advantage. My wagons sink where his passed easily. I crossed his Morass by a corduroy, otherwise I should have been

---

92. Dodge wrote the interlineations at a separate sitting. The first parenthetical note identified the watercourses correctly; French Creek was to the south.

stuck there yet. The scenery is very fine. I went again today to the top of the hill from which I had the fine view yesterday. Hunted a little today with Spauldings gun & had a long shot at a bear. I think a Grizzly but a very small one - Spaulding missed a deer. Five deer brought in today. The Elk and black tails have not come up yet. This must be a magnificent hunting [ground] in the fall & winter. The whole country is covered with dropped horns, elk & deer - All the deer seen and killed by this party since arriving among the mts are white tails. The canon of French Ck is very fine - walls about 1000 ft, & accessible only in a very few places. We have been passing constantly today over & by ledges of quartz, but no gold has been found today by us. Some of the quartz looks very favorable, but there seems little prospect of good placer or gulch mining. If there is gold in these Mountains in paying quantities it ought to be found on this creek. I would like to describe the parks through which much of our road passed today, but can not do justice. They are very beautiful. The timber on the sides of this Canon is better than any I have seen in the Hills, taller straighter and freer from twists. This is due to the protected position Quite a sharp thunder storm this afternoon, while we were down the Creek. Wrapped in our waterproofs we defied the rain. Freds horse strained himself in a mire yesterday. Today he exchanged with a soldier. He is learning to ride very rapidly - & went with me over some very bad ground today. Most of the officers at my <tent> camp fire at night. Distance 10 1/2 miles. Wood & grass very good & plenty. Water perfectly superb, as fine as I ever tasted, & cold as ice.

Monday, June 14. Camp Harney, Camp 17

Slept like a top. Broke camp at 6 a.m. Struck for Custer's trail again & followed it to the Stockade.[93] The country passed through

---

93. In *The Black Hills* Dodge describes in detail the structure built for defense by the Gordon party the previous winter (pp. 116–19). Photographs of the stockade taken during the Black Hills Expedition of 1875 are in Turchen and McLaird, *The Black Hills Expedition of 1875*, pp. 98, 99.

is most beautiful. Open glades in the midst of timbered hills, widening occasionally into parks. The grass is very luxuriant & the timber grows better as we go south. I was far ahead of the command, & constantly looking for a good place for my permanent camp. We struck French's Creek about 10 1/2 a.m. The valley <was> is lovely - a real park - long reaches of the loveliest sward covering hill, valley, & ravine. At irregular intervals huge rocks thrust their heads through the green turf, & clustered about each such group, as <chicks about the mother hen> if offspring of the granite is a group of pines towering to the skies. On every side the valley is shut in by hills sloping gradually towards the Heavens, their summits crowned with the dark green of the pine.

Here I proposed to make my camp. While riding around looking for a site which should fill all the requirements I saw some animals, & in a moment after, a man dashing amongst them ran them into a narrow gorge of the hills. I immediately recognized the inevitable miner. Under the circumstances I had rather not come in contact with these people, & shied off. The military have general orders to arrest all Citizens found on the Indian Reservation of the Black Hills. I assume that my special orders to escort the scientific people, exhonorates me from obedience to the general order, for if I have to race round the country looking for miners, I must neglect the true object of my trip here. Besides I have not men enough to arrest & send in all these parties without endangering my Command - Still I would rather not meet them. Foote, the Adjt, asked permission to go up & see them & I let him go. As he did not return in a reasonable time I went up to see what had become of him, & found him in a little ravine with six of these men. I rode up & one of the men called out, "How do you do, Colonel." He had seen me many times he said, but I did not recognize him. His name is Harrison & he knew me at Ft Larned.[94] I rode up, & after speaking to them asked, if they

---

94. Dodge had commanded at Fort Larned, Kansas, between March 13 and July 9, 1871.

knew that they had no business here. The spokesman answered promptly, "We do." "Do you know that the military have orders to arrest you"? "We do," he replied - I was pleased with the frank manliness of the fellow, & said, "Well I dont intend to arrest you" - "Thank you" he answered, "- I am very glad to hear it". After that we got into a pleasant conversation, & they took me to their claim to show me the gold. The first pan showed seven colors, the next twelve - & the earth was taken about 2 1/2 feet from the top - not near the bed rock. He told me that there were over 20 miners on the creek, that they had had a miners meeting yesterday to decide on all doubtful or conflicting points, & to settle the amount of land each man might claim - that their claim averaged three to five cents per pan from top to bed rock - that not a shovel full of earth was thrown in vain. They are building a waterway & hope to get in a flume in a week, when they expect to get from 20 to 50 dollars per day to the man. I brought off some of the gold, which I myself saw panned out, & brought in with me to send to Genl Crook - After a very pleasant interview I came away, leaving them very happy -

They had this morning set fire to the grass on their claim to facilitate their work in fixing stakes &c. While I was with them the wind arose, & the fire spread with great rapidity, so much so as to preclude any possibility of making a camp in that valley near it[s] course. So I determined to come down stream, & went back to meet the wagons. Hurried them up a little & got across the valley ahead of the fire, & struck down stream for the stockade. Arrived here about 2. pm. The wagons about half an hour later. The stockade which is about 400 yds from my camp was built last winter by the Miners whom Mix brought out this spring. It is 80 feet square with flanking projections at each corner. The upright logs are 12 to 14 feet high above the ground - not squared [-] the openings between the round logs are battened on the *inside* - not the best arrangement, but adopted for fear a resolute enemy might tear them away, if put on the outside. Inside are five cabins, strongly built, but very low, small and dark, and terribly filthy. The men deserve a great deal of credit for the amount of work done, & also for the practically sensible way in which all preparations for defense were made. The most serious <objection> lacks to the defensibility of the stockade are, first, too few loop holes - second, the loop holes are on <the> a level outside & in, & a dashing enemy might get possession of them - & third, that there are no barbette defenses[95] whatever. Still it is a strong work and a small force could make a good defense against any enemy not <armed with> ∧possessing artillery.

The camp is lovely—a level sward, thick turf, surrounded by low hills, & masses of rock the hills covered with pine. In front is the pretty little creek. Plenty of wood, splendid water and fine grass!! What more can the most fastidious "Camper" desire. We have turned Harney's Peak and its contiguous range, & are now directly south of them. The country is apparently lower <tho> (I have no barometric measurements of today) & the grass and timber are better than two days ago, tho the water is by no means so cold.

Yesterday when on "Prospect Peak", the Harney range appeared an immense mass of Mountains towering to the skies. We have been getting lower ever since, if going down stream is any criterion Yet when we arrive at them they *appear* crags, & buttes of a few hundred feet high. We will test this in a day or two. The country is full of quartz & veins of that mineral are every where to be found. There is no doubt <but> that this country is very rich in both leads and placers. Jenney will go wild when he arrives here, to find that the soldiers have panned out fifty times more gold today, than he has found in all the trip. He is terribly jealous and fearful that some one besides himself should discover the gold. I would not be greatly surprised if todays discoveries shorten our expedition.

---

95. Platforms or mounds of earth within fortifications, permitting gunfire over the parapets instead of through embrasures.

Trout goes back tomorrow with escort of 10 men & six wagons for Jenney & the Compy left behind - I shall send out a party in a few days, to the Red Cloud Agency - with mail - Fred has been rather under the weather today. Caught cold, dabbling in creek yesterday.

Miner came down this p.m. to beg rations - sent in 16 days ago for supplies, & has been living on venison, without bread or salt for that time. We gave him a meal, but could furnish no supplies. It is a very hard thing if the greed & rascality of the Indian ring shall succeed in preventing the miners from developing the immense wealth of this country. The Indians do not use it. There is not a trail to be found. The country is rich in gold, in timber and tho' the season may be too short for agriculture, it is a most glorious grazing country, & will furnish cattle butter & cheese for a nation. I shall arrest no man, if I can help it.

Distance today 16 1/3 miles. Total distance from Camp Jenney travelled by us, 70 2/3 m. Actual distance 68 miles

June 15, 1875. Camp Harney, Camp 17

Got up late - 7 a.m. Trout started soon after 4 a.m. to bring up Wessels & the scientists. Everybody being glad to rest, we did nothing today.[96] The Comps washed up and fixed themselves comfortably. Shall send in party to Ft Laramie as soon as possible. Wrote long letter to Genl Crook in afternoon giving him all the items. The camp is lovely - weather warm by day, but real cold at night, requiring 2 blankets & a comforter. Went to bed late the youngsters having rather sat up with me -

Wednesday, June 16, 1875. Camp Harney, Camp 18

Up at 7 a.m. After breakfast commenced moving Hd Qrs to the point selected for permanent residence - cross the creek -

---

96. Lieutenant Bourke availed himself of this free day to visit the miner's camp in company with J. Bratton, a pack-train employee. He "verified, if verification were needed, Colonel Dodge's report" of gold (Diary, USMA). The comment suggests that as General Crook's aide-de-camp Bourke felt it his duty to serve at all times as the department commander's eyes and ears.

about 400 yds off. Could do nothing at writing. Laid about looking at the working parties. At 2 1/2 p.m. Wessels reported with his Compy & the wagons came in soon after. They have come about 29 miles today. Jenney is terribly disgusted that we should have found the gold before he did - and Trout says all the scientific party were at loggerheads last night when he told them of the discovery & showed them the gold. Each abused the other and if you believe all, every man of the party is a d——d fool, for each says that of the other. Issued orders for Spaulding and Trout to start tomorw to try & find a good route to the bridge on Beaver Ck - also for a N.C. Off[97] and ten men to go to Ft Laramie for mail.[98] Wrote long letter to Genl Bradley - also wrote to Tooty & Father & Mother. Also wrote telegrams for Genl Crook[99] and for Tooty, to be sent to Genl Bradley. Made tracing of a map for Spaulding by which I am sure he can do his work

Jenney and several of the scientific people over to see me this p.m. Jenney is "scooped" - I felt sorry for him, & did not pitch into or crow over him as I might. But he is a "royal" ass - Trout informs me that one of Jenneys men, in a moment of confidence

97. Noncommissioned officer.
98. BHE S.O. 7, dated June 16, directed Captain Spaulding with twenty-five men to proceed to the Beaver Creek bridge, approximately fifteen miles below Camp Jenney, which the command had built on June 2. Lieutenant Trout was to accompany Spaulding as far as the bridge but was to proceed thence to Camp Jenney, where he was to collect the troops and stores at that point and return with them to Spaulding. Meantime, Spaulding was to dispatch a "reliable" sergeant with ten men to Fort Laramie with the mail. He was to remain at the Beaver Creek bridge until the infantry companies under Captain Burt arrived there, detaining Burt until all the troops at Camp Jenney had also returned with Trout. Spaulding with his company would then return at once to Camp Harney with the mail, leaving Trout to bring the whole train with the rest of the command. Trout was to follow the route to the Beaver Creek bridge opened up by him and Spaulding unless it proved impracticable for wagons. In that case, he and Burt were to return by way of Camp Jenney.
99. Widely reprinted in newspapers, Dodge's telegram was terse: "Harney's Peak, June 17.—Gold has been found in paying quantities on French Creek. Custer's report has been confirmed in every particular. The command is well and in fine condition."

told him that the scientific party had found gold some days ago, but that Jenney had bound them to secresy, & they were not to tell the military. The ass! ass! ass! There are private soldiers in this Comd who know more about gold hunting than he can ever hope to learn. I am very glad that we found the gold, tho' we are entitled to no credit for it as the miners really found it. See letter to General Crook[100]

June 17, 1875. Camp Harney, Camp 18

Up late because I was up writing letters until 1 am Sent Tooty check for $120 for June & July pay to servts & household expenses. Spaulding and Trout left about 8 a.m. Kept a man or two back to take up the mail. Hope they will get a good road. Had bough awning put at front of our tents, & am now enjoying its shade. Every thing quiet & all of us taking a good rest - for though one does not feel it at the time, a weeks march well fits a man for rest. Made last night a tracing of Custer's map for Spaulding & have given him clear directions. I cant see how he can fail, unless the country is absolutely impracticable. Mr. Davenport hired a man to take in his despatches to the Herald. He was to start yesterday morning, but alas, even the Herald sometimes fails. The man went prospecting & did not get back. So Old Joe the guide was subsidised to take in his telegrams ahead of time with the understanding however that they should not go before mine. Joe is to take in his & mine together.[101] Our new camp is as lovely an one as I have ever seen. Some rain in afternoon, & it tried to get up a thunderstorm but failed. Evening cold. Had a good nap in afternoon.

---

100. Below, pp. 102–7.
101. On June 24 the *New York Herald* reprinted (p. 7) a telegram from the correspondent of the *Chicago Inter-Ocean*, dated June 16 and announcing the gold discovery; a telegram from Jenney, dated June 17 and announcing his discovery of gold on Castle Creek; and a report of Dodge's telegram of June 17. The June 17 dispatch from the *Herald* correspondent was not published until July 1 (p. 4).

June 18, 1875. Camp Harney

Got to reading Mr Midshipman Easy[102] last night, became interested though I've read it a dozen times, & finished it before I put out my lights. Even then I could not sleep till about daylight. It has rained all day, a regular soft spring rain. The weather is somewhat too cold for comfort. Have had quite a levee today almost all being in to see me. Came near having a stampede this p.m. Jenney will not keep his stock tied up. He takes no sort of control over his understrappers. I ordered the Officer of the Day,[103] that when he found a horse loose, to have him taken up, find out who is responsible for his care, & tying up - investigate the facts and circumstances carefully & if the man is to blame to tie him up. Tried to write on my book today, but can't get started again. I think 50 or 100 pages will fix me out, & I must get at it.

June 19. Camp Harney

— Took a long ride this am with Old Bullock Hall & Foote to examine the country South West. It is more than beautiful. <The cou> It is very broken, & each stream appears to have thousands of tributary ravines, each of which is carpeted with splendid grass & looks like an eastern meadow, while the sides of the ravines and tops of all the divides is covered with thick pine. The scenery is charming & tho only wood meadow and rock go to make the variety, it is not monotonous. We travelled about 20 miles all told, a most excellent wagon road can be easily made - Pretty tired from my trip and went to bed early -

June 20. Camp Harney[104]

Lovely day. About 9.30 a party of us started on a sort of pic

---

102. The novel by Captain Frederick Marryat (1836).
103. The commanding officer of the cavalry company that served on that day as picket and camp guard. When the command was on the march, this unit served also as the pioneer company. Companies assumed these duties in regular rotation.
104. Dodge wrote "Camp Jenney."

nic to try to get to the top of Harney's Peak[105] Followed up a little brook for about 4 miles. At a distance Harney & the contiguous range appear to be very high mountains. The nearer you get the smaller they become Owing to the fact that these are more or less bare rounded blocks of granite the ascent is no childs play. We could tell nothing as to the best line of advance. After getting to the foot Hills everything was broken - huge masses of rock surrounded by pine, & on every spot where a little earth could be found the thicket of small pine became dense. Getting up as high as we could on horseback, we tried it on foot. I got high enough & quit. Foote & Davenport got some 300 feet higher to the top of the rocks which crowned our crag - to find themselves very nearly on a level with the highest of these mountains - There is not one of them 1000 feet above the valley say 6500 feet above tide but they are very difficult of ascent We all got home again by 1 p.m. after a pleasant ride & scramble - Took a good nap - Read Dickens - Chatted & gassed in evening - Went to bed 10 1/2 pm Country very pretty and wild from the numerous bare crags, & isolated rocks - More gold discoveries -

Monday, June 21

The longest day of the year & though a regular Sunday as all days are in this quiet wilderness, passed quickly & pleasantly. Did not go out. The day was warm & the air of that delicious softness, that soothes to lazy indifference <of> ^to all surroundings. Dr Lane came in early in afternoon. Capt Hawley with 2 Cos camped 18 miles from here last night, & will be in early tomorrow morning - Spaulding and Trout struck Camp Jenney on second day. Why they did not go to the Bridge on Beaver

---

105. According to Davenport, who published an account of the "pic nic" in the *New York Herald* for July 13, p. 4, the group included Dodge, Lieutenant Foote, Lieutenant Bourke, MacMillan, and Davenport, accompanied by seven orderlies.

"Saw teeth" of granite, near Harney Peak. (From Newton and Jenney, *Report*, opposite p. 70)

as I directed, I cant say.[106] My mail will not get to Ft Laramie as early as I wished - but it will make no difference for the letters. Read Dickens, & passed a pleasant day. Tried to write for my book but failed. My brain is too enervated for work. To bed at 11 pm -

Tuesday, June 22

Beautiful day. At 9 am I was much surprised to see Spaulding coming. Soon after Hawley arrived with the 2 Cos, 3d Cavy, which were put into camp. Burt with the big train with Trout and Kings Co of 3d are expected tomorw. Spaulding brought

---

106. In his written orders (BHE S.O. 7, June 16) Dodge had given Captain Spaulding and Lieutenant Trout the opportunity to select their own route to the Beaver Creek bridge. They had discovered a passage to Camp Jenney that afforded a steady, relatively easy grade, greatly reducing the difficulty of transporting supplies in wagons to Camp Harney.

a large mail, the first we have had since we left the Rawhide. It was very satisfactory to me. All my loved ones well - Not many letters but one from each point of interest. There are also a good many papers - I am very sorry to lose Bourke who will return by first train, to take a years leave of absence to try the Egyptian service.[107]

There was no official news of much importance, except that the Indian chiefs have returned from Washington dissatisfied & that we will probably have a considerable row this summer & fall.[108] It had just as well come now, & so far as I am concerned, it is the very best time. I have a good command, & unless Mr Lo is too smart for me & gets my stock, I am in a fine condition for whatever may transpire -

Jenney has been very ill-natured to Bourke and some of the other officers today, & accused Custer of having "salted" the gold diggings here.[109] The more I see of him, the more I am satisfied that his report, or the general purport of it, was decided upon

---

107. Bourke had received from Colonel William McE. Dye, of the army of Egypt, the offer of a position as major on the military staff of the Khedive. Dye, formerly a U.S. Army officer, had resigned his commission to join the Egyptian service. Bourke also received in this mail a note from his senior aide-de-camp, Captain Nickerson, advising his acceptance of the offer. Bourke determined to follow the advice and to return to headquarters at Omaha at once; eventually, though, he decided to remain with the U.S. Army (Bourke Diary, June 22, 1875, USMA).

108. The Indian delegation had arrived at Washington, D.C., on May 17 and, after airing many complaints and at last refusing to sign a treaty that had been prepared for their signatures, left the city on June 6. Secretary Edward P. Smith of the Office of Indian Affairs was able only to secure their promise to convene the Sioux bands and discuss the proposed pact. According to the *New York Herald*, informed persons in Washington from the frontier believed that "nothing can be done with the Sioux until they have had a sound thrashing" (June 4, p. 10), a remedy not easily administered. The same newspaper reported on June 24 that "prominent frontiersmen and army officers" predicted "great troubles" with the Sioux, Cheyennes, and Arrapahoes in the summer and fall (p. 7).

109. In a report of this date to the commissioner of Indian affairs, Jenney noted "considerable excitement among the soldiers and teamsters" at French Creek, but he characterized their reports of the richness of the gravel as "greatly exaggerated." He held to the view that extensive mining operations for gold were not warranted economically (Turchen and McLaird, *The Black Hills Expedition of 1875*, pp. 15–16).

before he ever came on the expedition. It seems almost impossible for a man to have anything whatever to do with the Interior Department without forfeiting his honor. Should he attempt to bolster up Winchel,[110] he will rue it the longest day of his life.

There are reports of Indians in the Hills. I must give special orders tomorw about the guards, & see that the Officer of the Day, attends closely to his work. Today, & yesterday we have been visited by flights of grasshoppers.[111] They are from the lower plains as they are full grown even to their wings - while those indigenous are not a fourth of full size, & have no wings yet. So far as I have seen this is the only drawback to the Hills. They have eaten everything at Camp Jenney, & the water there is so horribly alkaline as to make everybody sick. All are delighted to get away from that Camp. Have not been out of Camp today - Writing letters at night -

Wednesday, June 23

Foster[112] came in about 11 a.m. saying the train would be in. Not till dark however did the wagons make their appearance -[113] Wrote letters to Tooty, Father & Mother, Bird[,][114] Mix & Genl

---

110. A detailed account of N. H. Winchell's opinion that no gold was to be found in the Black Hills, and the consequences of his stating that opinion, is found in Jackson, *Custer's Gold*, pp. 108–9. Winchell's official summary of his findings is in Ludlow, *Report of a Reconnaissance*, pp. 1131–72.

111. The previous fall an infestation of grasshoppers had ravaged communities in Nebraska so severely that, by an act of Congress of February 10, 1875, the army was called upon to distribute food and supplies in relief.

112. Second Lieutenant James E. H. Foster was attached to Company I, Third Cavalry.

113. With the wagon train arrived the official photographer, A. Guerin of St. Louis, who had been detained by illness. See the *Chicago Inter-Ocean*, August 13, 1875, p. 1; *Chicago Tribune*, August 14, 1875, p. 2; and the congressional report, *Survey of the Black Hills*, p. 3. Guerin's photographs were later offered for sale by Robert Benecke of St. Louis.

114. Lieutenant Charles Bird, Twenty-third Infantry, was the regimental adjutant; he was stationed at Omaha Barracks.

Bradley. Issued camp orders for the care of the stock -[115] also orders relieving Bourke and Whitman and ordering them in.[116] I send escort of 2 N.C. Offs & 12 men, 1 wagon, 1 ambulance. This escort is to take the mail & also return with it -. Intended sending in 10 wagons but will wait till next week. Orders to Hall and his Compy to go on escort with Dr McGillicuddy. Burt & other officers owled me at night so that I did not get to bed until very late. Trout reports everything in and in good order ———

Thursday, June 24

Up pretty early. Settled accounts with Bourke. His mess bill was more, but I let him off with the $30 he advancd. Gave the final orders for the moves. At 1 pm Bourke bade us good by & started. He is an intelligent energetic ambitious officer & will make his mark in the world yet. - I am very sorry to lose him. Detailed Lieut Morton as Engineer Officer in place of Bourke & ordered him to go with Dr McGillicuddy on his topographical expedition tomorw. Had a long talk with Jenney. He wishes to remain here until about 15th July, then to push along the west slopes of the Hills to Bear Lodge Butte, thence around to the North and Eastward. He thinks he will not get through before the 15th October - Poor old man Tuttle is just getting over an attack of the *Jimjams* & is as invisible as Venus.[117] Jenney goes

---

115. In BHE G.O. 4, June 25, Dodge reminded his men "that the only danger to be apprehended is the loss of our animals, that for a stampede two or three Indians are as effective as a hundred and that our only security from loss is untiring watchfulness while the animals are out grazing. The nature of this country is such that Indians may creep upon the herd at any time. They may be expected at any and all times."

116. In BHE S.O. 8, June 23, Dodge directed Lieutenant Bourke to report to General Crook at Omaha and appointed Second Lieutenant Charles Morton to replace him as engineer officer. Lieutenant Royal E. Whitman, Company H, Third Cavalry, had been ordered to appear as a witness at a general court-martial to be convened at Fort D. A. Russell on July 17. Upon completion of that duty he was to rejoin the Black Hills Expedition.

117. A reference to the vain efforts by the astronomer to deduce the longitude of elevated points from occultations on certain heavenly bodies, which, when

off tomorw on a pack mule expedition to the North East. He is very decided in his opposition to gold for some reason or other - & I am very sure will not find a particle. Mr John Brown Jr,[118] son of he whose "body lies moulding" went off today - greatly to the disgust of Trout, who was bitterly opposed to his putting anything into the wagon. I had to "punch" Trout a little, as he was very unreasonable. My new guards are commencing well & if Mr. Indian gets any of my stock, I shall be greatly disappointed - not to say annoyed - I am doing all that can be done to keep it secure.

The wagons are being unloaded today - Have taken the Stockade as a store house & it makes a very good one - Ordered 3 wagons 2 packmules & 35 men with Dr McG. Coles asked leave to go along.[119] Wrote a little on my book.

Friday, June 25

After a great deal of "pottering round" Mr. J. got off about 1 pm on his journey with pack mules. He is very sneaking about this, & in fact about almost everything else, & wants to get off by himself, so that no one can know whether his report agrees with the facts One of his reasons for stopping back on Rapid Ck, as he told me himself, was that he wanted to work without a lot of soldiers watching every pan of dirt washed out. Dr McGillicuddy got off about 9 a.m. Hall & the Compy followed about 12 - with 3 wagons. Visited the stockade & examined the

---

the few opportunities for measurement occurred, were obscured by clouds. See Newton and Jenney, *Report*, p. 545.

118. Brown Jr., Jenney's general assistant, was one of the miners and laborers in the scientific party. T. C. MacMillan described him as "heavy-set... possessed of sterling physiognomy, has heavy hair, plentifully sprinkled with gray, and is altogether a Brown" (*Chicago Inter-Ocean*, May 29, 1875, p. 7). Brown Jr. was returning to his home.

119. Dodge had ordered a detachment of Company I, Second Cavalry, to accompany McGillycuddy; Second Lieutenant John H. Coale, whose name Dodge almost invariably misspelled (as Cole, Coles, Coales), was attached to Company C.

condition of store houses. Everything is very nice. Burt allowed the soldiers to ride in the wagons coming back, & several articles are missing. I told him his and Munson's Cos would have to pay for all shortages, & gave him a talking to for allowing the soldiers to ride, as it relieved the teamster from his responsibility for the contents of his wagon. The suttler complained that he also had been robbed, but as investigation showed that his employees were drunk I declined to do anything for his assistance.[120] The soldiers say his men gave them the liquor. The clouds looked very black in the afternoon, & there was every appearance of a real old fashioned thunder storm. It passed around however with but little rain - & no "Electric Phenomena". Have written some pages in my book today. It is terribly hard to get started again. Fortunately I have only to write description. The buffalo is my subject now, & anyone ought to make that interesting at least to sportsmen.[121]

Sent my rifle to blacksmith yesterday to get a new double trigger. He said I should have it today. Suppose he was too busy shoeing the horses & mules for the scouting parties.

Several offs to visit me in evening - Wrote afterwards To bed at 12 pm

Saturday, June 26

Fred made his first effort at shooting. He is naturally very timid - having been brought up entirely by women, & had as nervous a feeling about firing off a gun as I have about going into a dentist's chair. He fired eight shots at <a> pieces of paper - 5 with rest and 3 offhand - at about 30 yds - & rather to my astonishment

---

120. "Deacon" H. Willard, an employee of John S. Collins, ran the sutler's shop from a wagon that accompanied the Black Hills Expedition. According to Davenport, two former members of the recently expelled Gordon party were his assistants (*New York Herald*, July 8, p. 4). Dr. Lane reported in the *Chicago Tribune* that Willard was selling merchandise in exchange for gold at the rate of $18 per ounce (July 8, p. 2).

121. See *PNA*, pp. 140-59.

hit every time - He is delighted and talks about going out squirrel shooting If he manages to kill one or two squirrels within the next week he is henceforth a sportsman.

Rainy in afternoon. Went to bed, & slept through it Wrote a letter. Spent evening at Dr. Jaquette's story telling. To bed at 12. -

Sunday, June 27

Wessels & wagons got ready to start tomorw[122] Read our Mutual Friend all day to the exclusion of everything else. Wrote letters to Tooty and Father at night. Burt a very Singular animal - Asked me to detain the train till Tuesday, to enable him to get of[f] his infernal Newspaper letters -[123] Refused of course - Then he dammed up the creek in his pursuit of gold until our spring is overflowed - Ordered him to take his dam away

A lot of miners with 6 wagons arrived on the creek above us, today. Am going up to see them tomorw -

No Indians seen or heard of up to this time -

Fred killed his first birds today & is very proud in consequence. He is very eager I let him go alone, & he is very much elated -

Got chilled writing, & went to bed at 12 - after a good drink -

Monday, June 28

Wrote to Genls Crook & Bradley. Got mail off about 9 am Wessels started about 6. Had to go into Capt Burt this morning. He is so very anxious about his mining operations that he commenced them in Camp. Dammed up the creek so as to overflow our spring with backwater, & spoiled the water for drinking in the creek to all below him. As soon as I found it out I sent for

---

122. Captain Wessells with thirty privates and "a proper proportion of noncommissioned officers" was to escort the wagon train to Fort Laramie. On the return trip he was, if practicable, to bring with him the unused lumber that had been left at Camp Jenney (BHE S.O. 10, June 26).

123. Captain Burt's most recent dispatch, dated June 23, appeared in the *New York Tribune*, July 15, p. 7; the next one, dated June 30 at "Custer's Gulch" (i.e., Camp Harney) appeared in the July 12 issue, p. 7.

him & stopped his operations, much to his indignation & disgust - Wrote in my book more than on any day yet - Very warm - too warm for comfort or a good nap -

Dr. Lane commenced to mess with us at breakfast.

In afternoon went to look at Burt's gold mine - Am not surprised he was mad Had done a deal of work

Went visiting in evening & was up late ———124

[*The text that follows is written with the notebook reversed, beginning on the last leaf and ending on p. [69V] in the original pagination.*]

General Observations

The branch of the Beaver named Spauldings Creek is bordered above our permanent Camp (1<3>1)125 by high ranges of Hills - those on the west consisting apparently of one back bone with occasional outlying foothills. Those on the East consist of no less than six parallel ranges, rising one above the other until the final summit is about 2000 ft. The water from these elevations has cut narrow but very deep gorges through all these six ranges, winding and twisting most irregularly but finding its way at last to the main stream, through openings in width extremely disproportioned to their length & the depth & volume of water which must sometimes come from them. In front of these narrow doors the valley of the main creek is covered with debris of all kinds, drift wood & boulders of all sizes. In some cases the force of the water has been so great as to carry Boulders of 3 or 4 ft in diameter for nearly a mile out on the plain, while the sand and mud deposited by the abating current have built its bed many feet higher than the <adjoin> ⋀ underlying plain. In spite of these evidences of terrific torrents there is very little appearance of freshets

---

124. Pages [67], [68], and [69R] are blank.
125. Camp Jenney.

on the main stream The absence of drift wood can be accounted for by the fact that the valley is a favorite camping place of Indians & the driftwood might have been burned by them. But their presence would not account for the absence of drifts of small sticks grass &c lodged on the trees or against the bushes which border the stream. I suppose either that these freshets occurred ages ago, or that they are extremely rare The <se> foot hills are all underlaid by immense beds of gypsum & the water is consequently abominable. Coal, lignite was found on both banks of the Cheyenne in three beds - all thin however. Iron has been found in several places, near the Cheyenne & on Beaver near our first Camp on that stream. There is no appearance of mineral of any kind, so far, in the Black Hills proper. Mr Jenney states that we are Geologically going down & that the top of these hills is in the carboniferous. - The timber here is poor for purposes of lumber the pines rarely reaching a foot in diameter. The water is very fine - its temperature being 41.

— Written in Camp 13, June 11th a.m.

Copy - Letter Genl Crook

       Camp Harney on French Creek
          near Harneys Peak
            June 16th 1875

Dear General -

I am happy to inform you that we have arrived at this the 2d stopping point of the Exp[editio]n without loss or injury to man or animal. On June 4th I wrote to you by the train which returned to Ft Laramie for supplies. When that letter was written I expected to remain in Camp Jenney until the return of the train. The geology of that section was so simple however, that on the 8th Prof J. expressed a desire to move into the Hills. Most of my wagons had been sent to Ft Laramie so that I could not move my whole Comd. On 9th taking 2 Cos 2d Cavy & one of 3rd, I moved north up Spauldings Ck - a branch of Beaver, leaving Capt Hawley with 3 Cos 3d Cavy at Camp Jenney to take care of the stores. His position is a strong one. He has two unassailable redoubts, a howitzer & gatling gun. On 10th we turned the head of this stream (Spauldings Ck) and enterd the Blk Hills proper, on the divide between Spauldings and Red Water Ck, attaining a max. elevation of 7850 feet above tide water. I kept nearly east and about 11 am struck Custer's trail which I have followed since except occasional deviations The distance from Camp Jenney is 68 miles - Arrived at Miners Stockade or Harney City on the 14 after a most delightful march through one of the most beautiful countries I have ever seen. I left Prof J. & Capt Wessels Compy on a branch of the Rapid working up the geology of that section. They came up <on 16th> today - I am short of rations & transportation. Capt Spauldings Co and Lt Trout will return on tomorw for the supply train which they will meet at Camp Jenney

The Black Hills are of singular formation - a section of country forty miles wide from East to West and possibly a hundred from North to South. The western portion is a huge horizontal upheaval of formations above the primary the strata being nearly horizontal, the nearly level summit of this mass being about 8000 feet above sea level. From a mere divide to the northward (where we came in) this mass widens towards the south to 15 or 20 miles. The western face of this grand upheaval has been cut by water into parallel ranges, each to the east <being> rising above those to the west, until the final summit is reached after passing five apparently distinct mountain ranges.

The waters from the main summit joined by the waters which take their rise in or between these ranges have cut immense gorges from one to two thousand feet deep, through all the ranges, and finally debouch as tributaries to Spauldings Creek. The Eastern face of this immense plateau falls away with more or less precipitous plunges. In it rise all the streams which are tributary to the South Cheyenne from the Blk Hills - French Spring Rapid Box Elder &c - These cut their way through a country as broken as Arizona (though the summits are not so high, nor the gorges so deep) - On an average of 12 or 15 miles from the great back bone, granite begins to appear & as the streams approach the eastern Rim of the Hills, they force themselves through masses of primary rock in canons deep narrow & exceedingly tortuous. From the great western summit, the mountains on the east appear of great height. We have come down nearly 2500 feet to find ourselves at the foot of Harney's & other peaks, which we supposed towered above the clouds, & which turn out to be mere buttes of scarcely a thousand feet from the valleys. The tops of the Granite Mountains on the eastern edge of the Black Hills, are nearly 2000 feet below the secondary mesa of the western edge.

Almost at the moment of striking the granite, we commenced finding the gold, in most minute particles at first, but here on French Creek in abundance. Custer's report is borne out in every <respect> particular. Gold is everywhere on these eastern creeks if we are to believe the miners, & in profusion on this creek, for I have seen it panned out myself & enclose you the result of two pans which I had taken out especially to send to you.

I find that there are at least a hundred miners on these Hills & about 20 on this creek. I went into one of their camps on 14th & had a long talk with them. They say they can pan out four or five dollars per day to the hand, from top to bed rock. One party is building a sluice & they told me they would average from thirty to fifty dols per day to the hand "You cant throw a shovel full of dirt from grass to bedrock without being paid for it", said one of them to me. On the bed rock they have panned as high as 27 1/2 cts to the pan and claim that they average 5 cts all the time.

These men know that they have no business here & that they are violating the law, but they say that they will not go out unless forced out, & that if not put in prison they will return the moment they are released. I consider that the special orders to escort the Geological party, relieve me from the operation of the General orders to arrest miners. I have no force to spare for their pursuit, no guards to spare for their security after arrest - I cannot detach parties to <send> ∧conduct arrested <parties> ∧men to Ft Laramie, nor can I feed them here. In short I cannot arrest these men without imperilling the success of the expedition, & the safety of the Command, so I do not propose to arrest any one unless under special orders from yourself.

The country we are in is a perfectly magnificent one. The streams are pure & cold as ice, being from 39° to 42° by actual test. The soil of the valleys is a deep rich loam, capable of producing anything. The timber is excellent - grass most rich and luxuriant. There is only the possible drawback that the season is too short, to prevent this from being a splendid agricultural country. As it is now, it would furnish cattle butter & cheeze for a nation. Add to all these the undoubtedly very great mineral wealth, & the value of the country can be estimated The absurdity of turning over such a country to miserable nomads is too manifest for discussion - Besides the Indians dont want it. They never use it. There is not a trail of Indians in the whole interior of the Black Hills, except in the vicinity of the head of Spauldings Creek, where a few come in apparently for a week or two each fall to pick berries, and cut spruce lodge poles. This portion of the country has not an Indian trail, and Custer was never more right than when he said they held on to it from a dog-in-the-manger spirit.[126] My own opinion is that they do not hold on to it of their own accord (except from the natural <d> indisposition to give up any portion of what they consider their territory) but they are put up to this opposition by interested agents, who hope to have the manipulation of the millions of dollars which the Govt may pay for the land, if the Indians only make row enough.

All the power of the Administration cannot keep this country in possession of the Indians, and I confess my sympathies are all with the miner and settler.

126. See the interview with Custer in the *New York Herald*, May 22, 1875, p. 4.

The country is too glorious an one to be kept from development & while I will obey orders & arrest these men if necessary, I shall never injure one in person or property - None but a ring ridden nation would ever think for one moment of leaving such a paradise in the hands of miserable savages even did they use it, which is not the case ——

Our recent discoveries have I think set a limit to our stay in these Hills. The Geology is too simple for any extended labor (the west being a huge secondary mesa and the east primary rocks undoubtedly full of gold.) & Prof. Jenney can have no reason for any extended stay in one spot. I shall have to remain here until about the 1st July, to await the arrival of my supplies. After that I think a tour around the northern portion of the Hills will be all that is necessary. We ought to be through by Sepr 1 - unless the Prof has some private reason for staying out later

Something has been said of putting a Military Post in these Hills. There is no need of any post towards the south, for as I have said <the> Indians apparently never come here.

Between the steep ravines, which the streams have cut in the great west mesa, and the canons by which they force their way through the eastern granite rim, is a beautiful broken country, full of parks - This is very narrow, averaging but two or three miles, & extends apparently nearly the whole length of the hills. A post on this belt, would thoroughly block any North and South travel of large parties & if located not far from the point where I came in, say on the head of Rapid Ck, would as effectually block any east & west travel. I think the whole problem very simple & a 3 or 4 Co post, would be as effective as 40 Comps I hope you will come in & look for yourself.

It is early spring here yet. The smaller birds are beginning to hatch, but I saw on the top of the Mesa a fine pack of Spike Grouse not yet paired. The Elk and Blk tails have not come up yet. Not one has been seen since we came into the Hills. The valleys are full of White tails however & we have had no lack of venison. One night we had 15 in camp killed that day. I have not seen a mountain grouse. One of the men shot a Ruff grouse the New York partridge. Bourke is doing admirably working like a beaver & I am sure will have a fine map. This camp is not over 80 miles from Camp Sheridan - Red Cloud -[127] and there is a direct trail. If you want to join us, that is the best way. We shall probably leave here by or before 10th July - working to the North and East. Trout is invaluable - The Command is generally very efficient, & I am well satisfied with it ——

RID.

June 22, 1875

The mail brings us information that the Indian Chiefs have returned from Washington badly snubbed, & in an ill humor, which means war, & the death of many good men. From the newspaper reports of the conferences, there is no doubt that this end is intended - The long peace has given too much facility for the examination into Indian affairs by outsiders - Professor March's reports, & the affidavits of Genl Bradley, Mix & other Army officers have caused more or less inquiry into the conduct of affairs & this must be stopped.[128] Mr Commissioner Smith, has been very determined with the chiefs. He must hold his

---

127. The Red Cloud Agency was adjacent to Camp Robinson, not Camp Sheridan.

128. Othniel C. Marsh, professor of paleontology at Yale College, during a fossil-collecting expedition in 1874 in the vicinity of Red Cloud Agency, grew convinced that the administration of Indian affairs there was marred by frauds and abuses. He undertook to collect the evidence necessary to place these matters in their true light, and in 1875 he issued several strongly worded reports accusing the Office of Indian Affairs and the "Indian Ring" that allegedly profited from its corruption. Lieutenant Colonel Bradley, Captain Mix, and other army officers supplied statements to support some of Marsh's claims. The campaign by the scientist culminated in a letter of July 10 to President Grant summarizing his charges; see the *Chicago Inter-Ocean*, July 14, 1875, p. 1. The result of all this agitation was an inquiry conducted first in New York and later, during August, at Red Cloud and Spotted Tail Agencies. Only a few of Marsh's sweeping charges were sustained, but the publicity and investigation they stimulated did result in the resignation of J. J. Saville, the Indian agent at Red Cloud Agency.

place, which he earned by selling Indian pine lands, & putting the proceeds in his pocket - The Indians begin to know too much. They must be incited to a war, & a new deal made all round. The President therefore snubs them. They are offered 25,000 for a territory worth as many millions -[129] If it is theirs the offer is an insult If it is ours, it is a steal. Whatever it be, it is intended to force the Indians to war. The Indian Ring is in danger. Nothing but a war can save it, & a war we will have. Their ill-gotten gains have been cemented in the blood of many a good man before now, & many another good man will go down before their rapacity Blood is nothing to them, so it is the blood of other men, & so long as they can sit in the seat of power, & pocket the money that ought to go to the Indian. <t>They care not a fig for war & rapine - for ravished women & depopulated settlements. They go to church regularly, are immaculate in dress, & conversation, & with the mass are "honorable men" -[130] That such a country should be ruled by such men, is enough to shake our faith in republican institutions, in human nature, & almost in God himself -

Item for my Book -
Conclusion on Indians[131]

Again, a long interval of peace has given the Indians knowledge of what they ought to have. They begin to complain that they are cheated & starved. The piping times of peace are not favorable to the giant steals of the Indian Ring. There are too many intermeddling outsiders, too many officious & evil-disposed

---

129. The proposed treaty presented to the Indian delegation at Washington, D.C., named "the sum of $25,000 which has been appropriated by Congress for the purchase of presents" in return for their surrendering various privileges of hunting and occupation guaranteed them by the treaty of 1868 (*Chicago Inter-Ocean*, June 4, 1875, p. 1).

130. An allusion to *Julius Caesar* III.ii.88.

131. Although Dodge's work-in-progress did conclude with a spirited denunciation of the federal government's Indian policy and a series of recommendations for improving it, the passage that follows was not included in *PNA*.

army officers making affidavits of what they see, & otherwise unsettling the ordinarily quiet security of the Ring. This must be stopped. Somebody must be hurt. Some temper & a public opinion must be created against the horrible savage. So he is inveigled to Washington snubbed abused & insulted until it is highly probable he may be foolish enough to try the issue of arms - and with what result. Some few good fellows & valuable citizens "pass in their checks" Some homes are ruined - some women ravished - some babes brained against burning door posts - but the Indians are subdued & the Ring taking charge again commence anew the old System sure to be safe in their steals for some years to come -

---

Camp Jenney. June 8
Long. 104° 19' 30"
Lat. 43° 49' 40"
Variation above tide water

Camp Harney June 25, 1875
Long. 103° 44' 45"
Lat 43° 46' 20"-5
Variation 15° 40' 30" E above tide water 5620 ft.

Soil of valleys excellent - Plenty of rain - No wind No dust - Climate superb.

Develop the ideas -
Black Hills an oasis < in desert > - Approaches through alkaline deserts, sage brush - horrible water. Describe Hills - if possible - Grasshoppers.

July 1
　　Discoveries of gold still continue - It is everywhere in the creek bottom, but there is still the Doubt "Will it pay?"

No one will make fortunes in the gulch mines, unless very [much] better diggings are found than have been found so far - The quartz leads look very promising, but we have no means of testing their value -

―――――――――

This country <will be> ̭ⁱˢ a magnificent one for sheep.
It rains so frequently that irrigation would not be necessary. The climate is superb - a little cold

Journal Three:
June 29–July 20, 1875

3
June 29th, 1875
to
July 20, 1875[132]

Tuesday, June 29, 1875. Camp Harney[133]

Mail arrived about 11 1/2 a.m. - Corpl Irwin in charge apparently about half drunk No letters from any of the dear ones except Sis Molly,[134] who writes from Salem. Letter from Genl Bradley. Soon after the mail was opened, Davenport the Herald reporter came to me with two letters one from Ford, tel[egraph] op[erator]. at Ft Laramie[135] & one from Collins['] book keeper informing him that the tel. despatches sent in by D[avenport] had not been received - That something was wrong - and he asked me to

---

132. This manuscript journal consists of seventy-two pages. On the bottom side of its cardboard pad, Dodge has written in black ink "Black Hills [/] *1875*"; below it, in pencil, is an encircled "3." Except as noted, all entries are in pencil. The heading is written on p. [1R].

133. On p. [1V] is a listing of rainy days between June 29 and July 20, not reproduced here, and below it the phrase "at [*unrecovered*] all day." The entries begin on p. [2].

134. Mary Helen Dodge (b. 1835), Dodge's youngest sister, was unmarried. Dodge assumed the responsibility of providing for this "unfortunate" relative (Dodge to J. D. Glenn, Fort Sully, January 13, 1884, Graff Collection, Newberry Library). A nephew of Dodge's once referred to Sis Molly as "peculiar" and requiring circumspection in the assistance given her (R. B. Glenn to Dodge, Danbury, N. C., n.d., Graff Collection, Newberry Library).

135. John W. Ford, the telegraph operator, was a civilian employee of the Quartermaster Department at Fort Laramie.

investigate - It appears that though Davenport hired Joe Merivale to take his despatch in for him - offering $100 if 24 hours ahead of the mail - Spaulding preferred giving the chance of earning that money to Corpl Irwin - My mail and Davenports were given to Spaulding who left 17th (see diary of that date). At Camp Jenney Spaulding gave this special <ly> package mine & Davenort's mail, into the care of Corpl Irwin, with the promise of $100 if he delivered it 24 hours ahead. Trout corroborates all this. I then sent for Corpl Irwin and 5 men of the escort. Corpl I. <says> ∧ stated that he carried this special package in the bosom of his blouse until he was driven by fear of its getting wet, to open the bag & put it in with the regular mail. At Beaver he met Capt Burt, who asked to examine the mail. Corpl I. took it to him. Opened it & left it lying on the ground in possession of Capt B while he went to see about his horses. That when he came back, Capt B. had got through examining it. That the special package appeared not to have been touched, & that he did it & the other mail up together - That Capt B. asked him to remain to enable him to write a letter & that in compliance with this request, he stayed there 4 1/2 hours longer than he wished.[136] That when he arrived at the Niobrara he again opened the sack, or canvas in which was the mail & taking out the special package, started for Ft Laramie On his arrival there he went at once to Mr Collins['] bookkeeper who on opening the package told him that some important papers were missing - He declares that no one but him self & Capt Burt touched the mail from the time that Capt Spaulding put it in his hands until he gave it to the

---

136. The June 23, 1875, issue of the *New York Tribune* printed two brief articles, both under the heading "By telegraph" and sent from Fort Laramie on June 22. One, dated June 16 at Camp Harney, summarized events since June 8, including Jenney's explorations on Castle Creek and the main command's reaching Camp Harney. The other, dated "Camp near Harney's Peak" on June 20, described the mining activities in that vicinity. Captain Burt had been away from the main command since June 5 and so could not have written these dispatches from firsthand knowledge.

clerk. Three of the soldiers with Corpl I state that they were with him continually except when on guard, that no one touched the mail except him & Capt Burt. The other two did not see Capt B. open it, as they were on guard - I then sent for Capt Munsen. He was on guard & did not see Burt open the mail - No officer was present - Burt was next sent for. He acknowledged opening the mail - but denies having <touched> taken out anything except two letters of Dr Lane to the Chicago Tribune. At his request I sent for Davenport and Corpl Irwin. Davenport & he soon got into hot words - which however stopped very soon. (Corpl I. had been sent for again by me - to explain why he had the special package in his breast, as testified by Capt Munson & which he said was only a temporary arrangement for fear some one might get at it -) Burt examined him, but soon got into a snarl, the Corpl insisting that he left the mail with Burt, the latter denying that the Corpl went away while the mail was being opened -

Joe Merivale examined says he was present when the mail was opened. That it was untied by Corpl Irwin that Capt Burt run over the letters, took out two, which Joe heard were Dr Lane's - that Corpl Irwin then tied up the mail again, that Corpl I. did not leave while the mail was open, & that from the opening to the closing again was not over 3 or 4 minutes - Now who took the letters? Either Burt or Corpl Irwin.

Burt was, some 3 weeks ago, foolish enough to threaten in the presence of Bourke, to take Davenports letters out of the mail. He is a rival correspondent, & he had opportunity - Threat, motive & facts are against Burt - Per contra, his honor as an officer, & standing as a man - and the little likelihood of his selling himself so cheap -

Corporal Irwin is a drunkard not above a bribe - & someone may have induced him to fail to deliver the letters - Davenport offered $100 for the delivery - Neither Burt nor MacMillan have any money to spare to pay for non-delivery. It is all a snarl now, though the weight of evidence is against Burt - Yet I dont believe Burt did it - & I suspect, it may be ever so wrongfully, that MacMillan is at the bottom of the disappearance and that Corpl Irwin is the agent —— I can do nothing but wait - Burt appears to be greatly troubled, & if guilty, acts innocent remarkably well - Corporal Irwin looks guilty & acts the same - & is very impatient of cross questioning - The affair has created a great excitement in camp - Almost the whole day has been taken up in investigation. Wrote several pages in my book this morning before the mail came - To bed late -

Wednesday, June 30, 1875. Camp Harney

End of the fiscal year. Uncle Sam short of cash only partial payment to be made for June - When I woke up it was raining heavily. Has rained at intervals all day - & until after 2 Oclk quite hard. At 3 went to the Co[mpanie]s and mustered them without inspection. It was not raining, but looked very suspicious. Wrote a good deal today in my book, & will be able to finish the buffalo in another good days work. More miners reported arrived, making near 100 on this creek. I forgot to mention that Genl Bradley said in his letter recd yesterday, that 2 cos of cavy were to be sent up to clean out these miners. I shall be glad to have them cleaned, as they induce my men & the teamsters to steal provisions &c - to sell to them - & I am not convinced that some of them might [not] want some of my stock - I'd rather risk ten Indians than one white thief - No additional light on the lost mail matter. Burt seems quite downhearted & I've no doubt he is so - Must get out & take some exercise -

Thursday, July 1, 1875. Camp Harney

Ordered the horses for a ride but it looked so much like rain that I gave it up - Wrote for an hour or two, & then read the papers. Nothing of news. All quiet in the Black Hills. Wrote at night - To bed 12. pm

Friday, July 2

Burt & Dr. Lane went off today on a prospecting expedn. Went out for a ride with Spaulding, Foote, Bullock & Fred. Had a delightful day. Got the joke on Spaulding, who got lost - rather turned round. Rode through very interesting country. Found a quartz lead which looks more like gold, than anything I have seen. Dr. McGillicuddy & party returned in evening They have had a good trip - Heavy rain with hail at night - Wrote letters to Genl Bradley and Genl Crook, dated tomorw - Old Joe Merivale asked permission to go to Red Cloud Agency - Gave it and will send a mail by him - Told Genl B. about the Burt trouble and asked his assistance —— If the abstracted letters have been found at Ft Laramie, it will show that Burt had nothing to do with the abstraction -[137] I think the Inter Ocean man, MacMillan, and Corpl Irwin are the people to blame. Went to bed 1 a.m. -

Saturday, July 3, 1875

Old Joe came at 9 am, & said he would like to start at once. Told him he might at 12. m. Finished letters to Genls Crook & Bradley. Wrote to Father, Tooty, Bourke and Comdg. Off Camp Robinson[138] Signed Muster Rolls and Post Returns. Wrote several pages in my book, & finished up the Buffalo, except statistics of the hide and meat business -

As if in response to my suspicion of last night the Inter Ocean [man] came over this evening, to see me about the loss of Davenports mail - He disclaims all knowledge, & says that had he bought Corpl Irwin, he would readily acknowledge it, now that[139] the fair fame of an officer is involved. H<is>e is a very nice gentlemanly fellow, & I believe he is telling the truth. Munson tells me this p.m. that he heard Corpl Irwin tell Spaulding that the two letters missing, were found by him in the regular mail, the day after the fuss, & that he (Corpl I) delivered them to the proper parties. If this is true, it entirely relieves Burt of all suspicion in, or connection with the affair & shows that Corpl

---

137. Captain Burt had left Fort Laramie on June 13. He could not have hidden the missing letters there, since at that time they had not yet been written.
138. This was Captain William H. Jordan, Ninth Infantry.
139. Dodge mistakenly wrote "than."

Irwin was either bought by some one to take these letters from the special package & put them in the general mail, or he did it of his own accord, in his maudlin drunken usual condition. My plan of keeping quiet will I sincerely hope develop the true facts, & I can congratulate Burt, on the present favorable aspect of his case. Had one or two interesting talks with Dr. McG. on the subject of mapping this country - He has ten times the sense that Jenney has. He says that Morton will do very well. All the youngsters have been to see me today. Morton has not got his notes worked up. Dr. Jaquette brought in the first strawberries of the season today. Went down to see the mining operations of the men - some of them seem to be doing very well. Visited the store rooms. Trout has all in excellent condition. Hall came to tell me about the impudence of the Trader and wanted to tie him up. After hearing his ∧H.'s story, I told Hall that he was all wrong, that he must give up the stove the cause of quarrel, and must not permit any camp follower. I alone do that. He went off disgusted, but I think convinced - Read some of my Book to McMillan & Munson. Both Complimentary Got $50 from Trout today. He would not take a check for it. James wanted to have a settlement. I think he has mining on the brain, & after getting his money will leave. I rather hope so. He is of little account - certainly not worth $20 per month - Ordered Company Inspections tomorw a.m. Joe left with mail at 12.30 -[140] Has been a cool and pleasant day. Ther in a.m. about 10 - 63°. To bed 12 p.m. Nap in afternoon ——

    A miner came in today with about $10. in very nice looking gold. Have arranged to buy $20 worth from him through Munson.

    Paid Fred his allowance for July - Have not yet been able to get my rifle fixed. Shall be dead broke, if it cant be done here - & must send it in to Ft Laramie - Many officers out today on hunts & riding parties -

140. Joe Merivale, bound for Camp Robinson and the Red Cloud Agency.

Sunday, July 4, 1875. Camp Harney, D.T.

Raining when I woke up. Had to countermand inspection. Orders issued for Capt Hawley & 45 enlisted men to start tomorw escort to Scientific's 4 wagons - Also to Foster to take 20 men & map the country far west on the Camp Jenney road - 1 wagon.[141] Rainy at intervals & very cold all day. Highest ther 52° - lowest between sun and sun day 40°.[142] No 4th July worth a cent. The scientists made a huge bonfire at night & the youngsters not to be outdone got permission to send up some rockets. When the third had gone off however, I found such decided symptoms of alarm among the stock, that I stopped it - MacMillan Inter Ocean man, came and begged my manuscript about Buffalo. He wants to put it in his paper as extracts from a forthcoming work by Col Dodge. I gave it to him - for I can take no harm from having a little eulogium & puffing in advance.[143]

If the buffalo part takes, I have every reason to congratulate myself, for I think it the least interesting part of my book. Wrote a little today - started on Wild Cattle -[144]

Spaulding says that Corpl Irwin told him that he himself found the Herald's missing letters in the regular mail at Fort Laramie, & took them to the bookkeeper at Collins - As soon as Burt comes in I will send for Corpl Irwin and finish the thing up -

If this cold rainy weather holds on much longer I will have to modify my opinion of the perfect climate. Though the rain is good for the grass. Made map of this camp and vicinity, which I think good. Got to bed 11 1/2 pm -

141. Captain Hawley, with Company A, Third Cavalry, was to accompany Dr. McGillycuddy, who was allotted two of the four wagons. Lieutenant J.E.H. Foster with his detachment of Company G, Third Cavalry, was to study the topography independent of the geological surveying party (BHE S.O. 11, July 4).

142. That is, the lowest temperature between sunset and sunrise (day) was 40°.

143. Dodge's discussion was published under the title "The Doomed Buffalo" in the *Chicago Inter-Ocean*, August 5, 1875, p. 2.

144. See *PNA*, pp. 160–64.

Monday, July 5, 1875

Capt Hawley got off with the Scientifics at about 9 a.m. Foster with his twenty men left by 8. All are comfortably off & I hope will have a good trip. They have 10 days rations - Spent the morning making a map of the vicinity of Camp Harney. I made one last night, but it had several serious errors, so I discarded it. I think I've got a nearly perfect one now. Wrote some in my book, & took a short nap. It was raining in the morning or I would have gone out riding. Cleared off before 12 & is pleasant day.

Tuesday, July 6, 1875

Cold last night - but slept well, by addition of overcoat to my bedding - Clear warm day. Started out at 10 a.m. with Fred, Foote Spaulding & old Bullock for an investigation of the canon of this Creek. Rode down it some 6 miles - Found the canon very deep and crooked - Had a long shot at a deer running. Evidently shot it through the ear. It went off shaking its head. Turned off the canon to the right, & came into a lovely park country - Followed it to the south east for some 4 miles - Had a 600 yds shot at a Black Tail Buck - Put my bullet between his legs, not hitting him - As we did not care to see the Cheyenne we turned back. The country is one of the most beautiful & picturesque in the Hills - so far as we have seen. Getting into the canon again on our way home, <we> I came on a White-Tail Doe, & shot her through but too far back - She did not run, but could do so, & I put three more bullets into her before she would lie down. Bagged & brought her in - My first deer on this trip - & my first white-tail in several years - all my hunting in the Dept of the Missouri being among Black Tails —— Vegetation on creek very eastern in character - wild cherries, hazelnuts, thorn apple & gooseberries growing together - We found also some magnificent ferns over two feet high - The timber is very fine in places - The pine, the largest of it, is a very light yellowish red, with a thin bark - not scaly, or in thick scales like that about in here — It may or not be the same tree - Had a splendid dinner

& being tired, lounged about read Great Expectations. Had my deer skinned & hung up. Trout set his saddler to work on a scabbard for my hunting knife & to fix my bullet pouch. No mail - & all rather disappointed - Read & lounged until 11, then went to bed - Has been a lovely day, and is a pleasant night, warm for the hills - I being now under only 2 blankets & a comforter.

Wednesday, July 7, 1875

Up on time - lovely a.m. - After breakfast cut up my deer - sent ham to Burt, another to Spaulding - Went out to practice with my rifle. Am *off* in shooting for want of practice. Trout fired the rifle several times - after he had the double trigger fixed - & thought it shot to the right. A fair trial however convinces me that the sights are exact for line shooting - All my shots were excellent line shots, but all but <one> ₍two₎ a little high. Would have taken game every time. Nap in afternoon Lovely day - warm & lazy. Went down to look at the miners. We have got a sluice box in, & started on making runs. We will now soon know exactly what is to be expected from Black Hills mining on French Creek. Two miners left yesterday for Ft Laramie - disgusted - They say they have prospected the Hills thoroughly, & are satisfied they wont pay. They tried to live as teamsters but failing, sold their blankets to the Herald man & "cut out" - Many a man will be disappointed like these, but no one will take warning or advice. Each must see for himself. *Sluice box* 3.25

Thursday, July 8, 1875

About 11 1/2 p.m. last night when I had finished my diary and had done a really good night's work of some 10 pages on my book, I heard far off a sound as of horses feet. I got up & stuck my head out, but could then hear nothing. When I laid down I heard it again. Finally after near 15 minutes it became so distinct that I got up, & this time on thrusting my head out I found several horsemen not far from my tent. I challenged & Jenney answered. He dismounted sent his escort to the Compy & I gave him a shake down on my floor. - It is singular & difficult to account for my hearing the horses steps so far off. The road is soft the thick turf scarcely beaten. They came at a walk, and yet I must have heard them fully a mile off, & my ears are none of the best. Jenney was very communicative and very much pleased with his success on his trip. He has found a better country & more gold, even than here. He says we are in the poorest part of the Hills, except in timber alone. We had a long talk this morning. He is learning rapidly. He said he was much pleased with the work of the soldiers here, & that if I would permit him, he would utilize their labor — I told him that I was not only willing, but that I had often wondered he had never thought of it before. That he had it in his power by showing interest & sympathy in the work of the men, to convert every soul <d> of this command into his active & valuable assistant. That he could only see with one pair of eyes, while they could see with 400 pairs & that the exertions of all properly directed, would teach him more of the country in a week, than he unassisted could find out in 3 months. He appeared much struck by this view & said he would do all he could hereafter to interest the men in his work.

After the mail comes, I am to send off a good party with him - Burt & Munson are wild to go. I copied my last nights work & finished the subject of wild cattle. Spent an hour in Burts tent this pm Saw Marcy's book for the first time, & discovered that he has got my Black Beaver story.[145] Must write to Potter[146] & see who it belongs to. If it is Potters story I will hold on to it, for I have got a better story than Marcy's.

 145. Randolph B. Marcy, inspector general of the U.S. Army, was the author of *Thirty Years of Army Life on the Border* (1866). In that work he recounted an anecdote of Black Beaver, a Delaware chief and trusted army guide, in which the Indian comically revealed his inability to credit claims that a "talking wire" (a telegraph) was in use by the army. For Marcy's version of this story, see *Thirty Years*, pp. 84–85; for Dodge's, see *PNA*, pp. 273–74.
 146. Colonel Joseph Haydn Potter, who commanded the Twenty-fourth Regiment of Infantry, was at this time stationed at Fort Brown, Texas.

Brought the book up, & read it at night - It is very interesting in its facts & knowledge, but dull in detail & manner of telling - The day has been pleasant, but a long one to me. I am getting tired of this camp. My watch broke down yesterday, & I am in a bad way. Jenney's party all came in this p.m. out of provisions & looking rather forlorn & hard worked - Had a pleasant party at my tent in evening - chatted & told stories - <Read Edinburg> Read Blackwood's Magazine all afternoon till dinner. Found it very stupid, or I am stupid. Too heavy for my digestion — To bed about 11 1/2 pm -

Sluice box, faithfully worked by 5 men - only $1.10 don't pay -

Friday, July 9, 1875

Had old Joe up this a.m. (California Joe) & a long talk with him about getting wagons from here to Spring Ck and Rapid. He says it can be done, without much work, but seems to think it impossible to go up either Spring Rapid or Box Elder. I must go out & do some looking about for myself - Jenney is very anxious to move over to those creeks with troops. He needs the Infantry Cos to do the work, that his new fit of sensibleness enables him to see is to his advantage.

No mail - something must be wrong.[147] If not in tomorw will send out. Wrote some little but have been very good-for-nothing [-] lounged, read novels, wrote snatches now on description of Bk Hills now on something else. In short my mind was in a lazy or at least a fickle mood, & I accomplished nothing satisfactory.

It rained hard for two hours this morning, & I suppose that had something to do with it - for I am constitutionally opposed to work on a rainy day. I suppose this comes from being brought up with "*Niggers*"[148] Took a walk in afternoon, after dinner with

---

147. Captain Wessells with Company H, Third Cavalry, had been rationed through July 7, but he did not arrive at Fort Laramie until July 5. His command began the return march four days later.

148. Dodge was raised on a farm in rural Surrey County, North Carolina.

Trout & Fred - admired the cattle - sat with the Dr. for some time - Had short nap before dinner - I do wish the mail would come so I could decide on something - Jenney brought some very fine looking quartz from last trip - I learn that 26 miners go back tomorw - satisfied with the prospects - No work, no pay -

Saturday, July 10, 1875
Rained hard nearly all night. I was awake just often enough to hear <it> & enjoy it. The pattering of rain on tent or roof is to me the most delicious of lullabies — Tent is excellent. Does not leak at all - tho no fly is up -

Wrote well this morning on the book - getting off about 10 pages of Elk very comfortably.[149]

No mail. Recd. a pencil note from Lt Foster - out surveying. He reports Indian sign in plenty, & that the prarie has been fired all about the Cheyenne - There is also news or a report coming from the miners who came in yesterday or today, that the Cheyennes had stolen all the Stock at Ft Hartsuff on the Loup,[150] & that Genl Crook had ordered all the Cheyennes out of the Dept & ordered the troops to kill them wherever found. This letter & rumor coming on my lack of mail, set me up a little, & I ordered Capt Russell & Co. to start tomorw am to unravel the difficulties, bring in my mail party or at least see what the trouble is. - He takes 60 men and 3 wagons 10 days' rations, & 10 forage at 3 pounds per day per animal.

16 miners with two wagons came in today - 26 miners said to have left disgusted - Has been a pleasant day - Jenney & quite a party around my camp fire tonight -

---

149. See *PNA*, pp. 165–76.
150. Established in September 1874, this post was approximately ninety miles north of Grand Island, Nebraska. Its strategic purposes were to intercept bands of Sioux Indians that were raiding settlers in the Loup valley and on Cedar River, and also to protect Pawnee Indians who lived on their reservations in that vicinity.

Sunday, July 11

Jenney very uneasy at losing time - so to comfort him I ordered the two Infy Cos and 6 Caval[r]y to start with him tomorrow morning -

Went out myself in the morning with Foote & Fred & old Bratton the packer to look out a road for them. Went about 10 miles & found an excellent route that far. They go on to Spring Creek to a point about 25 miles from here. Jenney intends to put in sluice boxes & test those diggins thoroughly[151] On my return issued the necessary orders, & got all ready for the start - Made up my mind to make one more effort to find Harneys Peak - So ordered an early breakfast tomorrow.

Spaulding set up with me at night - to the sma' hours

Monday, July 12

Burt and Comd got off about 7.30. Soon after started with Trout Fred Foote ∧ & Old Bratton for Harney's Peak. I had seen what everybody said was the peak & taken careful bearings so was sure of no failure.

Travelled nicely to the first range, & crossed it with some difficulty, which was rewarded by the sight of the noble peaks, which we believed to be Harney, directly in our front - After immense difficulty & fatigue, succeeded in gaining the base of the perpendicular rock of the most southern of the Peaks. Trout rushed up on foot, but I preferred trying the other which appeared higher, & up which I could ride - At last I reached the top, to find myself at least 100 feet higher than Trouts peak. Although it was cloudy - indeed raining a little the view was most superb. I got out my compass, & commenced to get bearings,

---

151. According to the *Chicago Tribune* (August 10, 1875, p. 2), with the assistance of the infantry companies Jenney dug a ditch on Spring Creek 900 feet long, carrying 800 miner's inches of water through a sluice 65 feet long. The sluice was capable of washing all the dirt that twenty or thirty men could shovel into it.

<the> when happening to look behind me to the North West, I was disgusted to find a peak yet higher, & which from its marks was undoubtedly the true *Harney*.

It was not more than 3 miles off, but was separated by profound canons. I made a strenuous effort to get on to it, but the ground was so difficult, & the ravines so deep & steep, that I was forced to give it up, for fear we would not get back to camp before night -

Harney's Peak is undoubtedly the highest point on the eastern edge of the Black Hills - but it is so very singularly situated that it cannot be seen from the South or West - We started to return 1.30. It rained in showers every little while - & we had to go through dense thickets which ducked us in spite of our gum coats - The route was so very bad coming down that we had to walk nearly all the way - & also in the gorges, the bushes were so thick that riding was out of the question. I was pretty nearly broke down, not tired, but from lack of wind - We reached Camp 4.30, after a most fatiguing trying but very satisfactory day. Considering everything - I now know where Harney's Peak is & can go to it if I wish - but I don't think I will wish — Just as I started out this a.m. I recd a note from *Burt* saying that the notorious Carpenter[152] had arrived bringing intelligence that Genl Crook & the Paymaster would be here today.[153] Didn't believe him & went on. On my return I got a letter from Russell detailing Carpenters news - but found no Genl Crook - I expect they will be here tomorw - Delany's[154] pony was stolen two nights ago

---

152. "Captain Carpenter" had organized, chiefly in St. Louis, an expedition of miners to the Black Hills, announcing rather blusteringly his determination to arrive there despite whatever interference the army might give. In an interview with the *St. Louis Daily Globe*, concerning Carpenter, General Sherman had assured the reporter that "enough forces will be sent there to cappture every enthusiastic and adventurous miner caught loitering in the vicinity" (*ANJ*, May 1, 1875, p. 596).

153. In fact, Crook and Stanton did not reach Fort Laramie until July 20; they left there the next day, bound for the Black Hills Expedition.

154. Second Lieutenant Hayden De Lany was attached to Company C, Ninth Infantry.

Granite forms near Harney Peak. (From Newton and Jenney, *Report*, opposite p. 72)

& today was found in a miners camp. I ought to go for them someway, & think I will — Dr. Jaquett went with Burt at his own request. After dinner had a nap, & at night copied up my work of 9th. Kept me up till late. Carpenter brought 44 men with him, & says that there are thousands of miners on the road here - Old man Bratton a very intelligent man - Has been a miner all his life - Several times worth $100,000 - now my packer - True American - & true miners fortune -

Tuesday, July 13, 1875

Woke up rather late somewhat stiff after yesterdays jaunt. Mapped out the discoveries of yesterday. Took all the morning, as my previous map was incorrect. I should have said I was waked up very early by a noise in my tent, & opening my eyes found a young snow bird had got in, & was amusing himself eating the flies which congregate near the ridge pole - Had no objection to that, but he was so familiar, lighting on the bed, & so noisy, that I could not get to sleep. So got up & let him out. It was just after sunrise & a bright beautiful a.m. When I woke up the second time it was raining, & that was kept up all morning.

Burt sent in an Orderly with some letters, & a report of the Lightnings ^(yesterday) striking his son, two men & a horse,[155] all of whom had taken refuge under a pine tree, to escape a heavy storm of rain & hail - The horse was killed. Burts son & one of the men, Welch - were struck in the same way, on the cheek, the fluid passing down the body, & out at the sole of the foot, tearing a hole like a rifle bullet in the shoe. They were partially paralyzed afterwards, & each had a blister on the sole of the foot like a burn - but were this morning doing well. The other man escaped with only a knock down. It was a very narrow escape all round ———

The man Carpenter who arrived yesterday with his miners has filled the camp with all sorts of rumors about Genl Crooks coming, & the doings of the Indian Commission. It is not necessary to record them, as they are only rumors - Took a good nap in the afternoon. At night wrote for some hours, & pretty nearly finished up my Elk business - I shall have to modify my expressions about this climate - There is decidedly too much rain - Went to bed late -

While we were on the top of the Mountain yesterday we had a little rain, but not enough to prevent our admiring the appearance of the clouds & storms below us. We could see half a dozen storms going on at once in different sections & the rain, & lightning far below us. We heard but little thunder & no loud reports. I saw the storm cloud that burst over Burt, & knew it must be raining heavily, but <sa>heard no thunder. Burt says

---

155. Burt's eleven-year-old son was unconscious for more than an hour after being struck; one of his eyes was permanently paralyzed (Mattes, *Indians, Infants, and Infantry*, p. 202).

20 trees were struck in an area of 2 acres. I was 2000 feet above him, but not more than six miles away. Query - Does the sound of thunder only pass downwards, <or> and laterally? -

Wednesday, July 14

Quiet warm day - Wrote in the morning & finished up the elk - Was visited by a Capt of a mining party, who was drunk & terribly polite. He bored me for half an hour & left. Had a nap in afternoon. Visited Spaulding & other officers & gassed - Nothing new, & no rain today - Took walk with Fred after dinner.

Thursday, July 15, 1875

Pleasant day but somewhat cloudy in a.m. About 9 1/2 am mounted our horses - Fred Trout Foote and Dr. Lane & started up the creek. Visited the mining operations first. Harrison's party is doing well. - They have got in a good sluice box & are working hard - The clean up of yesterday's work was a little over thirty-one dollars. They are all sanguine. Went on to Trainor's claim. He has only a cradle, & 2 men besides himself, but thinks he has the best claim on the creek - The strippings are at least six feet, but his gravel averages 10 cents to pan. He has a ditch ready & says he will begin to sluice as soon as the others of his party return from prospecting. About one hundred men have left this creek in the last week, & have scattered over all the Hills looking for something better. Miners are coming in at a great rate, & there must be 5 or 600 in the Hills - No effort is made to stop them. We saw a great number of men - in different parties - but very few are doing any work - Continued up the Creek for about 9 miles from Camp, then struck north. Struck Custers road in about 2 miles at the big bend. Crossed it & continued N. E. until we also crossed Burts trail. I then turned sharp to the east, crossed the Creek, & struck into a canon by which I believed I could make a near cut to camp. Succeeded admirably, & found a good route. Corrected my map of that country.

Left Trouts' compass on top of divide, and had to go back for it. A red squirrel had the temerity to show himself & I shot his head off, tho' he was high up in a pine -

Overtook Trout and the Dr. who had gone on. Trout had shot the head off a spike grouse & killed a young chick - The Dr. had let his horse get away from him, & was footing it manfully, having sent the orderly after horse. When we arrived in camp found the orderly but no horse. Blew him up. Sent party with orderly as guide to look for horse, & they brought him in just at dark. We got back at 5. pm after a most delightful jaunt. Saw 4 deer - but got none -

Found Newton and McGillicuddy home. They have had a hard trip. The country passed over by them is very rough but they have many discoveries - a new creek with a fine cascade of 50 feet, the principal one - Morton is doing nicely, & is very much interested in his work. McG says he has a good map - They start again in a day or two to explore the Canon of French -

Sanders, a hunter & guide[156] came in from Ft Laramie today & says that Genl Crook is not coming - that the paymaster is in St Pauls, Min[157] attending a Court Martial & that Wessels only crossed the Platte on Friday -

A little rain at night

Friday, July 16, 1875

James waked me up this morning with the mail - & a very disappointing one. A very satisfactory letter from Father & Mother was really all. Nothing from Tooty either to myself or Fred - Nothing from Genl Crook & only a mere note from Genl Bradley - But he sent me a batch of papers, & I have been reading them all day - & tortured my eyes - Foster goes out tomorw with

---

156. James Sanders, an old plainsman, had accompanied the expedition in its early stages.

157. Dodge first wrote "Wisconsin" and later "St Pauls Min" above it, neglecting to delete the first place name.

the Scientists to work up French Ck Canon. After that they return here & we will all leave soon for a camp on Spring Creek -

Foster brought me in a good map of his last scout. He does remarkably well for a beginner - & will make an excellent map maker if he sticks to it - Davenports letter in the Herald is very excellent - better than those of Burt a long way. He piles on the flattery to me pretty thickly, but takes his spite out at Jenney -[158] The latter brought it on himself by acting like an overgrown boy -

Beecher - Tilton a fizzle - & the American Rifle Shots beat the Irishmen -[159]

Miners coming in droves - They are evidently not to be interfered with. Rain all day, sometimes very hard. It is rather too moist for a fine climate. Chatted & read till late. Sent mail to Infy, & Jenney -

Saturday, July 17, 1875
Ther. 8 am 60° - 12 m. 67° - 12 p.m. 52°

Rain again & could not ride. Foster & McGillicuddy got off about 10 a.m. to explore French Ck Canon. Worked on map and

---

158. Dodge refers to Davenport's dispatches of June 2 and 4, published together in the *New York Herald*, June 20, 1875, p. 6. Under the subheading "COLONEL DODGE," Davenport wrote: "The government is fortunate in having selected for the command of this expedition an officer of the ripe experience and thorough knowledge of the Indians and their country possessed by Colonel Richard J. [sic] Dodge. A character combining enterprise, discretion, fearlessness, judgment, mildness, and tolerance, if it is not rare is certainly valuable. Without incurring needless risks, Colonel Dodge would shrink from no necessary responsibility which duty might impose, and the qualities required by the exigencies of a position such as he now occupies are as various as those which I have mentioned."

159. For the past six months the press had covered the trial in New York of Reverend Henry Ward Beecher, who had been accused by the journalist Theodore Tilton of adultery with his wife. The plaintiff demanded damages of $100,000. On July 2, the jury being unable to agree on a verdict, it was discharged and the case was dismissed (*New York Herald*, July 3, p. 2). An American rifle team had been lavishly entertained in late June while on a visit to Ireland before a target shooting match in Dublin against representatives of that country. The Irish had been beaten by the Americans while on a visit to the United States in 1874 (*Chicago Tribune*, July 7, 1875, p. 2).

have got an excellent one of the vicinity of this camp. Russell came in with Co about 10 a.m. Has had a very pleasant time. Davenport came in very early this a.m. and came over to see me after breakfast - I complimented him on his letter, deprecating the compliments to myself. Found an attack on me in Chicago Tribune - a first class D.F. or rather uses me as a means of attack on the Inter-Ocean.[160] Took it to McMillan & told him to go for that fellow - & gave him also an extract from my written report - Burt sent the mail orderlies back and they arrived at night. Jenney also sent a man in who reported 11 at night - with information that he had struck big gold, and a telegram to Interior Dept, reporting the find - & requesting me to send it to Ft Laramie as soon as possible -[161]

160. In its issue of July 7, p. 2, the *Chicago Tribune* had published an unsigned dispatch from Dr. Lane, dated June 24 at Camp Harney and describing progress in the mining district since the announcement of gold there a few days before. Lane observed that the miners' first feverish excitement had abated considerably and that many persons—both those already on the ground and those bent on coming—were bound to be disappointed. An editorial in the same issue (p. 4) chastened "certain newspapers [the *Inter-Ocean*] that give the most glowing accounts of the new Eldorado," exciting gullible readers to waste time and money in a vain search. Dodge was not mentioned by name. What he found insulting—by "D. F." he likely meant "defamation" or a variant—must have been the *Tribune's* slighting characterization of the expedition he headed and its implication that his June 17 report of gold had been exaggerated or untruthful.

On July 8 the *Chicago Tribune* published another dispatch, dated June 30 at Fort Laramie and signed by "H. S.," that implicated Dodge by name. In this article the officers of the Black Hills command were said to have discouraged soldiers from washing out gold "from the fear that it would make them discontented." According to "H. S.," an officer with Dodge had written to a comrade "that it would be of no use to state the truth concerning the gold in the Black Hills, as he would not be believed; that no man had attempted to prospect on the bank of the creek without finding more or less gold" (p. 2). On one day the *Chicago Tribune* had pooh-poohed the rumors of gold's abundance, and on the next it printed a dispatch that confirmed those same rumors. Whatever the newspaper's inconsistencies, Dodge had reason to consider himself slighted or defamed by both days' coverage.

161. The original text of Jenney's telegram, dated July 17 and sent from Fort Laramie on July 26, is printed in Turchen and McLaird, *The Black Hills Expedition of 1875*, p. 41. The message, frequently reprinted in newspapers, began: "I have discovered gold in paying quantities in Gravel Bars on both Spring

Lawson applied for leave of absence, will send him with a party.[162] Visited the lower camp after dinner. Miners coming in by scores. Have had to order them out of camp, & from the vicinity of camp - to preserve the grass and water -

Sunday, July 18, 1875
Ther 8 a.m. 58° 2 pm 72 - 12 p.m. 62

Gave all necessary orders for the movement[163] & for mail party. About 9 1/2 am started on an exploring expedition. Spaulding Old Bullock, Trout Fred & myself - went to explore the canon I found the day before yesterday

It was a splendid canon. The rocks on sides were not continuous but were all the more picturesque & they towered to the height of fully 1000 feet. After a rather hard pull through thickets & over rocks, we just got to the beginning of the end - when Spaulding backed out, & turned back - with Bullock. Trout had half a notion to do so too but was ashamed. I went on & in half a mile more was rewarded by coming on one of the finest views of the Hills. We were all at once between Harney & a companion of almost equal pretension, & being so near I could not resist, but went at the companion. Harney was too far. In less than an hour, we were seated (not very comfortably for <it was> the top was a bare crag, fitted only for an eagles nest) on the very summit. The views were superb. I unfortunately had left my glass at Camp, so had to depend entirely on the naked eye.

& Rapid Creeks." See the *Chicago Inter-Ocean*, July 30, 1875, p. 8; *ANJ*, July 31, 1875, pp. 807–8.

162. Lieutenant Joseph Lawson, of Company A, Third Cavalry, was detailed on July 18 to command a mail party to leave camp the next day for Fort Laramie. Dodge granted Lawson seven days' leave with permission to apply to departmental headquarters for an extension of twenty days (BHE S.O. 15).

163. Headquarters, with Companies C and I, Second Cavalry, was to leave camp on July 19; Companies A, H, I, and K, Third Cavalry, with other personnel detailed to maintain the artillery, were to remain at camp until further orders (BHE S.O. 15, July 18).

Made several sketches - which amount to very little - as I only sketch to my own understanding. I, however, got a good idea of the geography of that part of the Hills. We were 2 1/2 hours in returning, & the way for part of the distance was very rough - so we could not have made over 8 miles - As soon as I got back went to work on my map. Laid down a little while before dinner - after dinner worked again, & have got a nice map - Several miners called about their claims & camps - I wont let them work claims just above camp, because I want good water for my comd. I do not permit them to camp upon it, for I want the grass for my stock. Wrote long letter to Tooty just after dinner. Went visiting afterwards. Wessels & Co arrived today while I was gone. Also a new Lieut of K Company, whose name I have not yet been able to fix —[164] Wessels and he came up to see me after dark - Gassed & chatted a while, when they went off & I went to writing Wrote to Father & Mother to Mose[?] about our express package - Short note to General Crook - & one to Bradley. Told him the miners accuse him of speculating on the ferry. He will be hopping. Two full blood Indians near Camp today. They were sitting near a citizen who was paning gold. I went up and spoke to them. They were very civil, but I had no interpreter to talk to them. They are with some whites & halfbreeds & are just harmless enough to bear watching all the time - Ordered some miners away - They being too near. They are watching a claim & promised neither to pan nor graze stock, until I and the whole Comd left - so I gave them permission to remain. Tired & sleepy at night, but went to bed very late, as I had much to do - This diary being my last act before going to sleep ——

Monday, July 19, 1875. Camp 18
Ther 6.30. 57°, 10 p.m. 52.

Broke camp 8.45 with 2 Cos. & Hd Qr. Spaulding took comd & train, via road to Custer's Park, & thence north by Burts road

164. This was Lieutenant Oscar Elting, Company K, Third Cavalry.

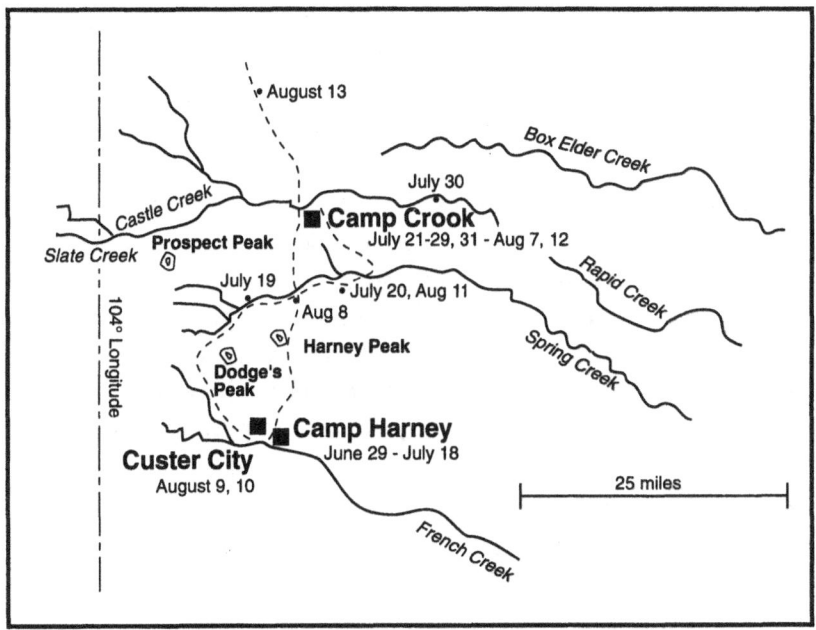

Itinerary, Camp Harney–Camp Crook, June 29–August 13

down a branch of Spring Ck. Foote Fred & I went over our trail of yesterday - over the mountain. I am not sorry I did so because, I got another idea of the mountain system - but it was hard work - The canons are immense - & the country as broken as any I have ever taken a horse over. After a deal of wandering over rocks and through brush, I got tired of the stream I was on, & struck across some low foot hills. After some time we came down to the Creek, & thence westward to find the road - Found it - sent an orderly to see where Spaulding was - & then turned north. Went about a mile and a half, & went into Camp, in a lovely valley.

There is something fascinating in the idea, that one steps where no foot of white man ever trod before. Yesterday I felt it on the peak of our discovery, which I shall name Fred's Peak, as he was first on top -

I was not so anxious to go up Harney's, which I could easily have done, for the reason that it had been ascended last year by Custer & party. Freds Peak is only second to Harney.

There is here in Spring Ck about three times the water there is in French at Camp Harney. Miners are everywhere. They seem to have sprung up as if from a seed sown by some Cadmus.[165] We have seen more than a dozen parties today - some going, some coming. In wagons, with packmules, & on foot - the country is filled with them. Camp Harney being in a sort of pocket, or out of the way, we were not aware of the stream that was pouring to our west. We are in it now, and it is a strong one -

Got along pretty well. Trout has had most trouble, as the Qr Mr always has if he is any account - One wagon overturned. The road is fair - Country lovely. Made 14 1/2 miles. Tried fishing, but I think there are no fish here. I did not see even a minnow. Saw no game at all. To bed at 10 ock p.m.

Tuesday, July 20, Camp 19
Ther - 6 - 60° - 3 pm 84° 3.30 62° 10 p.m. 58° ———

Broke Camp 6. am - started ahead of the comd & reached Burt's camp 8.30. Found all well. Spaulding and Cavy came in 9.20. The wagons did not get in until 1 pm Camped about 1/2 mile above Burt. Passed miners every half mile of the whole trip There must be an immense number in the Hills - but they are a lazy lot - Evidently the large mass of them are loafers at home - & came out here expecting to pick up gold without work - The usual picture is one man leisurely digging in a hole, while a dozen others are sitting around looking on, & commenting. After an hours march this am I found miners' camps, the occupants of which were yet buried in profound slumber. Eating, sleeping and loafing are the principle avocations & I am sure I today passed 50 idle miners to every one that was working.

165. In Greek legend, having slain a dragon that guarded a fountain in Boeotia, Cadmus sowed its teeth, whereupon armed men suddenly sprang up and surrounded him.

The general
There is not a sluice box on the creek. <A> ∧ miner registers a claim & sits down on it - until some man on a neighboring claim on the same bar shall have dug a hole, & panned out the dirt on bed rock. If not favorable the general miner pulls up stakes, & locates on some other bar, to wait for its development by same process. They are a lazy worthless set so far as my experience goes, & I have seen a very great many of them.

In coming into this creek we have entered a different country in many respects. The timber is not so good as on French - We have come down, I think somewhere near a thousand feet. The soil is equally good & the season is further advanced. The grass is heavier if any thing. The berries are ripe. The weather is much warmer the changes greater & more sudden. The nights are more damp. There was a very heavy dew this a.m. - It is a better agricultural country than French Ck & South - but not so fine a climate. This stream is at least four times as large as French & has much more fall, but the bottom is not so wide, & there is less arable land.

I took lunch with Munson who is a good fellow, & a Gentleman. When the wagons came in, I came over & selected camp. It is a very pretty & good one - as all our camps are in these Magnificent Hills, the very finest loveliest country I have ever campaigned in - We had fairly gotten into camp when there were premonitions of a storm. I laid down, read a bit & got to sleep, but was waked by the heat. Looked at the ther. & was astonished to find that it reached 84° A very short time after a thunder shower broke over us - & in 30 minutes the ther fell to 62 - 22° in half an hour ——

After a good dinner off a saddle of venison sent me by Burt, I had a fire built. California Joe came up soon after. He gave me very favorable accounts of our road tomorw - & wants to go with me. Told him if he would show me a good road, I would feed him -

Wrote a letter to Capt Hawley about Foster & his work. Soon after all the officers called & we spent a very pleasant evening.

The scenery along the road today was fine, especially some views of Harneys Peak and the neighboring mountains -

A good deal of game in camp tonight - both black & white tail deer

General course today a little east of North   Distance 10 miles - Had to cross stream a great many times   It canons several times & makes the road difficult   3 miles below this camp it canons again & is impassible for wagons -   We strike off here - a little east of North for Rapid -

Jenney stole a march on the officers in camp here, & did not tell them that he had asked for me to send in a mail -   He sent a man (soldier) out of Burts Camp to me, without asking B's permission - slipped him off in fact at night -   He is undoubtedly a low shabby fellow, with mean instincts -   Burt is mad as a hornet, & I would not be surprised if he gave Jenney a piece of his mind ——[166]

[The text that follows is written with the notebook reversed, beginning with the last sheet and ending with p. [68R] in the original pagination.]

Camp Harney
July 2, 75

Dear General -

After 3 weeks in the Blk Hills I am enabled to give you more satisfactory information in regard to their resources & value than I could in my previous letters -   Gold, is the most important question -   It is found everywhere in the granite region, so far as we have been able to investigate but not in such quantity as will warrant a rush of People   On all the streams tested, gold has been panned out in small quantities -   A sluice box run for about 4 hours today by 3 men, yielded $1.25 -   The earth was taken from the bank of the creek, without stripping from the top to

---

166. Page [59R], which follows, is blank.

3 or 4 feet down. My opinion is that no man will ever get rich from placer mining in the Blk Hills, but a considerable number of men may make fair wages.

The hills are full of rotten quartz veins, the rock looking very favorable We have so far been unable to assure ourselves whether or not it contains gold. One thing may be relied on[:] No such specimens as are reported to have been taken to Sioux City by miners from the Black Hills ever came from such ledges as we have found - No specimen found by us has shown any gold under the microscope but our specimens have generally been taken from the surface If many people rush in here there will be great misery & suffering. The placer mines will not pay a crowd - & the leads, even if they eventually pay, will require capital to develop. People who come here for gold will generally be disappointed

The country is one of the most beautiful I have ever seen. There is little variety in the scenery but wherever one looks the eye encounters charming bits of scenery, perfect pictures, similar it is true in general characteristics but constantly different in detail -

The climate as far as we have experienced is well nigh perfect. Some days have *felt* warm, but the thermometer has showed no higher than 78° since we got into the Hills - The evenings are somewhat damp & the nights sometimes rather cool for tent life - 3 or 4 blankets being decidedly comfortable We have had rains at least 3 times a week & 2 or 3 regular eastern rainy days when from morning to night it came down in a steady pour. You will see that there can be no necessity for irrigation The soil of the bottoms is a deep rich loam, as fine for agricultural purposes as any I have ever seen. The grass is magnificent, & set so deeply, & the roots so completely matted that our horses though tied to the same picket line for 20 days have not yet cut through the sod.

There is no dust, & we have not yet been troubled with any high winds - The grazing is splendid everywhere, even among the pines & to the tops of the hills - There is no finer country for stock raising in the world if we may judge by appearances -

Those who claim to know say that it is the finest sheep range they have ever seen & there are no burrs or briars to injure the wool. The water is unsurpassed, pure cold & abundant. The timber varies greatly. In some places it is very fine large straight stocks, free from knots & not windshaken In other places it is small knotty, & unfit for sawing - There *appears* to be much more good timber than there *is*, but there *is* an immense deal - I have found a few good hay bottoms where the grass is more than a foot high. These however are not frequent. Should a military post in the Hills be decided on, I recommend a large Mil Reservation both for lumber and hay -

The hills & valleys are covered with flowers. The number & variety of insects is wonderful yet there are in this vicinity scarcely any birds & no game at all - I took a ride today of at least 15 miles - saw one hawk, one robin, about a dozen sparrows, & 3 diminutive ground squirrels. Beautiful as it is, it is the deadest country I have ever seen.

The scientific party is very busy. Mr Jenney is out prospecting. Dr. McGillicuddy returned today from a seven days mapmaking trip - & starts again on 5th. They hope to be through here by 15 or 20, when we move to the north & west -

The Comd is in excellent health & fine condition. I have no trouble at all. Every one seem anxious to do his best when on duty, & the whole affair is so far a delightful pic nic (without the ladies)

A good many miners have come in recently. They think that an effort will be made to capture them & are scattered in the hills, where they will have to be taken like rabbits if taken out. We miss Bourke greatly. With kindest regards to Mrs C & all friends,

Most sincerely yours
RICHD I. DODGE
Lt Col 23 Infy
Comdg

Genl Geo Crook
    Comdg Dept
Not an Indian so far -

Two half breeds and an old Sioux named Robe-Raiser spent a week with California Joe on Rapid Creek, looking for gold. The old Indian told Joe that though fifty years old he had never been in the Black Hills before. He said that the Indians never come here, except occasionally to hunt, that when passing north or south in the fall the squaws come in for a few days to cut & trim lodge poles - During this time the "bucks" hunt. The reasons given for the Indians not coming here, are, 1 that there is nothing to come for, there being but little game; 3 that it rains very frequently & the Indians dont like rain - 4 That it thunders & lightens with terrible force, striking & overthrowing trees, & setting fire to the woods - The Indians don't like this - 2 That the flies are terribly bad, & torment their horses so they dare not turn them loose -[167] The old Indian said further that the Indians did not care at all for this country, & would have sold or given it to the whites long ago, if it had not been for the "squaw men" about the Reservation, urging them to make a big fuss & get a big price -

The Black Hills <were> undoubtedly ∧ once an Island, sur- (were)
rounded by deep water. In process of time the ∧ shores of this (water near)
Island were filled higher & higher by deposits torn from it, & other islands.[168] <While> The rains which fell upon this island, ∧ cut its surface into innumerable channels, apparently (before upheaval had)

---

167. Probably Dodge added the numerals 1-4 while revising the passage for inclusion in *The Black Hills*; see pp. 137-38 in that work.

168. At this point Dodge wrote an "X" in the left margin followed by the notation "next page." An "x" on that page, p. [63R] in the original sequence, appears before the passage "<While> . . . south," the latter portion of which is enclosed by a penciled line. The passage for interpolation is moved here to the point Dodge intended.

from <a general center to the outward>, about the center to the north & south. When these deposits had become many thousand feet thick they were by a great convulsion of nature, thrust up, the original Island probably going up with them, but not nearly to the height that the new elevation attained on the west -

The island now appeared as before in itself, but completely surrounded by an immense rim of secondary formation, the whole sloping from west to east. When the <old forma> general upheaval took place, the whole new formation, original island and surrounding rim, were tilted to the eastward. The rains which continued to fall had to cut new channels for themselves. Starting near the tops of the great western rim or the water tore its way down through mesa, ∧ these channels <tore their way down> ∧ the comparatively soft face of the new upheaval carrying with it immense quantities of mud & debris. This caught in the old channels or in the widened valleys & canons ∧ of the original island gradually filled them up, until the west side of the Hills is what we find it, an immense secondary upheaval sloping eastward, & getting thinner and thinner until we finally come to the primary rock of the original island. During all this time these new formed streams were cutting for <t> themselves new channels to the eastward. <Sometimes they use for a few miles an old North or South Channel of the island streams. But constantly forced eastward by the declivity or inclination, they force themselves> Constantly forced eastward by the new inclination, the waters are <forced in a> compelled in almost every direction by opposing mts, now using for a few miles an old <north or south> channel of the Island streams, now cutting its way by a deep & narrow gorge through an opposing barrier of mountains. The streams finally reach the plain having cut their way through from 15 to 30 miles of hard granite, through channels so extremely crooked that I can account for the course by no other hypothesis than that given. Not a stream takes its rise in the western rim, but cuts its way through the eastern mountains by canons from 500 to 1000 feet deep, & so crooked that at some time of its course it travels to every point of the Compass.

I modify the foregoing, by now thinking that, the original Island, was very broken, but with a marked mountain chain on its eastern side within an average of 15 to <2>30 miles of the ocean. These had been cut by water, & the drainage was from the principle heights. The highest part of the Island was then about Harneys Peak, & the principle streams flowed westward. The upheaval turned the waters back on themselves. The streams which start south from the vicinity of Harney's Peak, soon turn to the eastward - While those that now flow eastward from the western rim are so crooked, that they must in cutting a new way for themselves have used all the lateral channels into which their waters might have penetrated when dammed up -

See journal of 13 July for remarks on storms -

Govt in giving such small Salaries to Ind. Agents is actuated by same motives as U P R R, as told me by a prominent official. They give Conductors as small salary as possible - for as they steal all they possibly can anyhow, the less the salary the <y> less they cost

---

Game -
white tail deer - few

Spike grouse - very few
Squirrels - "few"

Birds - very few - large hawks Robins, blue birds,
Bee Martins woodpeckers - sap suckers, snowbirds, & sparrows -

---

Wood chucks - some
Ground squirrels - very small - plenty
Mice - abundant -

Insects - numerous -
  Flies of all sorts - bluebottle, small biting, & horse Flies [-] plenty.
  Butterflies moths not abundant -
              numerous
  Ants - <millions> ∧ - especially a red-bellied biting ant -

  Large wing cased bugs of nondescript character - of several varieties - abundant.

  Flowers - very plenty -
    Wild roses - all along creek
    - Tiger lillies - on side hills

  Many other varieties -
—— No snakes or toads - Some mosquitoes in day - but none at night -
No wolves - No skunks
Plenty of bull frogs in the streams - Only suckers & dace in Spring Ck as in French -

Rain in July—4, 5, 7, 10, 12, 13 16, 17, 20 -

  4, 7, 16-17, rainy days all day at intervals -

  The others showers more or less severe -

Journal Four:
July 21 – August 13, 1875

No 4[169]
21 1875[170]

Wednesday, July 21. Camp 20[171]
Ther. 6 am 57° - 3 p.m. 75° - 10 p.m. 60°

    Broke camp 6.20 a.m. California Joe on hand, but had no horse - nor did I have one to lend him - so he had to walk. The trail led in half a mile to a marsh, & I had to take to the hills - even so early - Went east for about 2 miles, & turned North up a nice canon which we followed for 2 miles more - Then up on to a divide. Joe wanted me to take a direction a little east of north but we were now in a fine park (which we call Foote's Park) & I could see the lay of the land. I turned well to the N West skirting the heads of deep arroyos on both sides - After some miles we struck a fine canon which led us directly down to Rapid Whole distance today 10 1/3 miles, and everything was in camp by 12 m. We have every reason to congratulate ourselves on our good fortune in finding so excellent a road - <It> & in

---

    169. This manuscript journal consists of seventy-four pages. On the bottom side of the cardboard pad, Dodge has written in black ink "Black Hills [/] *1875*"; below it, in pencil, is an encircled "4." Except as noted, all entries are in pencil. The text begins on p. [1R].
    170. The fragmentary text given here from p. [1R] is what appears on approximately the top quarter of the page, the rest having been torn away. On the reverse side of the leaf are a short calculation and the notation " <In> About 15 bagged his very first deer in Hills -." The entries begin on p. [2R].
    171. Dodge named this "Camp Crook."

so short a distance. Root, Jenneys H[ea]d Miner[172] told me yesterday that we could not get over to Rapid under 25 miles. I am on Rapid, in less than half the distance & with no trouble -

We have gone down considerably in altitude & must now be at least a thousand feet below Camp Harney. The grass is not so good being dryer - The season is here evidently much earlier and probably longer than in the French Ck Country -

We were followed over by a lot of miners, whom I suspect to be rather horse thieves than the O. M. - as Spaulding designates the honest miner - Very little mining work is being done here - the miners appearing to be the same lazy shiftless lot that we found on other creeks. There is no excuse for it here. The Rapid is the finest stream in the Hills from 20 to 30 feet wide - six or eight inches deep on the riffles - and running at tremendous speed. Mr. Jenney says the fall is about 90 feet to the mile. The timber is comparatively poor, & there are much wider areas of fire killed forest - indicating less rain here than in the southern higher portion of the hills - The vegetation is about the same, but there are more birds & less bugs. The common house martin is quite plentiful having nests in holes in the dead pine trees. Also there are plenty of the red-headed woodpecker, & I found a nest of the brown thrush - with three young   Hubert (our cook) killed a large rattlesnake, & Fred Spaulding & Bullock saw another very large one. So St Patrick did not visit this country as I was about to believe - The scenery today has been fine - but comparatively tame - We had one or two fine views of Harney's Peak. It is a glorious mountain from the North and East. From West and South it appears insignificant - We have a lovely camp near the Rapid. I found a good spring near us, so we are not using the Creek water, which tho' pur & sweet is warm. I bagged today

---

172. William H. Root, whose long experience as a miner included stints in California and Colorado. An interview with him eliciting his unenthusiastic assessment of the Black Hills as a mining country appeared in the *Chicago Inter-Ocean*, September 7, 1875, p. 3.

at a long shot - over 200 yards - a magnificent white tail Buck - The finest fattest deer I have seen this year. I cut him up this pm, & he is a glorious fellow - Eight deer killed today all white tails.

On arrival here & going along the creek to look for the best camp, I saw several suckers in a deep hole, & fired several rifle shots at them, getting two very fine ones - After the train was in I went fishing. Took about 20 fish, all dace but one fine sucker of near 2 pounds, which bit at a grasshopper & came to my basket - Sharp rain about 3 pm Took a good nap - Made some bait for suckers. Fixed my rifle, & was altogether very busy. Am delighted with my Camp & my day's work.

To bed about 11. pm.

Thursday, July 22, 1875. Camp 20
Ther 8 am 70° 5 pm 74° 12, 53°

Slept till 8. oclk. Went to see Trouts work on corral. Joe Merivale came in early and told us the Commissioners would soon be here -[173] They arrived about 11 a.m., with Egan's Compy as escort & Red Dog & a dozen other Indians en train to the Missouri agencies, to make treaty.[174] Dr. Hinman the man who has been lying so consumedly about the Black Hills seems to be the leader.[175] He is one of the Preacher Scoundrels who cloak their

---

173. Members of the commission to negotiate the purchase of the Black Hills by the United States had entered from Camp Robinson. Their errand was to locate representatives of Indian bands assigned to the several agencies, urging them to attend the conference being proposed for September. The members of the commission who arrived at Dodge's camp were Reverend Samuel D. Hinman, Abraham Comingo, and W. H. Ashby; persons who accompanied the official delegation included Dr. J. W. Daniels and John S. Collins.

174. According to the *Chicago Tribune*, August 10, p. 2, the deputation of Indians included Red Dog, No Flesh, Little Eagle, The-Man-Who-Kills-The-Hawk, and "eight other red devils with fantastic sounding names."

175. Reverend Hinman was in charge of preliminary arrangements for the grand council, which was intended at this time to be convened at Fort Sully, on the Missouri River; the meeting place was later moved to a site between Red Cloud and Spotted Tail Agencies.

stealings with their religion. I would not trust him an inch, just from his face, which is secret and crafty - never looks square. He has either lied most wofully, or been most wofully belied - Red Dog insisted on having a talk - I made all preparations and he began. "He was going with these good men to see the other Indians & try to induce them to sell the Black Hills to the whites He had been informed by the Great Father that the white men should be kept out of the country until it was properly purchased - yet he had seen that there were thousand[s] of white men in the Hills. He had been told that the soldiers would keep the miners out of the Hills, yet he saw the soldiers and the miners all together - & on good terms. - He demanded that I should at once remove all the miners from the Country, until such time as it was finally decided whether this is to be White or Indian Territory ———["]

I replied - ["]The white man's country surrounds the Blk Hills on every side but one. Heretofore the posts of the soldiers have been located solely with a view to the protection of the citizens. There are only a few posts & the troops at these cannot prevent the miners from coming in. They sneak in through the mountains or by the valleys - & the soldiers however they may work can only secure a portion of them. It is said that troops have within a few days been ordered from the posts to come into the Blk Hills, & take in all the miners that can be found. This is a matter for the chiefs above me - The U.S. wants to buy this country, but before doing so they want to see w<at>hat kind of a country it is & whether it will do for homes for white men. They therefore have selected some good men who are to make a careful examination of the whole country   I am sent with my command to see that these men are not injured or molested by bad people either white or Red men. I cannot arrest miners, for I have no troops to spare to hunt them up, no rations to feed them when captured, & no companies to send into the posts with the arrested miners - I have not therefore, nor do I intend to arrest or interfere with the miners. I am here for a particular purpose - & shall not do anything to interfere with it" -

There w<as>ere no violent manifestations of applause when I got through -

The party nooned with us, & Dr. Hinman & others took a toddy with me - About 1 pm all moved off & I hope got along well - Joe Merivale was wanted as guide to take them to the Missouri - so I directed Trout to discharge & let him go - James got more than unusually worthless today (which is saying a great deal) so I got mad & discharged him. Paid him to the end of his month - 6th August Trout goes tomorw morning with train to bring up Hawley & Comd - Took a soldier of Munson's Compy to wait on me.[176] Detailed a corpl & 6 men to go as escort to wagons - & detached another man from Munson's Compy on Hd Qr Guard. Rain in afternoon. Went fishing after shower. Bit well - got about 30 to my hook. Trout took 9 - I got 2 suckers on grasshoppers - Trout lost 2 - bad management - Does not understand the delicacies of fishing - Caught in a thunder storm. Took refuge in a miners tent. Burt got at me in evening about my Book. Read him some extracts - & he expressed himself as much pleased. Says he envies me not only the money, but the book itself - After that we got to gassing, & sitting alone - saw the sma' hours come in - I write this sometime towards morning, but as my watch has broke down, dont know the hour ——

Friday, July 23, 1875
Ther. 10 p.m. 62°

Neglected my ther[mometer] today - In fact could not make reliable readings as my tent had no shade & was intolerably hot. Got a bough awning over it by noon, & took a good nap.

176. In military parlance, "The C. O. of Company C, Ninth Infantry, will detail one private to report to Sergt. Molloy for duty with the permanent guard of these Headquarters" (BHE S.O. 17, July 23). The practice of assigning soldiers to act as paid personal servants to officers was often resorted to at remote army posts or on campaigns where civilian help was scarce. Although contrary to regulations, the policy was stoutly defended by representatives of the army. See, for example, the comments by Brigadier General R. B. Marcy in *Report of the Secretary of War* (1878), p. 58.

Wrote a good deal today on my book. Finished buffalo by adding some pages on the Bison or Mountain Buffalo.[177] Finished Elk by giving an additional story or two All together got in about ten pages today, which is good considering last night.

Trout got off 6 am with train for Hawley - Burt remained until about 9 am then cut out - After dinner went with Fred fishing. He had a rod, & after some preliminary pouting & disgust that everything did not go exactly as he wished, he settled into his business, & took a very handsome string of fish. One very fine sucker of at least 1 1/2 pounds - The suckers here are very curious They look exactly like eastern suckers, but are a delicious pan fish finely flavored & with very few bones for a *sucker* - They take grasshopper freely - even coming to the top of the water for one - It is the only place in my life where I have seen a sucker take anything but ground bait.

The Rapid is very pure & limpid, & flows over an even gravelly bed - or rather rocky bed. The suckers have no mud to dig into & have evidently got into the habit of living on bugs & grasshoppers - The difference of water & food makes it a different fish from its eastern brother. Returned after dark. Sat round the fire & had pleasant chat with Morton and Foote

Spaulding & all hands were out today hunting but got nothing - a couple of soldiers got a deer each. The beef came in today, about 12 m in good condition though one Compy complained of it - Made them take it - Kept the team here - To bed 11 pm

Saturday, July 24, 1875
Ther. 8 am 61° - 4 pm 66° — 11 pm 50°

---

177. See *PNA*, pp. 157–59. Dodge believed that a subspecies of the buffalo inhabited mountainous territories contiguous to the plains. He corresponded on this topic with Joel Asaph Allen of Harvard College, who had served as zoologist and botanist on the Yellowstone Expedition of 1873 and who published in 1877 a *History of the American Bison*. In a letter to Dodge of October 30, 1877, Allen expressed his view, later confirmed, that "the socalled 'Mountain Bisons'" were merely remnants of the great herds that had once roamed the plains (Graff Collection, Newberry Library).

Cool pleasant day with a little rain. About 9 am started with Fred & Foote to kill a deer. Went back on road towards Spring Ck. & turned up little stream on which I killed my fine buck coming over - Had gone but a little distance carefully hunting when I found myself within 100 yds of a fine buck which was feeding in the lap of a tree in such a way that I could only see the upper part of him - I fell off my horse took good aim & snapped - Tried again & snapped. The third time my gun went off & so did the deer apparently unharmed. I followed on his trail, about 400 yds & found him standing with his head down, & tail directly towards me. Again I fired at his latter end, & this time he went off with a leg broken. He took refuge in a little thicket, & on my approach attempted to get out on the other side, when I struck him in the top of the withers with another ball & dropped him. My first ball had gone straight through him too far back. My second went in within an inch of his anus & came out near the right shoulder. My third did not penetrate the cavity of the body but struck the back bone and turned out - knocking him however He was the mate to the one I shot on 21, hardly as fat but weighing as much & with a finer pair of antlers. They are however in velvet & can not be saved - Struck in on the creek above & tried fishing but without success Could see suckers, but they would not take the bait. Got in by 2 pm after a delightful ride tho' some of it was over pretty rough ground. The canons though impassible for wagons without a great deal of work, are so far better than those about Harney, as to be by comparison very good roads

Had a glorious nap, & most excellent dinner. Old Joe came to see me after dinner. He says todays buck will weigh 20 lbs more than the other. Spaulding got a fawn - Hall 2 deer, & the men 3, making in all <6>7 deer today. Gassed around the camp fire until after 10 pm - Have failed to write any today in book, though I have added something to my stock of knowledge. Quite cold tonight, but not damp. Talked map to Morton, & finally went to bed at 11 pm -

Sunday, July 25, 1875
Ther. <7>8.00, 55° 3 pm 68°, 9. pm 58

After Breakfast this am went to work on my book & stuck at it closely until near 3 pm Ordered the horses, & went fishing in evening. Went down creek, took 15 or 20 very good fish - 3 suckers of 1 to 1 1/2 pounds. Wrote in evening - finished 21 pages of Black tail today being about the best days work so far as quantity is concerned I have ever done.[178] I think too it is quite equal to my average -

Foote is to keep the thermometer hereafter. I shall make the Dr. keep it when he comes. Fred is disgusted with fishing caught but three minnows today, but had a bad rod and line. Broke my bedstead down going to bed - 1 pm

Shell drake & brood of young ones -[179]

Monday, July 26, 1875

Went out after breakfast for a fishing excursion with Fred. Went up the Creek for some distance but had ha[r]dly got to work before it came on to rain so hard as to spoil sport, so we came back. Took a nap & <read> wrote in afternoon. In evening Munson made his appearance with a Sergt of Mix's Compy, who brought me a note from Genl Crook.[180] <All> He & quite a party including the paymaster will be here in a day or two - There seems to be a revival of animosity to miners & the report now is that they will be taken out. It is a confound shame to the miner, & also to us, who should not be put to such dirty work. Ordered a sergt & 4 men to go & meet Genl. C. Hawley & the 4 Cos got in about 12 m - all in good condition. The mining prospects are better on Spring & French Cks. The cattle are all up - & we are intact except the Infantry & the

---

178. See *PNA*, pp. 177-85.
179. This line is written in the left margin, apparently as an addendum.
180. The message from Crook was dated July 22 at the Niobrara River (*New York Herald*, August 12, 1875, p. 6).

Scientific Party - Jenney is said to be growing crazy on the gold question - Wrote letter to Jenney -[181]

To bed quite late.

Tuesday, July 27, 1875

Up as usual, & went to work writing, & kept at it pretty much all day. Have finished Bl[ac]k T[ail]s - & made an alteration in the Buffalo, taking out the first two pages, & making them the basis of a general article on game - Ordered <old> ˄ California Joe to be hired from yesterday. Found nest of a curious woodpecker, which I am saving for Genl Crook. I finished my game article today at the expense of exercise. Have now 175 pages finished in the Hills - about a third of which <was> is the work of the last week I must go out tomorw either hunting or fishing - Spaulding and <Cowles> Coles went yesterday on a hunt to Box Elder - north. They returned this afternoon having bagged one Buck. They saw plenty of does which they would not shoot, & a grizzly which they could not get at -

No further news of Genl C. Munson went back to his camp. Sent a letter to Jenney by him. Had quite a meeting tonight. Every body congregated around the Dr.s camp fire & we gassed til 10 pm - Wrote some at night, did over 20 pages today - To bed at 11 pm

Wednesday, July 28, 1875

Got up at usual hour, & after Breakfast Fred & I went down the creek on a fishing excursion. We were very successful, Fred taking 43, & I 62 - 105 in all - two very nice suckers. Fred got hold of one but lost it to his huge disgust. It was very warm, & we returned earlier on account of the heat, to find Genl Crook in Camp. I found him on my bed taking it very comfortably Pollock is also here - (of 9th)[182]

181. This sentence is written in the right margin, apparently as an addendum.
182. Captain Edwin Pollock, who commanded Company E, Ninth Infantry, accompanied General Crook without his company.

The order to take out the miners is peremptory, & the Genl has ordered Pollock to establish a post at the stockade 2 Cos Cavy 1 of Infy - to work them up.[183] I am to give him the assistance of 2 Cos Cavy. The Genl proposes to issue a proclamation warning all the miners out of the Hills by a certain time, under penalty of being arrested & taken out -

The Genl seems well pleased with my Comd & complimented me on my letters to him. There is no eastern news. Tooty proposes to go East. The mail will arrive tomorrow with the paymaster -

In afternoon late, well after dinner, Dr. McGillicuddy & Foster came in. They have had a hard time, & lost 3 animals. About 11 p.m. I heard a clatter of hoofs & going out was met by Jenney's voice. He & Root came in after a 50 mile march, but what they marched for nobody can tell - I had quite a talk with him, & ventilated pretty freely my ideas about hurrying up. He agreed with me entirely and I hope we will now get along faster. The Genl wants to go on a hunt tomorw, taking all the Citizens, who are yet with the paymaster - I gave the necessary orders tonight.

There is to be no interference with my work in the Black Hills - & we are to remain as long as Jenney wants us -

Thursday, July 29, 1875

A very busy day. The whole camp was in a state of turmoil - everybody up. Burt & Munson came over with Paymaster Stanton, Mix on hand - pretty full of bad whiskey very early in the a.m. Pollock also & Jenney & Dr. McGillicuddy & Foster & Morton, all wanting something, & to be attended to before I left camp, which the Genl wished to do as early as possible - on a hunt -

In the first place, Genl Crook is ordered to take out the miners. He wants to do it without injury to them. He is about to establish

---

183. When established, the new post, Camp Collins, was garrisoned by Captain Pollock's company of infantry; Company E, Second Cavalry, under Captain Elijah R. Wells; and Company D, Third Cavalry, under Captain Guy V. Henry.

a post, 1 Co Infy, 2 Companies Cavy, at the Stockade Camp Harney, & on his asking Genl Bradley to recommen[d] a discreet officer to comd it, Pollock was selected. The Genl talked all this over with me last night. He has seen enough of Pollock on this trip to satisfy him that a mistake has been made in the selection P. is weak & vain, & very full of his own importance & as his duties are to be of a delicate nature, Genl C fears he has made a mistake in his man - Just after breakfast he brough[t] out to me pencil & paper, & asked me to write out a proclamation to the miners - Together we concocted a paper, & many copies were made which are to be sent out -[184] The miners are required to leave by 15 August - The Genl recommends a meeting at the Stockade on 10th of all the miners - to pass resolutions & make such arrangements as will best secure to <them> each his rights of discovery & occupancy - when the Hills shall be opened. The Genl, fearing Pollock, has asked me to be present at this meeting, & have a talk to the miners. I am to take such force as I deem necessary. I have agreed to be present, even though it interferes with my regular business - The Genl directs Pollock to obey my orders, & conduct the whole affair in accordance with my instructions -

This affair being off my hands, I gave orders for Jenney's outfit for a flyer into the North East of the Hills - a pack mule trip - Morton was fitted out the same way for the survey of the Rapid. McGillicuddy goes on a wagon trip up & down Spring. Foster goes with him.[185] Burt & Munson were sent off with a promise to get them off as soon as possible with Genl C. if I can. During all this work I was hurrying up the hunting party. There was

---

184. The text of Crook's proclamation, dated July 29, 1875, was published in the *Chicago Tribune*, August 14, p. 2. See also Parker, *Gold in the Black Hills*, pp. 207-8.

185. These arrangements were given official form in BHE S.O. 19, dated July 29. By that order Lieutenant Foster was placed on special duty as topographical surveying officer.

great trouble about messing the citizens -[186] but Stanton said he would arrange for them.

At 1 pm we got off - my mess arrangements - Trout and the Dr. turned out to browse until I get back. Genl & Cole with me on the trip.[187] Took Egans road & followed it to where he camped the 1st night from Crook in a regular pot,[188] from which he had returned 2 miles on his trail & taken another route - Followed on & just before night encamped on a small tributary of Box Elder. Nice camp as are all in the Black Hills. But the Citizens are hard up for eatables. <W> Our mess has plenty of everything. Mail today by paymaster. Three letters & a box of books from Tooty who is not at all well, & who had to leave on 13th. She has gone to Saratoga to Dr. Allen.[189] One letter from Father & Mother - one from Col Gantt -[190] one from Cath -[191] who is now well & happy - several others of lesser importance Tooty sent 2 pictures of herself to Fred and I each.

Several deer killed today - Genl got a doe - Had a good dinner by candlelight & went to bed late - Distance 10 miles.

Friday, July 30, 1875

All the party were up quite early & started off on their several lines of hunt, long before I was up. I had to look for another

---

186. Crook's party included as guests former major general William Sooy Smith, of Chicago, with his son; George Wilson, of Cheyenne; two men named Foster, from New York; a Mr. Campbell; and a Mr. O'Connor, from Washington, D.C.

187. During the hunting trip Lieutenant Coale, with one sergeant and eighteen men from Company I, Second Cavalry, served as escort to General Crook (BHE S.O. 19, July 29). The physician "turned out to browse" was Dr. Jaquette.

188. Apparently a topographical cul-de-sac.

189. Dr. R. L. Allen, a leading physician at this celebrated New York watering place, advocated frequent bathing in Saratoga's mineral springs and sleeping with windows left open. He also stressed the healthfulness of Saratoga during the winter months (Hugh Bradley, *Such Was Saratoga*, pp. 129, 348).

190. Dodge's old friend and hunting companion Thomas Tasker Gantt, who had served as judge-advocate in McClellan's Army of the Potomac, was at this time presiding justice of the Court of Appeals in St. Louis.

191. A cousin.

camp, & therefore could not hunt. Got my breakfast about 7 am & after commenced breaking camp. By a little after 9 we started down the creek. After scarcely two miles I discovered that the creek ran into a deep & difficult canon so I returned met the Comd & went into camp again scarcely more than a mile from my last nights camp - I then went out to kill a deer, but soon found that others were ahead on the direction I took. I saw only 3 deer all does. I shot & mortally wounded one but she got into a quaking asp thicket & escaped. I saw nothing else & returned to camp by 12 m, to find some of the hunters already returned laden with game Genl C. got 4 deer, Gen Smith 1 very fine elk, & 1 small deer. The others ranged from nothing to 3 deer each & one of the party got a splendid mountain sheep - with very fine horns — Our bag is 16 deer 1 sheep & 1 elk - very good I think so do all. I send most of it in tomorro a.m. by wagon. Stanton & Spaulding came in in afternoon bringing a wagon. Genl C. will remain 1 day more to give them a show. We all go out tomorrow Had a glorious day of it - Everyone in a high state of excitement except myself & Coles who didn't get anything Spaulding slept in Freds bed, He with me. Went to bed about 11 pm

Saturday, July 31, 1875

Up at daylight got Bkfast, & started with Fred & the 2 orderlies for the hunt. Had to go over the same ground worked over by the party yesterday, but by 12 m had succeeded in bagging (4) four fine deer, 3 bucks and 1 lovely little barren doe - Then retd to camp, & soon after Genl C. & Spaulding came in The Genl got nothing - Spaulding got one deer, as I told him by a scratch. Where[u]pon he challenged me to shoot at a mark. I regulated the distance 60 yds off hand, & I walloped him so bad that he had nothing to say.[192]

---

192. This trial of marksmanship, the first of several between various contestants, was summarized by Dr. Lane in the *Chicago Tribune*: "Capt. Spaulding is a very good shot, and he thought he would cool down his

The Genl is very anxious to stop a night at Burts camp to see the miners - & thought of starting tomorrow am, & pushing throug[h] to that camp in one day - As that would give us no chance to get our mail ready, I proposed we should come in this afternoon - He agreed at once. The orders were given to start at <5>4 p.m. I left a wagon, & a corpl & 4 men to wait for all those hunters who were then out. We started on time 4 pm, hunted, & took it quietly & were very happy till we got within about 4 miles of Crook - where there overtook us, about the most lively storm, a man would want to meet. The Genl was in his shirt sleeves, & in a moment "had a good <g> bath" as he expressed it. Stanton & Spaulding were also soundly ducked. The hail was quite large, the rain extra fast & incessant. My feet got a little wet, but Fred & I in our rubber coats defied the storm - The lightning was very vivid & near, & the people with the wagons behind said that a large tree was shivered after we passed & before they got to it - a close escape for somebody <Mr> General Smith was next to me in game today, bagging 3. I flatter myself I am a far better hunter than any of the party, & if I had hunted squarely yesterday I could have got many - The others of the party got 1 or 2 each - whole No[193] not known, as all are not in yet, but (13) thirteen had come in before I left making for the day and a half hunt, so far as heard from, 29 deer, 1 elk 1 sheep - This is extra good, & all are well satisfied - Mix was unusually mulish & perverse. He wanted to force the Genl by his trail on the return trip - which is most absurd.[194] He is getting almost unbearable & I lost my temper, which was foolish.

---

commanding officer a little; but after a good and fair trial, he now says that his own thermometrical conceit has fallen several degrees'' (August 21, 1875, p. 2).

193. Number.

194. By this time the route to Fort Laramie had been shortened from the circuitous one followed by Dodge and his command in May and June. Parties could now traverse the whole distance in six days. A cutoff at Beaver Creek permitted travelers from Fort Laramie to take a northeast course from that point

Am very glad to get back to home & a good bed. Very tired wrote no letters - will do it tomorro and send them to Maj Stanton tomorro evening - To bed about 10 1/2 pm Traveled today about 31 miles

Sunday, August 1, 1875

Up at usual hour to find Genl C's party nearly ready to leave. Saw them all off about 8 a.m. It seems now late at night as if they left here about a week ago. Spent the day writing letters. To Tooty - Father - Col Gantt, Thompson 3d,[195] Rice, & notes to others. Got throug[h] about 4 pm and sent all over to Burt's camp to Stanton by Hall, who goes as the Genls Guide. Had quiet day, & in evening several of the Offs loafed about my camp fire, & told stories until quite late - Read lots of papers. Letters from Morton & Jenney about horse thieves - all anxious to catch the rascals. Fred sent off lots of letters - a paper from Tooty, with Dr. Allens name on it, showing that she got safely to Saratoga. Pleasant day - Some men drunk - To bed quite late

Monday, August 2, 1875

Up late - feeling tired & with no appetite. The arduous hunting was too much for me, in my present soft & lazy condition. Spent the day reading newspapers, & writing letters. Wrote to Palmer, W. J.,[196] to Sis Molly & Cousin Cath Took a small nap or two. Got

---

through a long canyon to within a few miles of Camp Harney (*Chicago Inter-Ocean*, August 2, 1875, p. 1). Mix proposed a much longer route, which he had established with great difficulty in the early spring. This had followed a northward course from Fort Laramie, entering the Black Hills by a trail that had been used by an Indian commission in 1874.

195. Lieutenant John Charles Thompson, Third Cavalry, who was stationed at Camp Robinson.

196. William J. Palmer (1836–1909), president of the Denver and Rio Grande Railroad, was an old hunting companion and business adviser of Dodge. The two had met while Palmer was engaged during 1867 and 1868 in directing surveys of potential railway routes to the Pacific.

a long effusion from Mix in answer to a squib of mine on him He shows temper, & is evidently mad. The poor old fellow has lost his grip, & is not half the man he was five years ago -[197]

Not a thing doing. The men are gambling & getting rid of their money, & the officers loafing, reading &c. Must stir them up a little There has been no hunting since the paymaster came Cloudy curious day. Miriads of bugs in evening - & no birds to catch them as usual -

Tuesday, August 3, 1875

Fine day but very warm for the Hills. Ther. 86° at highest. Spaulding & Russell had a shooting match - 5 men of each Co. Russell badly beat - but tries it again tomorw. Wrote several letters - <one> to Jeff C. Davis.[198] To Joe telling him about his pay for Aug and Sept.[199] Sent check to Omaha Natl Bank for $200 - $100 to be sent in a N.Y. check to Father, the other $100 to <Joe> be paid to Joe.

Wrote 7 pages in my book on game - It strings out but dont progress as fast to a close as I would like. The two Doctors paid a visit to Burts camp. Returned in evening, no news, except that miners are going out quite fast. Pleasant evening - several officers around my fire. To bed 11 pm

Wednesday, August 4, 1875

Excessively hot day - far the worst to me that we have had. Ther 90.

Burt & Delany over from camp - about going with train - Had pretty plain talk with Burt - Had a billious attack & high fever -

---

197. In *PNA* Dodge recounts an incident of February 1867, while he was in command of Fort Sedgwick, Colorado, when he had sent a company of cavalry into the field under Captain Mix. A violent storm set in during their absence from the post, and they were able to return only through "the indomitable will and pluck of the Captain in Command" (p. 84). Mix died in 1881.

198. Colonel Jefferson Columbus Davis had commanded Dodge's present regiment, the Twenty-third Infantry, since 1866.

199. Dodge maintained two servants at his home at Omaha Barracks, a husband and wife named Joe and Laura.

Couldn't eat dinner. Foster & Dr. McG. got in in morning. Morton must be having a hard time - as he has not come in yet tho his rations have been up this two days.

Mail arrived. Letter from Father - but nothing from Tooty or[200] any of the family East - Wrote several letters in a.m. but was so really sick by dark that I turned in - Fred is a good sick nurse & kind & attentive as possible. <Broke my fever> Went to work to break fever - at once

Thursday, August 5, 1875

Passed a wretched night with high fever & half delirious dreams, in which I was incessantly struggling through hills & brush, & never accomplishing any distance - Took aconite[201] regularly, & broke the fever before daylight. Have had a wretched head, back & belly ache all day, though <it is> much better at night. Have been in bed pretty much all day - & in very considerable pain. Fred is very kind & attentive. Up in afternoon - in fact I found it more convenient to dress, as <the> it saved the trouble of dressing every time I had to run, which was very often - Am much better tonight - though my back yet aches, & my head is very full -

Friday, August 6, 1875

Much better today, up & about as usual. Wrote letters all the a.m. to Father, Tooty, & others Had map made for Genl Bradley, & gave him a long account of how to get here. Made out schedule of time, route & distances for Burt, which he will consider <contrary> ^in^ derogation of his dignity -

Morton & party got in after a d——l of a tramp - After reaching Head of Rapid they took a cañon thinking it a head of Box Elder.

---

200. Dodge wrote "of."
201. "The root or leaves of Aconitum Napellus...As internal remedy aconite very valuable in sthenic fever from any cause" (Wood and Bache, *Dispensatory*, p. 128).

It turned out to be a Head of Red Water, & after getting in they could not get out, except by going on or returning. They kept on to near the Belle Fourche then came around by Bear Butte & the eastern base of the Mts. to Rapid, then came up the divide between Rapid & Spring, one of the very worst in the Hills I think the whole party was a little lost - Old Joe included. I forgot to mention that a man of this camp was lost four days ago, having gone down the Ck hunting. Jenneys party found him out on the plain en route for the Missouri with gun but no am[munitio]n. Morton brought him in. He says he was nearly 3 days without anything whatever to eat, & tho' he shot all his cartridges away at game he killed nothing. - Just at night two men came in from Jenney to say that Mr. Newton the Asst Geologist is lost. Ordered Old Joe & party to start <to> at daylight tomorw to hunt him up -

Saturday, August 7, 1875

Busy day - Joe and party off at daylight after Newton. Just after Breakfast in came Foster & Dr. McGillicuddy reporting that they had lost their outfit entirely, & that Capt Tuttle had refused to come with them & started off east - None of them had had anything to eat for 24 hours - I at once ordered a N.C. Off[icer] & 4 men to go out on the wagon trail & hunt up & bring in all the lost of that party -

Spaulding & Colonel Bullock started this morning - (but first of all, by soon after 6 am the whole wagon train, except just enough for our use went in for supplies.)[202] I had finished all my letters & gave them to Spaulding who was to take them in for me, & he and Col B. were over at my tent to bid me good

---

202. The two infantry companies, under Captain Burt, accompanied the wagon train. To enable wagons to be repaired at Fort Laramie, Burt was to delay beginning his return until August 24. He was then to proceed via Camp Jenney to Indian Springs, at the head of Spaulding's Creek, arriving there on September 2. A party from the main camp was to meet him at that time (BHE S.O. 22, August 6).

by,[203] when I heard that Jenney had hired 8 of his special miner friends & was keeping them in the Hills as his employees, and that the other miners, those going out, are very angry at this partiality -

I immediately wrote a letter to Jenney, disapproving this act, & telling him that all the miners must go out. I kept a copy of the letter The original I sent to him by the men who came in to report the loss of Newton. I detained Spaulding, had another copy of letter to Jenney made & sent it with a letter of explanation to Genl Crook<e>.

There is a possible row on the tapis, but I can I think manage Jenney, & obey my orders at the same time. I have given each of Jenney's party, himself included, a pass to remain in the Hills. This to protect them from the Troops soon to arrive & who do not know them -

About <7>3 pm Capt Tuttle made his appearance - He had gone back to Burts camp, got breakfast & came on. About 9 am Mr Newton the lost came in. So now at night I have all the lost ones safe in the Camp, but have 2 parties out looking for them yet -

<The Civilian> The Scientists are all mad as March hares at Jenney, & loud are the swares "swored" at him today - By his tom fool arrangemts 3 of his party <with> went without food for 24 hours & slept without bedding last night. I have insisted that he come in, & will try to induce him to let me have the organization of his parties in future - If he dont, I will have to be hard on him

Jenney is the queerest compound I ever saw, & I really think he is cracked on some subjects. Newton who is a really good man & geologist says that Jenney will not attend to his work, & will not give him (Newton) time to attend to it. He races over

---

203. Captain Spaulding with a small detachment of Company I, Third Cavalry, was to accompany Captain Burt's command as a mounted escort (BHE S.O. 22, August 6). Upon his arrival at Fort Laramie, Spaulding was to avail himself of a month's leave of absence.

the country like one possessed, breaking down mules, & if I dont put a stop to it he will cripple me seriously. I am going to have a steady talk with him, & thereafter I hope things will run better.

King went out today & found a covey of young grouse - Ruff - Bagged eight of them. Sent me 2 - which is clever.

Russell & Hall ordered to go to Harney with me tomorw. Hall takes rations to 20th, as I will leave him there until Pollock comes.[204]

Sharp storm in afternoon with heavy thunder & high wind. Came near upsetting our Hd Qrs Tents, but the guard rushed out & saved us at the expense of a ducking -

Sunday, August 8, 1875

After very careful consideration, I had come to the conclusion that I must try a "coup d'etat['] on Mr Jenney. The time seemed ripe for it. His parties disorganized & in bad humor were doing little work, & throwing the blame on him. He must begin to know that he has not the peculiar faculty necessary for the management of men. I therefore today quietly & without flourish of trumpets, assumed the management of the whole outfit. Jenney's men as well as my own are to recognize me as head. To do this I issued an order organizing 2 pack trains placing one under comd of Morton, the other of Foster. This latter train will always go with Dr. McGillicuddy & the scientific people - but Foster is to have full military control, & is held responsible for the care & safety of the animals -[205] I took every pack mule away

---

204. Lieutenant Hall's Company I, Second Cavalry, was to take tents, company baggage, and rations; Russell's Company H, Third Cavalry, was to take rations only (BHE S.O. 23, August 7).

205. The first pack train, of seven mules, would be under charge of J. Bratton and would serve the surveying party of Dr. McGillycuddy. Lieutenant Foster, the acting topographical surveying officer, was given military charge and control over the escort and pack train. The second pack train, of four mules, would be under California Joe and permanently attached to the surveying party of Lieutenant Morton, who would have military control over it and the escort (BHE S.O. 24, August 8).

from Jenney himself. I then gave orders to Dr. Mc to Morton & Foster as to where they should make their next survey, & directed them on completion of the work, to report to me for further instructions. I expected that Jenney would be in a rare bad humor & that I would have serious trouble. About 12. m he came in on a canter. I took him into my tent, told him frankly all I had done & intended doing with his party. Instead of a dignified protest, or a passionate tirade against my interference (one or other of which I fully expected) he siezed my hand, thanked me for what I had done & said that he would rather I should direct, than direct himself. He was extremely complimentary - spoke of how much I had helped him, how I had thought for him planned for him, & that he had never followed my advice, but found it was the very best that he could have followed &c. He acquiesces cordially in my orders to his party - my cutting out the work for them - & says he will assist me with all his power. He is to stay more in camp, or go with Dr. McG, & locate his <g>Geology in future - He was troubled about losing his miners, but was entirely convinced I am right - He begged for 2 special ones, but I was inexorable. I told him that he might keep every man he had hired in the Hills, *before the proclamation of Genl Crook* for they, being at the time that proclamation was issued, employees of the Govt, were not "miners or unauthorized citizens" -[206] but that every man hired *after that proclamation must be discharged* ——

I told him I would give him all the soldiers he wanted, as assistants - miners or anything else -

He took everything admirably, admitting most frankly that I was right about the miners, & that I knew so much better than he, how to do the other work - It is not an easy thing for a young man to admit that he cannot manage an affair, or that he is wrong. Jenney has done both, & in so frank & manly a way, that he has

---

206. In the proclamation of July 29, General Crook had directed "every miner or other unauthorized citizen" to leave the Black Hills region by August 15.

rizen a hundred per ct in my estimation this day. He is a very curious compound. Many men inspire one with feelings or sentiments of repugnance or dislike, when they are present, which feeling changes when they are absent. Such a man is Burt. - He is so ill-natured & says so many ill-natured things that I feel like kicking him when he is in my presence, but when he is away from me, I rather like him - Jenney on the contrary manages to make one dislike him when away, but I defy a man to dislike him when present - My "coup d etat" is accomplished - I run the whole machine from this time, with Jenney's full approbation & consent, & I must do him the justice to say that he has acted like a gentleman & with much more sense & character than I gave him credit for -

At 1 pm Hd Qrs Staff & 2 Cos, Russells (3d), Hall (2d) started for Camp Harney 5 wagons - 1 Hd Qrs 2 each Co

The rain yesterday made the road bad up the canon. I came across lots, by trail. Arrived near Burts old camp 4 pm - the Infantry gone of course Camped on small stream near spring about 4 miles above Burts - All the miners gone except a small party of 3, just coming in. I sent for them, & had just commence[d] to question them, when the gun of one went off accidentally, & put a ball through the hat of another A very close shave - I blew them both up for carrying breechloaders loaded tho' I do it myself sometimes. They are going out after the 10th - They tell me that all the others are going - Lovely camp & splendid grass this pm Travelled about 13 miles - To bed about 11 pm One deer killed by a soldier of Russells Co -

Monday, August 9, 1875

Up before sun rise - & by a quarter to six was on the road. Arrived without event at the site of the new town. Found miners everywhere. Camps & wagons were in every available nook, & their animals covered the plain. It is said about 200 are collected here - all of whom propose to leave after the meeting tomorw - A more regular camp, in a most unsatisfactory position, suggested a possible arrival of Cavalry - Went over to it & found Capt Benteen 7th Cavy, with his Co. all the way from Fort Randall, & with orders from Genl Terry to take out all the miners he found in the Hills -[207] The War Dept & some of the higher off[icer]s do manage to mix things most abominably. Here are two Dept Comdrs ordered to take & keep the miners from the Black Hills. One comes in, sees the condition of affairs, & by a few judicious words does more <than he> in <a few> ^ten^ days, than he could have done with a Regt of Cavy in a season. The other sends one Compy a distance of 350 miles with orders to drag out as prisoners all he may find. By the best fortune, Benteen met Genl Crook on his way in, & is warned not to do anything - Had it not been for that accidental meeting, instead of a no. of quiet miners ready, if not willing to go out, & all while deploring the necessity, yet willing to accept it, & blaming nobody - I would have found several hundreds of prisoners, - angry, & ready to escape, & a Compy with its hands so full, that it is doubtful if it had succeeded in doing anything - Of course if I had found any prisoners, I would have released them, but the mischief would have been done -

I find French Creek almost dry - water standing in holes Benteen was here with Custer last year. He says that they had scarcely any rain, yet that French Ck was a fine large stream. We have had plenty of rain, yet French is dry. Inference - that the very light snow fall of last winter was exceptional - The grass here is parched & burned yellow - while on Spring & Rapid it is fresh & green - Spring is somewhat lower than when we went north - but not much -

I have found camped near Benteen, Mr Howard Indian Agent, with Spotted Tail, & several Indians. I went over & talked with

---

207. Captain Frederick W. Benteen had left Fort Randall with his Company H, Seventh Cavalry, on July 15. Benteen's orders from Brigadier General Alfred H. Terry, commander of the military Department of Dakota, were to remove from the Black Hills vicinity all the miners he found there, escorting them across the Missouri River on his return to the fort.

them. They are in on a visit, to look at the gold diggins - & see the Hills -[208] They return in a day or two - It is a little curious that the Cavy, though supposed to be excellent campaigners have apparently no sort of idea how to select a camp. Benteen's Camp is on a little knoll without a tree or shrub to shelter him - no grass no wood & no water near except the stagnant water of French Ck. <H> At about a mile off is a good spring from which he hauls his water in wagons - & near that spring is plenty of wood & good grass. Yet he has been several days in that camp. He has taken no pains to make himself comfortable in any way, & though he has unlimited space on which to extend his camp his wagons, his compy, & horses, & his officers tents are all jammed together, as if ground were worth $1000 a foot - He has not built an awning & though he expects to remain here 5 days more, he seems to propose no improvement - The new town has 2 houses of logs. I am told the settlers almost had a fight over its name, the Southern element of which there is quite a sprinkling, insisting on calling it "Stonewall" while the Yankee inhabitants insist equally on its name being "Custer" - The difficulty is postponed now that all go out —

2 deer killed today by Hall's men, & as I gave him a decided blowing up this afternoon, I got none -

Benteens Officers called on us this p.m. & stayed till after 9. Craycraft, &c[209] Travelled 18 miles today Found Burt in Benteens camp - seemed amiable -

---

208. Spotted Tail, with ten men of his band; E. O. Howard, government agent for the Ogallala and Brulé Sioux; and Louis Bordeaux, an interpreter, had arrived on August 8. A physician, Dr. J. L. Mills, and the Reverend Mr. Cleveland were also with the party. According to Davenport, at the first sight of these unexpected visitors "the hair of the brave adventurers"—that is, the miners—"literally stood on end." For a consideration, Spotted Tail granted an interview to Davenport; the text appeared in the *New York Herald* in both English and Lakota (August 26, 1875, p. 3).

209. Second Lieutenant William T. Craycroft, Seventh Cavalry; also with Benteen's command was Second Lieutenant Charles C. De Rudio, Seventh Cavalry.

Tuesday, August 10, 1875

Breakfasted late, 7 am - At 9 1/2 mounted our horses & went to the Town. At 10 the meeting was called to order Mr Chase in the chair.[210] It appears there were to be two meetings one of the miners of French Creek, the other more general. The first was principally occupied with the business of the new Town. On final vote it was named "Custer City." The streets are numbered one way. The cross are to be designated "Avenues" & are named after *distinguished* men. The principal Avenue on which is the City Hall is called "Crook Av". <There is> There are also Custer Av. Dodge Av. &c The meeting was very harmonious, but did not seem to be able to comprehend what <the> it wanted to do. <It d> The last thing done was to draw for lots in the new town,[211] & this with a few complimentary resolutions, to Crook & myself, was about all done - I was informed by a committee that General C. had authorized them to select six 6 miners, to remain here, take charge of the property tools &c that could not be taken out. The Genl had said nothing to me about it, nor had he written by Benteen as he might have done. I questioned the Committee very closely. Three men are said to have been promised by Genl C. Two of these (the other being absent) I questioned apart, & their stories tallied. Genl C. had told them that he could give no permission to <but> any one to remain here, but he would authorize them to delay going out, until he could see Genl Sheridan. I was in some quandary but finally decided to accept this statement.[212] If true, I do not interfere with the

---

210. According to newspaper correspondents who reported the proceedings, the chairman was C. L. Craig; John Maulux was chosen secretary. See *Chicago Tribune*, August 21, 1875, p. 2; *New York Herald*, August 26, 1875, p. 3.

211. Among Dodge's papers is a memorandum, dated August 10, 1875, and signed by Tom Cooper, town clerk, certifying that Dodge drew by lottery Lot 5, Block 16 in the town of Custer City (Graff Collection, Newberry Library).

212. The statement was accurate. The persons delegated to remain in the area to protect the rights of the departing miners were Dodge's acquaintance W. Harrison, A. Garrison, A. D. Trask, Samuel Shankland, A. Thompson, A. Allen, and J. Sanders (Parker, *Gold in the Black Hills*, p. 67).

programme of Genl C.[;] if false, the falsehood will come out in a very short time & can avail the miners nothing - I gave permission to six to remain. Their names are given to Hall, who will not interfere with them. They are not to mine or prospect.

Another class then claimed my attention - A number of miners are here who were brought in by contract, in the conveyances of others, & "dumped," as one may say. These though willing & even anxious to obey the order cannot do so for lack of transportation. I have directed all these to report to Lt Hall & register their names to remain in the vicinity of Custer, & not to mine or prospect. I have directed Pollock to treat these men not as violators of orders, but to send them out <under> as comfortably & as soon as possible.

I called at Benteens Camp again. He told me that he intended calling on me tonight, but he has failed. I guess he did not care to trouble himself - He is a true Cavalryman & would rather superintend the work of his stallion than attend to the courtesies of life - Nothing lost to anybody - but one feels degraded to think that he is socially on a par, with those who voluntarily make of themselves third class livery stable keepers - However if the Nobles & high gentry of England find their highest pleasure in doing the work of a stable boy, I suppose I ought not to growl at our Cavalry. There seems to be something demoralizing in the love of horseflesh. I dont believe a thoroughly horsey man can be a gentleman or a thorough gentleman a horsey man.

I returned to camp 1 p.m. & wrote a long letter to Genl Crook, <another> ˄and to Pollock & Hall each a letter of instructions - I had hardly got through these, before I was visited by a committee bringing the resolutions & proceedings of the meeting this p.m. These people have not at all recognized their own power, nor the effect of a series of well drawn resolutions on Congress. They have really done nothing today, to secure for themselves the benefits of their discoveries and their work. At one time I had serious thought of drafting the resolutions for them - but there are too many reporters about - To be effective they must at least appear the work of the miners themselves.

No fresh meat today. Fog & damp after sunset. Cold & raw at night, tho' clear - a very interesting day. Howard - the Indians Ag[en]t - I believe that Man a No 1 scoundrel that he is persuading the Indians to ask a large sum for the Hills, so that a quantity of money will stick on the way - Sent express to overtake Burt, with letters to Genl Crook. He started about 5 pm, & ought to catch B, by 9 or 10 am tomorw —

Wednesday, August 11, 1875

Frost on the ground this a.m. - Up early & got off 5.45 am Had to snub Davenport to make him stay back - I wanted to kill a deer & to be ahead. However found after a long time that I was travelling just behind a party going to Castle Ck for a wagon. Lovely day - tho' rather warm <af> in afternoon. Crossed Spring Creek, & tributaries making bad crossing 34 times in this days march Hall sent me a little venison - but grudgingly.

Went out after arriving at the camp ground, to try and kill a deer. Travelled about six miles without seeing anything - & returned disappointed to ham & bacon. Am camped about a mile from Burts old camp on Spring, on a splendid spring of water - clear very cold & abundant. Davenport & Lane went to Camp Crook this pm Root & Mallory two of Jenney's employees[213] passed my camp this p.m going in. Mallory left J. some time ago, but Root only today. He says he has no serious charge to bring against Jenney, but only leaves to get rid of a long & continuous series of petty annoyances, no one of which is much in itself, but all together have made his longer continuance with J. a load too heavy to carry - The last of the Castle Ck miners passed this pm - a party of 9 - all going out -

It is not nearly so damp & cold here as at last nights camp. A few miles makes a wonderful difference in temperature in these

---

213. T. H. Mallory was one of the original corps of Jenney's "miners and assistants" under the direction of William H. Root.

Hills. Distance today 21 miles - saw 3 harmless snakes, & the first turtle, I have found in the Hills - a small striped head, in Spring Creek -

Thursday, August 12, 1875

Left camp 5.40 a.m. & came to Camp Crook by trail, arriving here in 2 hours - to find this camp hardly up, none of the Offs having had their breakfast -

Gave orders for the move tomorw. Take Captain Hawley Lieut King with their Cos & Lieut Coles with his part of a Compy, & all the wagons

Trout & Hawley inform me that the Scientifics came near breaking up. Jenney insisted on having the pack mules, though to me he had agreed fully to my arrangements. Dr. McG. would have gone at once, & said he would not do another lick of work - He came to Trout, who went to Jenney, & informed him that he could not have the mules, that the orders of the War Dept authorized none for him - That I was disposed to do all I could, but had ordered the mules turned over to Lieut. Foster, & that Dr. McG. was going with Foster - Jenney yielded, & all is now quiet, & peaceable - All the parties are out. Jenney went with the wagons My Comd got in here before 10 am Took a nap, as a sharp rain storm prevented our going out. It cleared later in the evening, & Trout, Fred & I went fishing. We went on foot & near camp, but tho' all this is "fished out," we were successful I quite so. I took more than thirty fish, one sucker of near 2 lbs, 1 smaller, & a few very large dace. The others were variable some very small - Nice Dinner at 6 pm King sent me some grouse - Hubert dont know how to cook them but they are very nice - & its good to get back to beef again - The temperature here is very mild compared to French Ck - It is like a different country though only 30 miles apart -

Jenney has talked of going in soon -

To bed 10 pm -

Friday, August 13, 1875

Broke camp 7. am - Delightful day for the march, tho a little warm about 10 a.m. Had a good road for 10 miles, the same that I came over on the hunt with Genl Crook. <Ther> At my first camp on the hunt, I left that road, struck N. W. up a small branch of Box Elder, thence across to a larger branch, on which I camped. Tried hard to kill a deer. Shot at one, about 60 yds off, but could see nothing but its head, & missed that - Shot at him again running, & wounded him, but failed to bag him which made me mad & I started for venison. The Comd was not yet up, but I had taken Trout to where I wished to camp & sent him back for the train. I had a long & trying tramp sometimes walking but oftener riding - Had already tried west, & after losing my deer, tried east. Went about 3 miles down the Ck seeing no deer - then crossed & after some travelling came on a high point from which I could see three (3) elk and several deer disporting themselves in a Beaver dam. Had to make a long detour to get the wind right. Left my horse & worked the affair up "secundum artem."[214] When I arrived in splendid position near the dam there was nothing in it - I waited some time to see the last of the deer, slowly wending their way up the deep & nasty cañon in which was the dam in the dense thickets of which elk & deer had evidently ensconced themselves - I could do nothing - see nothing sufficiently clearly to shoot at it - Going down a little distance a deer was indiscreet enough to show itself, & I put a bullet through it. It turned out to be a barren doe very fat & nice - & though I was disappointed about the elk, I came back tolerably satisfied. I got into some terribly broken country. I am just on the happy mean between canons above & canons below. Today I saw two wolves - one of them the largest animal of that species I ever saw. I tried hard to get a shot at him but failed - I have not heretofore believed that there are wolves in the Hills - now

---

214. "According to art"—that is, through expertise.

I know it, & they are huge fellows. Timber wolves - as tall as a buffalo wolf - very much heavier - shorter ears, & slower motions - dirty gray in color.

Saw a pack of grouse today, but had no shot gun. Heard a plover - for the second or third time in the Hills -

Vast quantities of timber have been destroyed by fire - probably lightning. The country is not very broken along the route we have taken - but it is a little off - Springs everywhere - All the streams here are small but there are so many that it is not remarkable that Box Elder is a large stream lower down -

Had a nice nap in the afternoon, tho I did not get back from my hunt until 3 pm Enjoyed my dinner hugely - Just before it was announced Morton came in. He is running Custer's trail and says it is the crookedest thing on earth. Old Joe says a double S is nothing to it - Morton camped just above us - Had a nice party around my camp fire in evening. It is not so cold as last night, though we must be 5 or 600 feet higher - Rain all around us & at one time I thought we were going to have a bad storm but we escaped -

Foote saw a fine brook of Mallard ducks half grown. Didnt get any. Only 5 deer in camp tonight - very small for this excellent hunting country. Just as I am writing I hear the cry of Sand Hill cranes - To bed rather late - Distance 12 miles.[215]

[*The text that follows is written with the notebook reversed, beginning with the last sheet and ending with p. [68R] in the original pagination.*]

July 23. Camp Crook on Rapid Creek

Rapid is the largest stream in the Hills - Is pure delicious water soft & clear. It is about 20 feet wide by 10 inches deep on the riffles - & flows with great velocity. Jenney says the fall is 90 feet to mile. The timber is comparatively poor - nothing but pine & that not very good.

215. Page [67V], which follows, is blank.

We are in a fine open park or meadow, but the stream canons both above & below us —

I have not the exact altitude but we must be at least 1000 feet below Camp Harney - It is much warmer here, & the variations of temperature are not so great. This is the finest country for agriculture - that for stock raising - & dairy produce -

---

Snakes make their appearance - Two Rattle snakes have been seen - one killed - & I today saw a small water snake -
Birds - Robin, brown thrush blackbirds, catbird, Red headed woodpecker, broad winged black woodpecker & the common house martin which <buil> has its nests in hollow dead pine trees. There are also some very small sandpipers - & equally diminutive climbers & sap suckers. The men have a tame blackbird which they took from its nest lately & which is so tame that it flies all around into the tents, lighting on any man's shoulder or hat, & constantly begging to be fed - I have never seen so tame a bird -

---

We are not so pestered with ants, but there are miriads of bugs of all kinds -

---

I should have mentioned with birds, the bull bat or goat sucker, & the common leather winged bat -
No fish except suckers & dace. Both take grasshoppers readily from the top of the water. The suckers are better eating, & less bony than they are east.

  Spring Creek is considerably higher than Rapid I think.
  It has better timber - The birds about the same - Bugs ditto -
    The creek
<It> ∧ is four times the size of French & 1/2 as large as Rapid -
It also has only suckers & dace - Game rather scarce on both

Spring
<this> ₐ & Rapid - though red deer are quite plentiful <on Spring>. Spaulding found a covey of spike grouse today -

---

July 24 -

In hunt today saw one or two kinds of woodpecker common to North Carolina. also sparrows - & on the hills plenty of snow birds - <also> Cow birds are among the horses - Saw a curious fungus - deep red color - looked like a large tomato - On 25 Saw a shell drake on creek with a fine brood of 9 young ones as large as a <sp> quail ——

July 28

The best gold diggins yet developed in the Blk Hills are on Rapid Creek about 18 miles above Camp Crook - or a few miles below our old camp on Rapid where I left Jenney - About 60 miners are at work, & doing good work - sluicing &c

<29> Genl Crook arrived today -

July 30

The best hunting ground yet found is on Box Elder. Genl Crook & party bagged today 1 Elk 1 sheep & 16 deer - Lovely country - plenty of water - Sandhill cranes breed here - a bird very like the N. Y. partridge - Ruff grouse but much darker, found in the Hills - several have been killed -

Camp on Box Elder
    Hunting —
    Lightning in the Hills
    Buffalo bird
    Sand Hill cranes & young
    Ravens & nests in trees

July 20
I forgot to mention in the proper place, that we had quite a frost this am —

August 1
Our bag on the hunt footed up 1 elk, 1 sheep 37 deer

August 2
Miriads of bugs & insects of all sorts -

My curious woodpecker turns out to be Lewis & Clarks Woodpecker.[216] Those were remarkable men. They noticed everything and gave accurate descriptions.

Martins building for the 2d time - Carrying paper off to their nests ——

Genl Crook & miners See dates 9th & 10th

August 10
Interesting sight - Wilderness - Everlasting Hills - < Valleys filled with > Miners' camps dotting the foot hills - valleys filled with stock - The new Town. Miners, Indians, Soldiers - The meeting - the exodus.

Frost at our camp on French Ck - Aug 11 - am

Flies very bad - blue bottles - horse, & a small biting fly

216. George B. Grinnell, zoologist to the Custer expedition of 1874, identified "Lewis' Woodpecker" as "*Melanerpes Torquatus*." He added: "This woodpecker was by no means common... On the wind, their easy gliding movements and the dark greenish hue of their dorsal aspect made them conspicuous when flying" (Ludlow, *Report of a Reconnaissance*, pp. 1194–95).

August 13
  Saw two Timber Wolves -
Heard plover - also Sand Hill cranes at night

Heard the note of the bird called "Rain Crow" in N. C.

[*The list that follows is written on the inside back cover.*]

Sandhill cranes -	Catbird
Buzzards -	Snipe
Hawks - very large	Kingbird
Owls - Ravens	<mallards>
Shell drake	Small sandpiper
Mallard duck	Doves
Grouse	Larks
Buffalo bird	Blue bird

Lew[is] & C[lark]'s woodpecker

Red head   ''

Yellowhammer

Robin - Brown Thrush

Cat bird - Blackbird Cowbird

- House Martin

Rock

Barn swallow - sparrow

Snow bird

Leather winged bat

3 or 4 varieties Sap suckers - some very small

Goat sucker - or night hawk

Journal Five:
August 14–September 10, 1875

No 5[217]
Aug 14th 1875
to
Sepr 10th /75[218]

Saturday, August 14, 1875. Camp 21

Broke camp 6 am Had to rely on myself for route. General course today North. I wished to clear Custers Peak, & swing around to the West between it & Terry - The route so far as surface <was> ^is^ concerned is good - but the timber makes it utterly abominable - sometimes almost impassable. Trout came out strong today as a road maker. He had a pioneer party of 20 men, who worked almost every inch of the way. The pines were small & of very thick growth. When standing and green a regular lane had to be cut through them. When down, & dead they were even worse, being piled in inextricable confusion - on & across each other. However we worked away, cutting through dense woods, or bridging swamps & streams. It has been the

---

217. This manuscript journal consists of seventy-four pages. On the bottom side of the cardboard pad, Dodge has written in black ink "Black Hills [/] *1875*"; below it, in pencil, is an encircled "5." Except as noted, and for parts of a map drawn on p. [69V], all entries are in pencil. The text begins on p. [1R].

218. The text that immediately follows, comprising the remainder of p. [1R] and the whole of p. [1V], is not reproduced here. Page [1R] includes a summary of rainy days during August; p. [1V] is a hunting record that shows the numbers of animals bagged daily between August 14 and 31.

longest day of the trip, to me, & I am more tired than any day, simply because the march was so tedious & the long delays so constant. Arrived at a stream which I presume to be Elk Ck at 4.10. The wagons got in 4.45. Camped & very glad to camp Nearly eleven hours on the road & made 9 miles - & a perfectly satisfactory distance considering the difficulties. Did not hunt, but killed 3 deer. Might have killed more 12 deer killed today by the whole of us - Foote saw 2 elk - also a mountain lion. Bear sign very plenty - all in thick brush however.

Good camp, fine little stream, plenty of wood grass tolerable. 5 or 6 grouse bagged today - Ruff Rained on us a little & as I go to bed there is all appearance of a heavy rain - & raining now 9 pm - To bed early

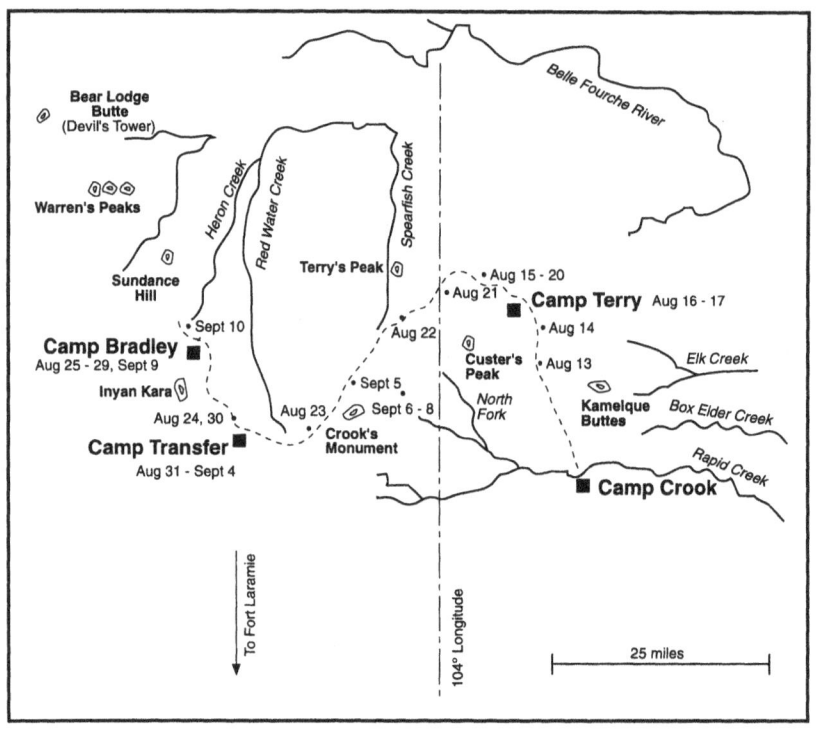

Itinerary, Camp Crook–Camp Bradley, August 13–September 10

AUGUST 14–SEPTEMBER 10, 1875   179

Sunday, August 15, 1875. Camp 21

Left the Comd in camp started 6.30 with Trout to look out a road - Found a good crossing of the divide, & sent Trout back to bring up the Comd. While he was gone I killed two deer which I bagged, & another which escaped into a thicket.

The route was much better than yesterday for several miles - but after that I was greatly troubled for the canons were very deep, & the timber very dense. Mounted a high bare hill to look, & came suddenly on 7 magnificent black tail Bucks - the very largest I have ever seen. Fred saw them before I did & called to me two or three times before I saw them - & before I could get a shot they were off. I fired at one running & I think hit him, but he got away into a dense thicket - I was disgusted, for I ought to have gotten one at least. I then went back to the train, after taking a most satisfactory survey of the country & satisfying myself of the course. Had lunch & a drink, & put Trout all right. Started up another high hill for a more detailed view, & came upon a fine white-tail Buck - which I killed & sent to the wagons - Got an excellent route up the divide - & returned after a five mile trip to find Trout going all right, but with a chronic disposition to keep to the eastward - & the east wall of the cañon on my right was an almost perpendicular wall of limestone - showing that we are nearly out of the granite. Kept well to the north west & got on top of a high divide, between the waters on which we camped last night, & crossed today. Elk Creek, and another creek, of which we know but little as yet. The canons of this latter creek are terrific. I kept on a back bone which seemed to promise a comparatively easy descent - but it kept getting higher & higher - so that finally I determined to get down into a canon - I tried it but soon found myself stuck. Could not get down even on horseback - Had to go back onto the backbone. The going down & back took time skill & work but Trout did admirably. Night overtook us while yet on the divide, so we had to go into camp. There <was> ˄ is no grass, & water <would> ˄ can only be had by climbing down and up a steep & deep canon. However, though we are now on "the Mountain high in Heaven blue," I have had worse camps.

We had hardly got our tents pitched when it came on to rain - & is at it yet. Regular eastern pour down. Fred and I have travelled at least 30 miles up and down mountains & my horse is very tired. I feel first rate - killed a Ruff Grouse on the Hill. Shot its head off with rifle. My bag today 3 deer 1 grouse Total bag of Commd - 10 deer, two of them black tails. Distance 8 miles.

Monday, August 16, 1875. Camp 22

Out early hunting road. Set Trout to work at 6 am, to make what I had decided on last night as road. Went ahead several miles - & met the first decided disappointment of the trip. Tried every divide & with great difficulty got into the Canon, but nowhere could I find a route practicable for wagons without very great labor. To crown all, I discovered that the Creek, on which I had set my hopes, had no bottom land. I[t] runs in a deep gorge with steep sides - & even had I got into it with my wagons there was no feed for my animals. After careful examination, & with very great reluctance, I was forced to acknowledge myself beat & to give the order to turn back. The only parties who seemed to relish the order, were the working parties, & I dont blame them. They have worked well & faithfully & if the road could have been made they would have done it. The country is the most broken I have seen. The canons are most irregular.

I feared it. The range of mountains culminating in Custer & Terry's Peaks is a center from which diverge streams in all directions except west. On South, tributaries of Rapid on S. East Box Elder, on East Elk - & the yet unknown creek on which I am now encamped On N. E. are innumerable ravines tributary to I dont know what and on the North, the deep canons of tributaries to Red Water take their rise - It is really little wonder that I could not get through. Yet as "hope lives eternal" I would never have been satisfied with myself unless I had tried all I could to make "the riffle" -

My animals have had a hard time, and luxuriated in the fine rich grass on which we are now encamped. I returned four or five miles on our yesterdays trail & camped on a small stream - tributary to what!! - Just before getting to camp, I left the road, & before going a half mile, struck a part of the herd of Black Tails that I saw yesterday. There were 4, and though the nearest shot I had was over 200 yds, I bagged three of the finest that we have yet seen - The last shot at least 300 yds was one of my very best - I got the 3, in less than 5 minutes that is I killed them, but as only one fell in his tracks, I had hard work to find the other two - One went 300, the other at least 600 yds before falling & both were found dead - the last shot in shoulder from the front, had 4 ribs broken, lungs perforated & hind leg badly hurt - yet twas only accident that I got him - he went so far. My bag has been the admiration of the whole camp. All the officers have been over to see them & they are really magnificent. Tonight I had them butchered, & distributed to all who wanted - 9 deer in 3 days

Only 4 miles today. Make Camp here for some days, until Trout returns with the remainder of the Comd. Mine the only deer bagged.

Very foggy this morning - Rained nearly all night but beautiful today.

Tuesday, August 17, 1875. Camp 23

Remained in Camp today to let everything rest. We have a nice Camp. I name it Camp Terry. Plenty of wood water & grass & all of the best. About 9 am Morton came in. He has been around Custer's Peak - & promises me a good route to Inyan Kara. It was where I expected to go when I started from Rapid, but my success emboldened me to try to get still further north along my route, which led to a retreat. I am much pleased with present prospects. Morton has got malaria & is not at all well. Trout starts tomorw for Camp Crook to bring up the two Cos. He is to make the trip there in one day & the return trip in two days.

Spent several hours today writing, & got off some 15 pages of Ms. about finishing up the Red deer -[219] Am very glad of it for it rather bored me. I cant get up much enthusiasm on White Tails, but have got a fairly good article.

Only one deer killed today by Old Erwin. Morton brought in three - but the Companies complain already of the want of fresh meat. I will try and kill some tomorw, as I go to hunt road. Copied at night, & went to bed about 10. Ice in camp last night. Ther. on going to bed tonight 40°.

Wednesday, August 18, 1875

Started 7 am with Morton & Joe to hunt up a road. Found a very good route between Custer & Terry's Peaks, to the west of where I tried to go. About 7 miles out came across Jenney & his outfit.[220] Gave them directions how to get to camp, & turned over to him a fine Buck that I had killed. After satisfying myself as to the route I started to return. Went more to the South & East & became thoroughly convinced that to get through these hills is a matter of accident as well as knowledge. Although but a short distance from the good route which I had found, I got completely entangled in a most abominable system of canons, through which I could get my horse only with the greatest labor & difficulty. So I finally got mad, & went back to the divide to find that Jenney had gone off too much to his right, & was fast entangling himself & party in the same canons. Went to the rescue at once & got them all out on my road, after two hours work - Got 2 red deer - only saw 3 - There are very few in this vicinity. I think the Blk Tails have driven them off. Found Dr. McGillicuddy & Foster in camp when I returned. They start tomorrow for Terry[.] Morton remains with me Ice 1/4 inch last night -

219. See *PNA*, pp. 186–90.
220. Although Jenney was no longer equipped with pack mules, on August 10 he and his assistants had been assigned a mounted escort of one sergeant and six privates from Captain Hawley's Company A, Third Cavalry (BHE S.O. 26).

Thursday, August 19, 1875

Morton went with Dr. McG. this time, as he had many sights to verify. They started about 9.30 for Terry's Peak - but will be back for rations tomorw or next day. I started out 9 am to look at a route that old Joe thinks is better than that of yesterday. It is better in grades, but the old route has the very great advantage that about three miles of the road is already made. Went over the ground on which I must make my road to Inyan Kara - & so far as I went, find it satisfactory. Then started off hunting - & worked most faithfully for two hours before seeing anything. Then two deer jumped from a thicket & made off up a hill. I fired at them running & dropped one. It bawled loudly whereupon the other one stopped & tho' I could see but a very small portion of him I fired. Foot & old Joe came up at this moment. Joe & I followed the trail of the second deer, & I soon found him quite dead. My rifle is lovely. I very rarely miss - in fact I have not missed even a tolerable shot, since I commenced hunting. Loading the deer on the horses, I sent Foote ahead in hopes he might bag a deer. He got a fine shot but missed. We saw no other deer. It commenced to rain heavily, & we returned home, getting to camp about 1.30 p.m. after a pleasant jaunt -

Rained steadily from about noon until about 4 pm Had my waterproofs along & did not get wet - Took a nap in p.m. Saw some ducks in a Beaver dam. They will soon be with us in abundance — Saw a beaver. Bear Signs very abundant but they remain hid in the thickets where we cannot see the animals themselves. Elk signs also plenty but no elk to be seen - Pleasant evening around campfire. To bed about 10.30.

Friday, August 20, 1875. Camp 24

Did not go out today. Expected Trout & the Comd which came in all safe about 10 a.m. Gave orders for the march tomorw. Russell & Wessels go with me. Issued rations to Comd. Borrowed 2 wagons of Jenney & sent them with one of mine back to last camp for the ammunition - which Trout had to leave. Morton,

Dr. McG. & party got into camp about 11 pm and stirred us all out of our slumbers, which was disgusting when we have to get up at daylight tomorw. Wrote considerably today - on Antelope.[221] Cant tell how it will compare with the other writing.

To bed late -

Saturday, August 21, 1875. Camp 25

A day of misfortune - Up at daylight, & got all the Comd off in good season, under the guidance of old Joe. I went with Fred & the orderlies on a hunt, & worked faithfully for some hours, seeing only the retreating flag of a fawn, as it scuttled away in the thicket. Came far ahead, & was enticed by the gamy appearance of the country into going into a canon up which my road is to run about a mile below where the road strikes it. Saw no game, & in crossing a bad bog covered with fallen timber, all leading our horses, Fred's horse in a plunge forward struck him with his fore foot on the hip, & hurt him quite seriously - so much so as to alarm me very considerably. After awhile however he got over it, & we mounted - We returned up the canon to where the road was to come, & struck back hoping soon to find the wagons. Had to go clear back to the pond to meet them, & found that Trout had been knocked down & nearly killed by a tree falling on him. Went to the ambulance to see him - He was very cheerful & manly tho' evidently badly hurt. We came on and camped at a spring I discovered 2 days ago. - As soon as the tents were pitched the Dr. undid the bandages which the Hosp[ita]l Steward had put on Trouts ankle,[222] & we found that the poor fellows foot was terribly broken. The foot was turned completely sole up. The ligatures holding the inner bone of the leg to its place in its socket were torn completely apart & the outer bone broken. Though the skin was not broken, the appearance of the

---

221. See *PNA*, pp. 191–98.
222. Assistant Surgeon Jaquette and Hospital Steward James Lehane had been assigned together to duty with the Black Hills Expedition (*ANJ*, April 24, 1875, p. 580).

leg made me sick, & I had to leave. It appeared that if the skin were cut around the foot would drop off. He is laid up for six months, & is possibly a cripple for life. It seems selfish to think of my loss in him, when he has such loss himself, but I had rather lost any six of my Officers than him.[223] He is so cheerful & manly under it, that he has won all our sympathies. I would not have had it occur for any money. He is the best officer in his place I ever knew. The accident has cast a gloom over the whole camp. Fred is all right tonight tho complaining a little.

Distance 8 miles - Road fair, but heavy work.

Sunday, August 22, 1875. Camp 26

Started 6 am with wagons and pioneer party, leaving the Cos in camp, Foote acting Qr Mr, & running the train. I went ahead hunting. In half an hour bagged a splendid buck. Went off on what I expected was the course. After a dilligent search through a dense thicket of quaking asp, & pine I came upon 8 splendid buck elk. The thicket was so abominable that I could not get a sure shot though I was not more than 80 yards. Aimed the very best I could, & fired - The buck fell forward but recovered & walked away. I fired four shots, hit 4 times - put two bullets in one elk which went off bleeding very freely. I trailed him for a long time, but the ground was so tramped up by elk that I could not keep the right trail. To my thorough disgust failed to bag even one tho' I know I mortally wounded 2 and hit three - Gave it up and went on. As it was getting toward 10 am I thought I had best get back to the train. Turned towards the creek & after hard work pushing thro' thickets arrived at it to find that the wagons had not come down it. Struck up it looking for wagon

---

223. In his official report, Dodge observed that Lieutenant Trout's accident "came very near depriving the service of one of its most valuable officers" (Turchen and McLaird, *The Black Hills Expedition of 1875*, p. 58). In fact, Trout was so disabled by his injury that eventually, in July 1879, a Retiring Board found him incapacitated for active service and granted him leave of absence until further notice. He retired from the army on March 15, 1883.

trail, but had to go clear back to where I had last seen it, to find that it had turned in directly the opposite direction from what I had understood Joe. Pushed on after <it>, & overtook it at water about 12 m. Joe knows of no water further west, so I went into Camp - After resting an hour, I took another horse, & started with Joe to look out our route for tomorw. Went out at least 6 miles. The big Canon "Morton's"[224] is very near us on <our> the west. We hunted a road to it, and tomorw will take up it. The route is good, & work very little. Our route today has been a marvel of engineering & Joe deserves great credit for working it out so well. A short distance to either right or left would have plunged us into canons. Trout stood the march well & is quite cheerful. He shows great pluck and manliness - I forgot to say that we found no water on tomorw's march except a pond about 2 miles ahead. We may have a dry camp. Distance today 7 miles. Saw ducks, grouse & Sand Hill cranes today -

Monday, August 23, 1875. Camp 27

Broke camp 6 a.m. Our trail led too much to the south, but there was no help for it, as the hills & canons were inexorable. We followed down a branch of Rapid for some 4 miles, then turned up another branch to its head, crossed a divide followed a canon down, & in something <over> ˄near <a> 2 miles came into the Big Canon - Morton's - Turned up this. About 3 miles up came to forks. Old Joe was bent on taking the left hand branch, I equally on the right - as the canons were taking me too far south all the time. Just at the forks found water in a little side spring. The fork followed looked unfavorable at first but soon widened out into a good bottom. Two miles brought us to a broad meadow like expanse, the main stream of which led too much to the north for me. I noticed a little depression to

---

224. The canyon was named after Lieutenant Morton because of that officer's having entered it and then been unable for two days to find a practicable way out.

the west, & pushing through a belt of woods came to another meadow like expanse which as we went down rapidly narrowed into a very crooked canon, which every moment looked as if it would shut in on us - We persevered however & were rewarded by debouching on to the Red Water just at the mouth of Custer's "Floral Valley." Just below were most lovely springs, & as I was afraid of tiring Trout I camped. The road has been very crooked but excellent. Distance 15 1/2 miles —

We are all elated at crossing the country so successfully - Bagged 2 deer this am, within a mile of camp & before I had half finished my first pipe. Excellent camp. We are very near our camp of 10 June

Tuesday, August 24, 1875. Camp 28

Broke camp 7.30 am, as we were to have so short a march. In one mile & a half we made our old camp of June 10, "Floral Valley," where we had the snow storm. Came over the ridge, & went down to Indian Springs,[225] 7 miles. Found the water very alkaline & the grass dried up, and determined to push on in search of something better. Went back nearly on the same course we came down making a V three miles in ∧ each of the legs & only one mile across the opening. Had some trouble with Old Joe. He would not do as I wished. Had his own ideas of the country & was determined to carry them out, though without insubordination or disrespect. I however am as obstinate as he - though when I stopped to lunch, he came near getting the train entirely off the course I wanted it to go — Arrived in time - tho' not soon enough to save a good deal of work for the men. Gave him a good blowing up, & it evidently did him a power of good, as he has been very apologetic & conciliatory in his manner ever since. Took the guidance into my own hand, & brought the

---

225. This is the springs that Dodge had named on June 10; Captain Burt had been ordered to arrive here with the pack train on September 2.

Comd onto a fine rolling Prarie & about 2 1/2 p.m. found a small stream of water & encamped. It is probably the most elevated camp we have made in the Hills. I do not know how high - but the trees & bushes begin to show the "sear & yellow leaf" -[226] It is already autumn here - I walked out a mile or so, with my rifle. Except the quaking asp, the flora is very much like western N.C. on a small scale - Flowers are in very great profusion. Huckleberries are ripe, but they are small scrubby things hardly worth picking. I saw also some holly, the first I have seen in the Hills - & many very familiar plants whose names even I don't know -

Shot a deer during the walk but could not find him. Returned to camp, got the Hd Qr Sergt[227] & his dog to go with me, & we found him quite dead. Trout stood the march splendidly, & is very cheerful. Just at dark we were all electrified by the report that a mail had come. It was soon brought down & opened in my tent, & was apparently very satisfactory to all. To me very much so except that there is a prospect of my losing Morton, whose wife is about to be confined - He has permission to go in - Letters from Father & several to Fred from Gracie,[228] Ma P & others. Tooty had arrived at Utica in good health & after a short rest had gone on to Saratoga - Ma P was at Richfield. Grace was going to Long Branch -[229] Long letter from John Connolly, who certainly writes better than I expected he could, & with more gratitude than I thought he possessed -[230] My letter to Adair returned through the dead letter office. Note from Jenney who is at Floral Valley, & goes down <the> Custers Trail on Red Water

226. See *Macbeth* V.i.23.
227. Sergeant Molloy, Company C, Ninth Infantry.
228. Grace Paulding, a younger cousin of Dodge's wife. She later married a West Point graduate, Second Lieutenant Louis P. Brant, First Infantry.
229. The two ladies were visiting resorts at, respectively, Richfield Springs, on Canadarago Lake, New York, and Long Branch, on the New Jersey shore.
230. Dodge's entry for September 2 suggests that during the Civil War Connolly, even then an old acquaintance, had been a Confederate prisoner to whom he had lent money.

to what he expects to be a gold field Nice camp - Good water & grass & wood. Distance 17 1/2 miles

Wednesday, August 25, 1875. Camp 29[231]

Three months today since we left Fort Laramie — Broke camp 7 a.m. Followed down the creek for about 2 miles then across a high open prarie. Soon the ravines began to encroach on us, & we were forced to cross some quite deep ones. Two or three had water. The whole country is of the Red bed & gypsum formation, & the water is very poor - alkaline & though beautiful to look at very trying to the bowels - Tried hard to get at the very foot of Inyan Kara ("The peak that makes the mountain") but its base is so cut by deep ravines through the Red Beds, that I had to get away to the N. E. & camp on the alkaline creek though I <know> ^am sure^ there is good quartz water within a couple of m[ile]s. Will look for it in a day or two. Went into camp 11 am Very pretty camp though wood is scarce and water poor. It is however as good as I dared hope.

Ordered the teams back to bring up Hawley & Comd, wrote him a long letter of instructions. It will require two trips to get him up. He is to be at Indian Spring with his whole Comd on 2d Sept. Wrote to Pollock Issued an order relieving Lt Hall and Compy from duty with this Comd & ordering him to report to Pollock for duty. Ordered him to send his two wagons up for rations. Will return three - (3) Am glad to be rid of that company Hall is an ill-conditioned shirk, & the Compy the most insubordinate, undisciplined mob I ever saw in the Regular Service. My command is stronger without than with the Compy. I was thinking seriously of sending it in with Burt. This opportunity comes very apropos -

Saw plenty of deer sign today, & could certainly have bagged one or more but that I dared not leave the Comd for I was anxious

---

231. Dodge named this Camp Bradley.

to go just <to> in a certain way, & could not trust anyone to take the lead. At a small creek saw several mallard but was too lazy to get out my shotgun. A fine large flock of sage hens, put some life into me, & I got it out pretty quick. Took a pot shot on a part of the covey and bagged 4, & 1, as they rose - making 5. As they are large fine birds, this was very good. They flew to an immense distance & I saw no more of them - Foster starts out tomorw on a surveying expedn down this creek of which we know nothing. If it is Bear Lodge I wish to go down it - Have offered Pollock 50 bee<ves>f cattle Distance today 9. miles - Fish in this stream —

Thursday, August 26, 1875. Camp Bradley, Camp 30

Train started very early this am for Terry - also a det[achmen]t of a N.C. Off. & 4 men for Pollock. After breakfast started out on a reconnaissance with Foote, which we soon converted into a hunt. Stalked a deer, & got within 30 yds & was taking sight when another deer suddenly sprung to one side, startling mine which made a motion to one side just as I pulled the trigger - My bullet was "Dodged" & I minus a deer. I was sure of it. "There's many a slip" &c -[232] Saw 3 deer but had no other chance. One of the men bagged a magnificent Black Tail today. The Dr. got some fish - dace - Had our sage hens roasted for dinner They were delicious — Corpl came in bringing note from Jenney. He has lost my packmule. D—— him. Heavy shower in afternoon with sharp thunder & lightning - Went to bed in good season Foster & Old Joe left this am for a survey of Inyan Kara & Bear Lodge Creeks -

Friday, August 27, 1875

Heavy rain at intervals all night. Got up late. The day cold, raw, & with occasional showers, sometimes heavy. Devoted the day to writing, & did remarkably well. Finished the game animals

232. Betwixt the cup and the lip.

of the plains, having completed 234 pages of MS. on[233] these alone. Will now go to work on the game birds - which will probably give me an additional 100 pages.[234] My book grows wonderfully, but I fear I have not time to complete the 2 volumes by the middle of Decr at which time I want to go east to arrange for the publication. Have not been out of Camp today scarcely out of my tent.

Trout doing splendidly. He does not want to go in. Shall remain out if he wishes. Driven to bed early by the cold -

Saturday, August 26, 1875

Had to go hunting today. T'was a case of "groundhog"[235] "Our Mess" has by the neglect or economy of Hubert run out of all meat but ham. No bacon, no venison & the beef herd yet a long way off. I started about 9 am determined to bag something. Going up the creek I found ducks & went after them on the principle that a duck in hand is worth a deer in the mountain to a hungry man. Shot very well & knocked down 16 ducks & a heron, but because I had no dog I only brought in 9 of the ducks Left them lying in plain view in beaver dams. Of course the beavers having dammed everything there was no necessity for my doing it - Had a very long ride. Saw plenty of sign of elk and deer, but not a single animal. Where they have gone to is impossible to say. Got back about 4 pm after a very hard and unsatisfactory days work, to find that Jenney had got into camp with his party. He started down Red Water but saw so many Indian signs that he determined to get back to the protection

---

233. Dodge wrote "in."

234. In addition to his discussions of game animals, Dodge eventually added four chapters to the section on game. These included "Wolves, Jack Rabbit, Rock Rabbit, and Prairie Dog"; "Other Animals"; "Game Birds of the Plains"; and "Fish and Fishing." See *PNA*, pp. 202-31.

235. A "ground-hog case" is defined in the *Dictionary of Americanisms*, ed. Mathews, as "a desperate case or plight, one in which there is no alternative but great effort." The earliest usage cited by Mathews is from 1885. A second instance of its use in 1875 is in the *New York Tribune*, June 21, p. 2.

of greater numbers - He agrees with me in my future programme for our march, which is fortunate, as I had it fixed anyway.

Got a good view of the Big Horn mountains today. They are entirely covered with snow. Huge masses of white from summit to plains line. An expedition there will have to hurry up its work.[236] Snowed up 28. Aug. Has been quite cold & windy today. This Inyan Kara oūntry is simply a slice of the plains sandwiched between mountain ranges - The climate is plains & bad - To bed early, very tired -

Sunday, August 29, 1875

Up at usual time. A doubtful kind of day, might be good or very bad. So though fresh meat is an absolute necessity, I dared not risk a long tramp after deer, but about 10 am went up the creek for more ducks. Fred went out, though he had one of his bad Paulding head aches. Ducks were few & far between, but managed to get 9 - 3 mallard & 6 Teal - lost one of each - saw them fall but could not find them - Oh! for Bunkie.[237] Returned early, & with the Dr.s assistance loaded nearly 200 cartridges - so am set up for a little while - Gave all necessary orders for the move tomorw. Jenney & Foote went on top of Inyan Kara. Found Custer's name deeply cut in the rock on the very top. Had to punish a man today for the first time since I have been out - Sitting down & reading on post

While at dinner, we were visited with a sharp wind which came near demolishing the camp. Tore up the Hospl tent, & destroyed some of the property. Wrote at night about eight more pages in "Game". Dont like its connection with preceding but cant do all artistically when am in camp - Fred all right tonight - Went to bed quite late -

---

236. Dodge alludes to the reconnaissance of the Big Horn and Yellowstone region then being undertaken under command of Major G. A. Forsyth, Ninth Cavalry.

237. Dodge's pointer bitch, left behind at Omaha Barracks.

Monday, August 30, 1875. Camp 31

Started from Camp at 8.30. The wagons got off an hour later. Went up the creek, but got no ducks. Struck off to the east, to find out something about the country. It is a curious one. Following up one of the miserable little dry arroyos that are tributary to the Inyan Kara, one first comes to huge and deep canons. These passed to beautiful valleys, more or less wide & with side hills varying from a bare slope to 2 or 300 feet - Hundreds of these valleys go to make up the miserable little stream of Inyan Kara. In all my experience, I have known of no more beautiful country, nor a more bountiful provision of lovely valleys rich in grass, going to make up so poor a result <as these>.

Crossed Custers trail well up on the divide. Passed for miles through one of the most lovely hunting countries I ever saw, without finding anything whatever. It was a dead country, & but for an occasional snowbird lifeless. Coming back to camp in disgust, Cook the orderly called to me & pointed.[238] Dismounting I went in front of him and looking in the direction of his finger saw through the thicket 200 yards away, a splendid Buck. I could get no rest, from which I could see him, so after careful aim fired offhand & *missed*. The deer did not move. Putting in another cartridge I was getting ready to fire when he started directly away from me - Determined not to lose my only chance I took quick sight & fired, & was not a little gratified when I saw him on the ground. The bullet entered very near the anus,

---

238. According to Dodge, Private Charles E. Cook, who was attached to a cavalry company, was "ruptured" and therefore unable to do hard service on horseback. In 1876 Cook was transferred to Dodge's regiment, the Twenty-third Infantry. Cook served as his orderly during the Powder River campaign of that year, and in a journal entry of November 26, 1876, Dodge characterized him: "Cook is a character... He has not the slightest idea of politeness - no bump of reverence - never thinks of saying 'Sir' to anybody, & speaks of officers as Crook & McKenzie without a thought of giving them their official title. But he is perfectly invaluable - a splendid hostler, a fair cook an eye like a hawk for game[,] is thoroughly honest - that is he would only steal for me, if I needed anything. He never forgets or loses anything - is always rough & always ready for anything -" (Graff Collection, Newberry Library).

& broke the pelvis. We butchered & put him on a horse, & continued our route to camp. Coming down a wide ravine, a fine buck sprung from a thicket about 75 yards from me & made off at the very top of his speed. I jumped off my horse - bleated to him - to which he paid no sort of attention, & when he was about 130 yds from me, & going like the wind, but directly from, & considerably below me I fired. He ran a hundred or so yards & fell dead. The bullet struck him in the middle of his belly, & came out in the neck. He was just lighting on his fore legs after a bound, & my bullet passed between his hind legs. Lt Foote saw the shot fired, & Dr. Jaquette examined it after. It is one of the remarkable shots of my life - He was not the largest, but by all odds the fattest deer I have killed this year - I can say a good day, 2 splendid bucks, & both running -

I have been very boastful of my shooting tonight, & we have all had lots of fun.

Poor Fred is getting tired. He will never make a sportsman. It isn't in him. He has very little taste that way - He gets awfully tired following me about & I have had to scold him a little tonight for being discontented. It is doing him good, & whether it did or not he is in for it now —

My camp is the same as 29. Brought Jenney with me. To bed 10.30

Tuesday, August 31, 1875. Camp 32

Sent out Corpl & man to bring Hawley to proper camp. After breakfast started with Fred & Foote out to look for a camp. Came <ag> across ridges, northerly to a large valley, followed it up to water & good grass - then going up a lateral ravine struck my road in Foot's canon. Sent orderly back to bring up Comd & camp it in the proper place, & went on after Hawley. Found that Sergt Davis[239] did not make any cutoff as I directed, but went

---

239. Sergeant Davis, Company C, Second Cavalry, was quartermaster sergeant of the Black Hills Expedition.

all the way round by Indian spring. Struck a fresh trail of wagons on my road going to Indian Sps, & soon after overtook a man who turned out to be a messenger to the Herald Cor[respon]d[en]t.[240] He had come up with Lt Kingsbury from Capt Pollocks Comd[241] with Hall's wagons after rations. He camped at Indian Sps, & remains there tho' my orderly told him we were camped at this place. The Corpl & man were found & taken up to the divide with orders to bring Capt H down the valley to this camp. We then started for camp. Before very long I saw a deer on the side of <the> a hill, & fired a long shot. It went off apparently unhurt. Just then I saw another lying down, & taking careful aim fired. It also went off. I went to the place & after a little search found both, one (the first shot) quite dead, the other I settled with a ball thro' its head - The first had been shot as accurately behind the fore shoulder as it could have been placed with the fingers. The other a little too far back. About 3 pm Capt Hawley came up with his Compy[.] Wagons came up late, 4.30. We have a very nice camp for our transfer.[242] Good water & grass. Open valley with heavy pine woods on each side.

Had good nap in afternoon & a splendid saddle of venison for dinner. Davenport wanted escort to take him in. Couldn't see it.[253] He goes to Red Cloud Agency, to the Indian Council.

Jenney over at Hd Qrs & we had a pleasant evening. To bed about 10.30 pm

240. This person was said to have made the 180-mile journey from Fort Laramie in four days.
241. Second Lieutenant Frederick W. Kingsbury, Company I, Second Cavalry.
242. Dodge named this place for rendezvous and transfer of goods Camp Transfer.
243. Davenport left Dodge's camp on September 3 and made the seventy-mile trek to Pollock's camp alone. There, he wrote in the *New York Herald* (September 19, p. 6), he was entertained in "noble chevalier style" before joining a party of five persons bound for the Red Cloud Agency. Davenport covered the grand Indian council for the *Herald*.

Wednesday, September 1, 1875. Camp 32

Started out about 9 am to hunt up Burt & the train. Foote with me. After a long ride we found them a mile below Cold Spring,[244] in camp & very comfortable. We had a pleasant visit Got a mail - tho not a letter for me from any "home bodies". A long & gossippy letter from Col Gantt - & a shorter note from Genl Bradley. He sends lots of papers Blackmore was to arrive in N. Y. by 15 ult, & thought he could reach Ft Laramie by 20th, but had not arrived when Burt left - I still have hopes that he may join me within a few days - If so, I will take him back to Rapid, & have a *geloorious* hunt -[245]

Killed two wolves today. The first a coyote, I butchered. The first shot hit him in the fore leg, & while he was worrying over that the second shot went through his flanks. He rolled over but getting up started to run across me, when a third shot broke near the shoulder the foreleg that was hit before. He turned tail & made off at speed. A fourth shot shot broke a hind leg, at which he rolled over & howled, but got up & made off again, when a fifth shot broke the other hind leg. At which he howled still more, & sat up on his one fore leg, until the 6th shot went through his brain. I never saw an animal try harder to get away.

The next one was a large buffalo, or prairie wolf. He was about 150 yards off & running across me, & I knocked him at the first shot. After leaving Burts camp we had a heavy thunder storm with considerable rain - but had our waterproofs - Just after the worst was over passed a large pine which had just been shivered with lightning. It was torn to fragments. Found Andrews and [*blank space*] in camp.[246] Letter from Pollock as broad in cheek

---

244. The site of Camp No. 12, on June 9; Captain Burt with his command was on schedule.

245. The press of business kept Blackmore from visiting the United States in 1875.

246. Captain William H. Andrews, Company I, Third Cavalry. His unnamed companion may have been Lieutenant Royal E. Whitman, Company H, Third Cavalry, who had been away from the command on court-martial duty.

as himself.[247] Morton's wife has had her baby & is doing well. So I will not lose him - Saw a small herd of antelope today far off. They had been frightened by Jenney's party, & were running away. Saw no deer. Had no time to hunt. Rode at least 25 miles today, & am tired. Andrews & others at my tent tonight. Jolly time. To bed late.

Thursday, September 2, 1875. Camp 32
An eventful day. Burt arrived with the supply train - Lawson & Whitman accompanying him - <An> Soon after King came in with the two Cos from Terry, & except Russell and Wessels, we are all united again -

Trout is a wonderful fellow. On the arrival of the train he took to his crutches - hobbled to an ambulance, was driven down & himself took account of all stock I have been writing letters all day. One to John R. Connolly, about the money I let him have when a wounded prisoner. His letter to me was based on something I said in my letter of Feby last to Aunt Mary. I therefore sent the letter to him, under cover to them, asking them to read it. I also wrote a letter to Uncle Nick - Wrote a long letter to Col Gantt - principally about the death of Frank Blair -[248] but on all sorts of gossippy subjects. It may be fancy, but I think I write to him better than anyone else. Wrote also to Father & Mother, & to Tooty - scolding her a little for not getting treatment. Have not been out of camp today, & my rifle is getting rusty -

We received all sorts of nice things by the train and I made such a dinner Potatoes, onions tomatoes all went to help out the beef - also pickles butter milk &c - One does not know how he misses these things, until he gets them again after a deprivation

---

247. A photograph of Captain Edwin Pollock that shows his wide-set features is reproduced in Hughes, *Pioneer Years in the Black Hills*, following p. 29; a suggestive earlier photograph is in Hedren, *Fort Laramie in 1876*, p. 172.
248. Francis Preston Blair had served in the Civil War with the Missouri Volunteers; he died on July 9, 1875.

Everybody around my camp fire tonight & we had a jolly time. Foster and old Joe got in. I cant go with wagons to the Belle Fourche west, & I'm glad of it. Shall take a hunt on Rapid - Wrote at night to Tooty & to bed quite late. Burt is specially amiable.

Friday, September 3, 1875. Camp 32

Soon after breakfast the Herald man Davenport came to bid me "good by" He is off for the Indian Council, near Red Cloud. Shortly after Burt (whom I authorized to go to the Council) came to do likewise, also Kingsbury - By 9 ock all these were gone, & about 12 Whitman and Dr. Lane started in the other direction for Russells camp, with a wagon load of stores & vegetables. We are getting well reduced. Wrote letters & read papers all day. Trout has been working like a beaver. Long letter to Genl Crook - (copy in end) -[249] Dr. McGillicuddy Morton & party arrived late in evening nearly starved - but glad to get back. They have been very successful, & come loaded with information Sat late at camp fire with many of my offs & Old Joe

Saturday, September 4, 1875

Jenney & his party started about 10 am Coles & his Compy went with him. Have only 2 available Cos, & they are very small King shot a fine buck elk today quite near camp.

Wrote letters, took a hot bath, had my hair cut read newspapers & *loafed* generally -

Sunday, September 5

Munson and the 2 Infy Cos started on the return trip. Morton made application to go in, & I let him, tho' I did not want to.[250]

---

249. See below, pp. 206-8.
250. Lieutenant Morton, whose departure meant the absence of a topographical surveying officer when the Black Hills survey was not yet complete, was relieved from duty with the expedition and authorized to report to his post, Sidney Barracks (BHE S.O. 32, September 4).

Deacon Willard the Trader packed up & left. The Comd is so sober, he is nearly broke — McMillan the Inter Ocean man went also. So we are nearly out of reporters -[251] Sent in my art[iller]y, & all the surplus am[munitio]n by Munson. About 9 am Foote & I started with 2 wagons, part of Hd Qr Guard & a Sergt & 10 men on a hunting expedition - & are now encamped at Joes Spring 23 1/3 miles from Camp Transfer, on the Terry road. Nothing seen yet. Tomorw we go on to Rapid Ck some 5 or six miles east in a direct line - about 10 by the road -. I send the Sergt to make Camp - Foote & I will hunt across. Foote saw 2 of the cattle I turned over to Pollock. That party will lose them all.

I made an [un]accountable blunder in my course this morning. Went down the Creek we are regularly camped on - & added some 6 miles to my day's trip. Rode the big horse, a stumbling brute & am pretty tired - To bed early - on ground.

Monday, September 6, 1875

Foot & I left camp at 6.30 am giving directions to the Sergt to move camp to a fine spring 7 or 8 miles east. Sent Joe to look for the mule lost by Jenney. We hunted through a lovely country for game, but in a couple of <hour> miles the canon which we were following became very steep deep & crooked, & the timber all fire killed -

However we pushed along & about 8 a big buck got up on a hill side, & ran into a thicket. He stopped about 200 yds off & though I could see but a small portion of him I fired. He went off, I put in another Cartridge. The hill was so steep that he could not run fast, but to counterbalance the brush was so thick that I could only get occasional glimpses of him but I determined to give him one more - & taking good aim fired. The deer disappeared, but the bushes were so shaken, that I was sure I had

---

251. Of regular correspondents only Dr. Lane, for the *Chicago Tribune*, remained, though in the course of the summer letters had been published from Lieutenant Coale and Dr. McGillycuddy, both of whom were still with the command.

knocked him down - Sent a man up, who found him quite dead - shot quarteringly but through the heart. This was a very remarkable shot. The distance was at least 350 yds - Yet I took exactly the same sight that I would at 35 yds. Foote said today, "I begin to have a superstition about that gun. I think if you only pull the trigger it will kill the game whatever the distance & whether pointed at it or not." It is in truth a remarkable gun, the very best by all odds I ever saw. There is no waste of time or geniu<u>s in guessing at distance. In antelope shooting I elevate sometimes, because the distances are so very great, but this is the second deer I have killed at 350 yds or over - with the usual and regular fine sight. Going on the creek we were on ran into another & a few moments after we found ourselves on Custer's trail - coming north on Rapid. Coming up the stream we soon found ourselves at my Elk ground ₍of 22 ult₎. Foot & I separated & went through. Naturally I worked to the spot where I had shot the 3, Aug 22, & on arriving near, ran onto the carcass of one which however, had of course become food for bears & birds. He was within 150 yds of where I had most assiduously searched. From the position where he was found, he is the one of the 3 I thought least hurt, & I am now convinced that I killed all, tho I bag only this His antlers were very fine so I brought them in. I was provident today & brought along a pack mule - If I had bagged all 3 elk on the day I killed them, I doubt if I could ever have got them to the wagons. It is an awful thicket - Sent a couple of men & pack mule to camp. Bagged another nice buck & as the day was very warm came to camp - getting in about 2 pm - Foote had arrived an hour before. Joe did not find the mule. It is undoubtedly dead -

Nice camp at a most glorious spring. Tomorw we try again for elk. To bed 9.30 pm

Tuesday, September 7, 1875
Up early & off before 7 am & hunted hard & faithfully all day - that is until about half past 1 pm. Went over a great deal of

lovely ground for Elk, but saw not a single one Foote & Joe saw two Elk a buck & a doe, but I got not even a glimpse - Bagged three (3) deer - only saw 4 all day, & the 4th was with the last I shot.

The country is very broken, & covered with dense thickets, so that it is almost impossible to get ∧(at) the game. Horseback hunting is too noisy, & the stoutest man would soon tire out on foot

Wolves gave us a serenade tonight, the first we have had in the hills. Move back tomorw. Bear & elk sign very plenty - The animals cannot be found.

Wednesday, September 8, 1875

Got out by 6 am today determined to have a good hunt, - and a good hunt we have had with little result. Went north after black tails & elk. Bagged 1 B.T. quite early, & had a long shot at a large B.T. buck, & think I hit him but he got away. Went down the big canon, turned up a side west canon & came to camp through a lovely hunting country, without seeing a thing (except a fox which I shot) simply because we had the wind in our backs Found where several elk had been scratching & pawing and our approach had undoubtedly driven them to cover. We have been very unlucky on the hunt in the wind. Start whatever direction we may, the wind is sure either to be flawy, or to go directly against our success. Camped at Side Hill Spring. There is a great deal of beautiful water in the Big Canon, low down. We lunched at a lovely spring, & so many came together that in 2 miles from the start, the stream is as large as Rapid - Got in from an interesting trip about 2 pm - Had a long delicious nap - Had a pleasant evening by the camp fire. Thundering & threatening storm as I close this —

Thursday, September 9, 1875

Commenced raining about 10.30 last night, & kept at it all

night. Had breakfast put & the mules turned out.[252] By 6.30 am it had ceased & we got up & had bkfst, but the mist covered everything - so that we could see nothing, & the bushes were so wet that hunting was not to be thought of, except at expense of a ducking.

Made up my mind, to go back to Camp Bradley today. Started 8 am. Arrived at Floral Valley sent Joe with a note to Capt Hawley, directing him to move camp down to Inyan Kara. Followed Custers trail, & am sorry I did it, a more crooked way was never discovered - Arrived in camp at 4 pm after a hard days march of 30 miles - Has rained & misted all day - so we did not hunt. Have not fired my gun today - nor seen anything but a hawk to fire at - Found all right in camp. Fred well, & has enjoyed himself.

Trout getting on splendidly & all glad to see me - Had a nice camp fire, & enjoyed it

Went to bed about 9 pm, after giving orders for a short move tomorw.

Friday, September 10, 1875

Broke camp 9 a.m. & moved about 3 miles north, to a lovely little valley where I camped. This move was only preparatory as I expected to <go> have to go tomorw a considerable distance for water. Sent Joe out to explore the proposed route - Let my horse rest today, & was somewhat disgusted when a few hours later King came in with 2 deer - & 6 Ruff grouse.

Had a good nap, & wrote some - but unsatisfactorily. Joe returned just at dark with information that no water is to be found on my proposed route. So I am forced to go for some distance tomorrow on Custers trail. High wind last night & this a.m. Lovely night - one of my prettiest camps Water good & grass

---

252. This statement is garbled in some way. The word "put" occurs at the end of a line in the manuscript; perhaps Dodge forgot to add a word like "away" at the beginning of the next line.

most excellent - The grass in all this vicinity is unusually fine, & the Officers are delighted that their horses have had the benefit of several days on splendid "*Gramma*" I have not seen this grass since soon after I left Cheyenne ——

[*The text that follows is written with the notebook reversed, beginning with the last sheet and ending with p. [60V] in the original pagination.*]

August 14
 On Box Elder & Elk Cks the deer are very plenty but very small - A very great number of barren does - Sand-hill cranes on Elk -

August 15
 Came on 2 Sand hill cranes feeding on side of a mountain - no shot - Fred's orderly saw an animal which from description must be a Lynx - Another barren doe today

August 16
 Two of the Bk Tails bagged today covered with long coarse reddish hair very thinly set. The third had shed this coat, & was covered with a short thick coat of mouse colored hair He, tho' not the largest or fattest, was the *oldest* and was getting his winter coat early ——
Night of 17th ice 1/8 inch.
 " " 18th " 1/4 inch - & very heavy white frost which curious as it may appear, has had no effect on the flowers or shrubs -

August 19
 Another barren doe today. Bear & Elk signs abundant. The animals themselves hid in the thickets. Elks capacity for hiding very wonderful for so large a beast — Two remarkable shots today - The first at a deer running, 100 yds - dropped her in her tracks - The other 120 yds could only see part of its flank. Bullet went in at lowest rib, out at shoulder, same side -

August 21

Trout broke his leg - Fred hurt by his horse - Miriads of blue bottle flies & insects of all kinds - Camped near top of divide between Terry & Custer Peaks. Several hundred feet above Camp Terry. Course W. N W.

August 22

Saw Sand hill cranes Young ones large enough to fly. They pair — Saw several broods of Mallards, nearly grown, & a flock of 4 Teal the first I have seen in the Hills - The heads of Rapid Creek are a succession of Beaver dams, which are the resorts & breeding places of numerous water fowl - Shot 3 elk bagged none. Rather disgusted but if I had killed them I could not have got them to camp.

August 25

Camped under Inyan Kara Water alkaline - All the maps erroneous - Sage Hens today for the first [time] - Country bare of timber - soil red beds & gypsum - Called "Camp Bradley" Splendid *Hop* region - as fine wild as I ever saw cultivated.

Fish in stream. Wood plenty but rather far off - grass good Fair camp - The country is really a strip of the plains inserted between high mountain ranges -

August 26

Fine spring in Mts 2 1/2 miles east. Country very broken, & cut up by gullies in the red beds. Looks like a huge N. C. old field. Grass very fine. Black and cow birds very abundant Trout wants to continue the trip. Plucky but indiscreet. He may do so if he wishes.

August 28

Mallard, shovel bills & teal quite plenty. The first breeds here, the others just arrived from the north. I hear plover every night and tonight heard a regular Jack or English snipe. Yellowlegs, sandpipers &c are coming on rapidly - Saw Big Horn Mountains are completely covered with snow - this 28 Aug[253]

August 30

Tributaries of Inyan Kara Ck, very remarkable in length numbers, and lovely valleys towards their heads - Jenney & Foot ascended the Inyan Kara Mt yesterday. Country about here in valleys covered with Hop vines - the very finest I have ever seen wild. Foote says No 1 hops even cultivated -

August 31

Great variety of birds about Inyan Kara - many of them entirely new to me. Wished for a "Baird & Cassin" -[254]

The heads of Inyan Kara Creek, are splendid large valleys, - & that they so "peter out," and result in so insignificant a stream - would be remarkable in any but a limestone, gypsum, red-bed formation.

September 1

Cold Spring - fine cool & abundant in June, now perfectly dry. - An arroyo a mile south, dry in June, now a nice running stream - Burt is camped on it. Jenney saw great abundance of gooseberries on mountains near Cold Spring - Saw several grouse, & Lewis & Clark's woodpecker, but did not have my shot gun.[255]

---

253. On the page that follows, p. [71R], Dodge has sketched two maps. The first, at the top of the page, shows the relative locations of Camp 30, Camp Bradley, and the watercourses and mountains in the area. The second shows the relative locations of Camps 30, 31, and 32, and Red Water Creek.

254. Baird, *Catalogue of North American Birds;* Cassin, *Illustrations of the Birds of California, Texas, Oregon, British and Russian America*.

255. On the three pages that follow, pp. [69V], [69R], and [68V] in the original sequence, Dodge drew four maps and compiled a hunting record. The map on p. [69V] is carefully drawn, with watercourses shown in black ink and all else in pencil; it locates Cold Spring, Burt's Spring, and Indian Spring along Spaulding's Creek and shows several trails connecting that creek and a point "B" in Transfer Valley. The two maps on p. [69R] relate to Floral Valley. The first, at the top of the page in its reversed position, shows Custer's trail,

All the portion of the Hills west of Spauldings Ck, & north of the great divide is nearly worthless. The soil is the washings of red beds gypsum beds &c The water is very bad. The timber is scarce, but what there is is pretty good

---

All elk out of Velvet, by end of August —
2 red deer - killed 31 Aug in velvet - 1 killed 6th out of velvet 1st of Season

Camp Transfer
10 miles fr Inyan Kara
Sepr. 4, 75

Genl Geo Crook

Genl - Since my last letter this Comd has worked its way slowly northward until N.E. of Terry's Peak where we found the country impassible for wagons I then turned to the westward, passing between Terry and Custers Peaks and keeping S.W along a huge divide, the only practicable route. Struck our entering trail at our camp of June 11 - Thence I marched N.W. to Inyan Kara where my camp now is. The supply train arrived on 2d, and I am now reloading & preparing for our final round before finishing our work. I have kept 2 parties of surveyors under Lts Morton & Foster in the field all the time, & have materials by which we can make as perfect a map, as can be made without surveyors compass & chain. I am very sure that no part of the wilderness is as well known as the Black Hills now are. My route from here will be to the N.E. along the base of the Crow Peak Mountains One of my parties has already reached the Belle

---

"Springs," "Transfer," and "Floral Valley" and also traces three trails, two passing through the valley. The second map on p. [69R] shows Floral Valley and a trail along a watercourse to its east. The hunting record, on p. [68V], details animals taken on September 1 and 6–8. Beneath that record is a map showing Custer's Peak, Terry's Peak, a camp, a trail leading between the camp and the two mountains, and another trail that joins it.

Fourche surveying Inyan Kara and Bear Lodge creeks. I have designated the 20th Sepr, on which day all the parties are to concentrate near Bear Butte on the N.E. of the Hills - I anticipate that the work in the Hills proper will be done by that time. If not it will be finished very soon after. One party will then run down the Belle Fourche to its junction with the South Cheyenne The other with the Hd Qrs will move along the N.E. & E. base of the Hills joining the inside work with the streams outside - Mr. Jenney desires to return through the "bone fields" and I expect to strike from the mouth of Rapid to about the mouth of Porcupine Ck on White River & return to Ft Laramie by way of that river and the agencies.

You requested me to give Capt Pollock all the assistance in my power. When I went over to the Miners meeting on 10th, I took with me 2 Cos Cavy one of which I left there with instructions to report to Capt P. on his arrival. Finding that the work of the expedn took me entirely away from the vecinity of Capt P, & that it would be almost impossible to act with him I believed that your wishes would be best carried out by relieving one of my Cos permanently. Company I, 2d Cav under Lt Hall was therefore relieved from duty with the Expedn & ordered to report to Capt Pollock. I have issued rations to that Co to the 10th Oct, and also gave Capt P. 10 beef cattle My Comd being now supplied with all necessaries for the time that I propose to be out I have relieved the 2 Infy Companies & ordered them to report to Col Bradley.

I am truly sorry to have to report that Lieut Trout was struck by a falling tree and had a bone of his leg broken. This occurred on 21 ult. He has evinced the most cheerful & plucky spirit since the accident & attends now to all his duties as usual. He did not wish to leave the Expedn. The Dr. did not recommend it, the air & climate evidently having the most beneficial effect - so I do not send him in - To a man of his disposition nothing would be so trying as inaction, & I think he has the best chance for a prompt recovery in the fine climate & occupation of mind that his daily duties give him - I would like extremely to have my map of the Black Hills made up under my own supervision - If therefore there is no objection to the plan, I would be very greatly obliged if Lts Morton and Foster, both of 3d Cavy be ordered to report to me at Omaha on the completion of this expedition.[256] The Engineer Dept may make (or would if they knew of it) some objection to this, but as I am responsible I ought to have the making of my own maps. Lt Bourke being also in Omaha, all the officers who have acted with me in the surveys will be on hand, & I do not fear other than a good result - The miners went out in excellent humor, & were much gratified at your courteous & considerate treatment. Had however you not most fortunately met Capt Benteen there would have been great trouble, perhaps bloodshed. They were greatly incensed against him for indiscreet remarks & threats alleged to have been made by him So far as I saw or heard, he acted & spoke with entire propriety - The hunting is good, the game is not nearly as plenty here, as where I took you. In ten days of the last half of August I bagged 16 red and 5 black tail deer. No elk yet.

> Very respy
> Yr Obdt Svt
> Richard I. Dodge
> Lt Col 23 Inf
> Commanding

Elk Shaking over by 31 Aug. The first red deer found out of velvet bagged Sepr 6 - <th>

No elk here about since where I shot the 3, since - very shy -

---

256. Lieutenants Morton and Foster, and also Lieutenant Foote, were later ordered to report to Dodge at Omaha (BHE G.O. 6, October 15; *ANJ*, November 6, 1875, p. 196; December 11, 1875, p. 280; January 1, 1876, p. 332).

Begin to get in droves by Sepr 1 - Each sex by itself -

September 7

A buck and doe Elk found together for the first time this season. The buck also whistled, which is a symptom of running. It will commence very soon —

September 8

Elk scratchings getting plenty - We must kill some soon - They are getting careless. Pine in this section quite poor.

Black Hills favourite place for migratory birds to stop - Numbers here in Sepr that do not breed here — (Sepr. 8) ——[257]

[*inside back cover*]

Animals

Bear - several species -

Elk, Black Tails, Red deer

Ground hog, Wolves, Foxes -

Red pine squirrel - very small

Chipmunk, or ground squirrel

Lynx - Cougar or Mt Lion -

Mouse - Buffalo.

Birds

Kingfisher

Yellow bird

---

257. The text on the inside back cover is written with the notebook reversed; on the back cover, written right side up, is a list of dates not reproduced here.

Sage Hen

Buzzard

Heron

Teal

Shovel bill

(Migratory birds)

Reptiles

Rattle snakes, garter snakes
water mockasin - Bull frog -
striped head turtle - saurians

Journal Six: September 11 – October 19, 1875

Saturday, September 11, 1875[258]

After Joe's unfavorable report on route yesterday I determined to follow Custer's trail north, until I got beyond the abrupt canons & then strike east - Broke camp 6.30 am <after> and followed Custer's trail - Left the train to Foote & Joe & went off to the left hunting. Bagged a fine buck antelope after a beautiful stalk Went in behind or to the west of the Sun dance Hills - struck there a very bitter alkaline creek & followed it down to where the trail crossed it - Had lunch, got out my shot gun & started again, after giving directions as to how the Comd should go, for at this point I left Custer's trail. I went on to the north struck a ravine which I followed down, found water & soon after Beaver dams on which were ducks. Bagged in an hour 9 ducks & 2 grouse, spike tails - The train not appearing, I went in search of it. Had a long search & finally discovered it going down the very creek we had left. Got back to it in time to turn it into a nice camp, though the water is none of the best. Comd made today about 21 miles. I must have made 35 - Fred stuck by me remarkably well, but his "botty" is a little sore tonight - To

---

258. This manuscript journal consists of ninety-four pages; a few additional leaves at its front are missing. On the bottom side of the cardboard pad, Dodge has written in ink "Black Hills [/] *1875*"; below it, in pencil, is an encircled "6." Except as noted, and for parts of a map drawn on the inside back cover, all entries are in pencil.

On p. [1R] Dodge compiled a hunting record, not reproduced here, which summarizes daily results of hunting and fishing on September 11–18, 22, and 24–27. The text begins on p. [1V].

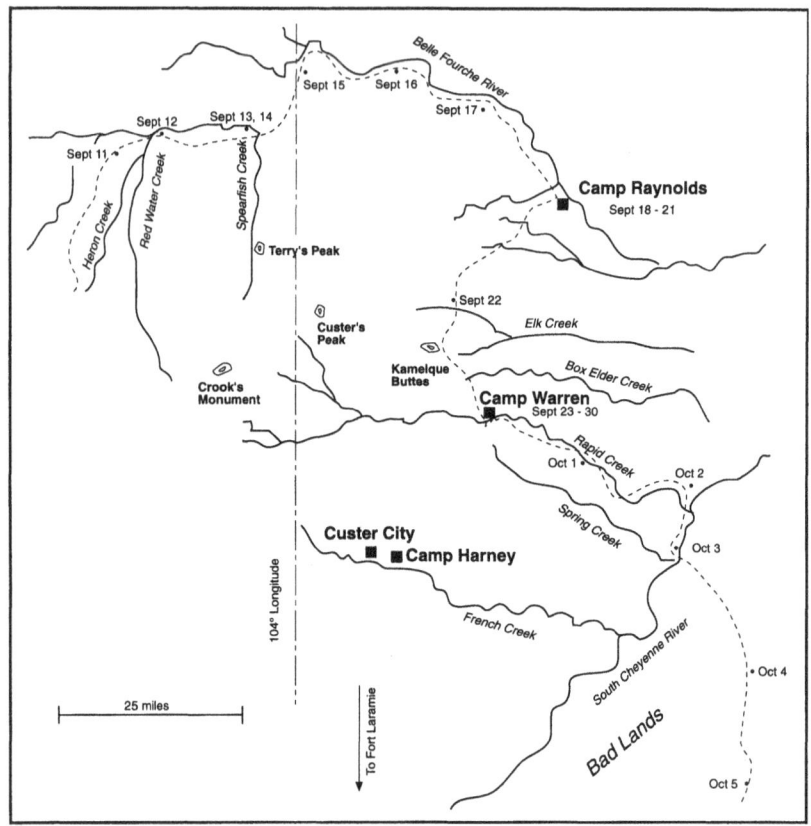

Itinerary, September 11–October 5

bed early, well satisfied with the day's progress, & hopeful for tomorw -

Sunday, September 12, 1875

Broke Camp 6.30 am. Went out with Joe on proposed route, & found it impracticable for wagons. Sent him back to take the Comd across the creek, & by a more northerly route. He was very successful in executing my orders, & we made a short march of about 10 miles without trouble or difficulty though the country is one of the very worst to travel in with wagons I have ever seen - By 11 am we arrived at Red Water (much to the discomfiture of Joe who had insisted it was 25 miles off) at a point scarcely a mile below where we would have struck it had we been able to go the way I wished. It is a large fine stream 30 feet wide by an average of 20 inches deep & very rapid. There are a good many suckers in it but apparently no other fish. We have a most excellent camp, <tho> not much wood, but the grass & water are perfect Sent Joe out this p.m. to look for tomorw's route. He returned at dark, has found an excellent route & it is only 10 miles to "Spearfish". So we are all elated. Bagged 1 spike, or willow grouse coming along, also 1 Mallard in this creek before the Comd came up. Had a 500 yd shot at an antelope - another equally long at a deer, both running & both misses - Had hardly got the tents pitched before it commenced to rain - Had a good nap. Late in afternoon went out with Fred, & bagged 3 fine suckers. There are a good many but they bit very badly To bed rather late

Monday, September 13, 1875

Broke camp 6.30 am. Went ahead with King to find some lakes which were said to be ahead. In about 2 1/2 miles came upon a very lovely little lake, evidently fed by springs of pure water. It was surrounded by tula grass. The open water was about half a mile <wide> ∧long by 200 yds. wide. The swamp in the tula grass nearly doubled these dimensions. There were numbers of ducks on it - but after knocking down six, & bagging but one I gave up in disgust -

The outlet of the lake is a small stream of beautiful water, which I did not taste - Went on, struck a small creek coming down from the west side of Crow Peaks. It was a succession of beaver dams, on one of which we found a few ducks. Here I bagged a mallard and 2 teal - & burst a cartridge in my gun, rendering that barrel useless. <I forgot to say that before getting to the lake> I then took to my rifle, and went off around the east side of Crow Peaks after deer - Went through a lovely hunting country for miles beautiful oak woods, without seeing a deer, or even a track. Was cut off from my projected hunt by a huge canon coming down from Crow Peaks, & had to come back towards the road. En route I bagged 2 grouse - ought to have got more - Overtook an ambulance in which was a man who had fallen from his horse & badly hurt his arm - Came down a tremendous hill to the valley of "Spearfish," found another pack of grouse and bagged 3 - Went onto the creek for ducks, but found none, as it is too swift for a duck to hold his grip in. It is a lovely stream hardly so large as Red Water, but from its great rapidity carr[y]ing more water. I had given Foote & Joe instructions about Camp, & my tent was pitched when I got in - We are in a lovely spot. The valley is a mile wide. Near the creek is timber - Oak ash Elm Box Elder & rarely a cottonwood - The water is splendid - clear pure and soft. We are now nearly on the plains level & the weather is warmer. I was greatly disappointed that there is no game, but it is on the great N. & S. line of Indian travel, which accounts for this — Fine wood grass & water. We lay over here tomorw. Soil fine - Winter grapes to be found - Delightful evening - To bed late -

Tuesday, September 14, 1875

<Broke camp 6.30> Didnt break camp, but slept peacefully until 7 a.m. After breakfast Foote & I rode down the Creek to its junction with Red Water, about 5 miles The latter is much the largest creek - carrying at least one-half more water. The two creeks when joined make a large fine body of water This stream is the best in the Hills for a Military Post - at least so far as I have seen. The day was lovely, but uncomfortably warm. About 5 1/2 pm a very heavy storm passed to the eastward of us, evidently hail. We escaped with a sharp blow, which lasted more than half an hour - after which the evening was as lovely as could be desired by the most romantic young lovers a splendid full moon & balmy atmosphere -

The country here is very bare of game of any kind. I saw today but three ducks two of which I bagged - not another shootable thing, except a rattlesnake & I bagged him with a fishing pole - We fished for a long time in the main stream below the junction. There are a great many suckers, some channel or Lady Cats & some white fish (called hickory shad in N.C., and herring in some other parts). There are also a few dace. I fished very faithfully & used all my skill, and I fear not a few bad words - but got only 1 cat, 6 suckers, & 3 dace. Foot was worse off for he displayed unexampled patience & got nothing in return. When we got back we found that the men had made a seine of mosquito bars & taken some 40 suckers, 18 at one hawl - among them a red sucker, with a long nose, mouth far under it, & very fine scales. I have never seen it before Orders to move tomorrow at 6.30 as usual -

Wednesday, September 15, 1875

Broke camp 6.30 a.m. Had some trouble crossing creek, so did not get fairly stretched out til 7 a.m. Passed over <p>a portion of ground visited by the storm of yesterday afternoon - Though after 8 a.m. the hail yet covered the ground in some places to the depth of several inches - & <were> many of the stones were of the size of hazelnuts.

The streams on that side were tremendously swollen, making some of our crossings difficult - & changing the pure sweet water of our mountain creek, to a dirty white alkaline compound. The fish would not bite. We came down stream striking the main creek or river about a mile below the junction It turns a little west of N., receiving three tributaries <on> from the west, the third of which changes the whole character & appearance of the stream. Down to this junction the stream is deep, rather narrow for the water carried, very swift with frequent deep holes, & low grassy banks - After striking the stream spoken of, it spreads out into a wide channel, is quite shallow, nowhere more than 3 or 4 feet. Every body is exercised to know whether that tributary was the Belle Fourche or not. - There are good reasons on both sides, but there is no use speculating when we will know of a surety tomorw. Got 3 grouse, all I saw, & one cat, all that bit. It is a miserable country for game. We are quite out of the Hills & on the plain. I can hardly realize it - & look back on the black mass with longing regret. Distance about 13 miles - Good camp - plenty of everything - Lovely night -

The valley passed down today - Morton's Creek is one of the very finest for a post I have seen in the Hills. Splendid water, & soil - excellent building stone - timber & limestone convenient, & elegant hay bottoms. Water power sufficient for all sorts of mills.

Thursday, September 16, 1875

Broke camp 6.15 am. Had a poor day. Troubled with my old enemy, dysentery all day, & feel weak & good for nothing. Under such circumstances everything goes wrong, I found a fine pack of sage grouse, & got but one shot & one bird. The others disappeared in the most misterious way, though carefully marked down. This is the disadvantage of having no dog. Had a running shot at a fine buck. Think I hit, but did not bag him. Found a pack of willow grouse in a thicket, got two snap shots, & no bird bagged. Got to camp disgusted & tired, & very weak in front and rear -

Went to creek with my rod, & had lots of good bites, & succeeded in losing more fish than I ever recollect, on any other occasion - Secured 4 cats (one very fine 3 pounder) 3 whitefish, & a dace. Lost more than twice as many. Such is luck - when it sets in bad, everything goes wrong - We have had no end of argument (& betting among some) on the vexed question - "Is this the Belle Fourche or not?["][259] The question is not even yet definitely decided, for there is still a chance that it comes in tomorw. All I can say is that the maps are all wrong, not one has his own ideas & insists on beating that into the others ——

259. For a further account of the betting over the identity of this watercourse, see Dodge's additional entries for September 16–18 at the back of this journal (p. 248).

About 16 miles today. Good road. Camp good - on high bank of stream Red Water or Belle Fourche we dont know which -

Friday, September 17, 1875

Broke camp 6.20 am Dysentery a good deal better tho' it seems to be beginning again tonight, just as I am going to bed. Nice pleasant day - Travelled down the Belle Fourche - decided at last to be such. Crossed Custer's trail about 3 miles from our last night's camp. It is not within 4 miles of where he puts it on his map -

Bagged 3 willow grouse. About 11 1/2 came into the valley to look for a camp. Saw an antelope a long way off. Fired 3 shots at him, each at a thousand or so yards & came so near him each time that it was a marvel how I missed him. He soon joined 3 others. I fired at the lot several times running at immense distances & wounded a buck. The herd ran near the head of the Column, and the Sergt Major killed one.[260] Joe's dog caught my wounded one, but could not hold it, & was beaten off - Returning to the bottom I saw another, & getting behind a hill fired at about 600 yds - He was so far off that he did not run away, though the bullet once covered him with dust. On the 3d shot he fell with a broken back, from a ricochette shot - The longest successful shot made on the trip. Marched 12 miles. Went fishing after getting into camp, but was not very successful. The river is wide & shallow & stands in great pools. The fish are too much diffused - Took 4 very large white fish - I have always had a prejudice against this fish though he bites well. We had them for dinner & they were delicious - I was too weak from yesterdays trottings to work much. Came back early & took a good nap. River turns too much to the south from here. Expect to reach our <pes position> ∧ supply camp tomorw, when we will lay over a day or two. To bed early.

260. This was the First Sergeant James S. McClellan, Company H, Third Cavalry. The journals of McClellan, which include graphic accounts of the Big Horn expedition of 1874 and the Powder River campaign of 1876, but not of

Saturday, September 18, 1875

Troubled with my complaint all day. Broke camp 6.30 Had a pleasant march of about 12 miles, to the junction of Bare Butte Ck with the Belle Fourche The day was very windy. Had a long shot at an antelope & missed him. Three others ran from behind a hill & past me within 300 yds I selected a splendid animal, & my first shot turned him out of the herd. Followed him a long distance, getting a shot once in a while, but unable to put my bullets where I wanted, by the wind. Sent back to old Joe for his dog, but before they arrived had bagged him. He had two shots directly behind the fore shoulder, but both rather too low - one in the leg - one in the loin - one through the side - & the last, 6 in all in his rump. Yet before receiving the last he seemed able to run any distance I could not catch him with my horse, nor would he let me get near enough for a sure shot. I secured him at last by stopping and watching him until after going at least a mile he laid down. Even then I had to shoot running - Was too sick & wornout to fish this afternoon.

At night copied what I had written on Sage Grouse. Saw plenty of willow grouse today, while I was after that confounded antelope. He lost me a fine opportunity, the best I have had, for there were quite 50 birds - Shall remain here until Jenney & the other party arrives. Have a good camp, good grass & plenty of wood - Dr. Lane caught some fish this afternoon -

Sunday, September 19, 1875

Remained in camp today waiting for Jenney & the other party. My bowels still trouble me greatly. If not better tomorw must take some medicine, a thing I hate to do.

---

the Black Hills Expedition, have been edited by Buecker, "The Journals of James S. McClellan"; see especially pp. 21–22.

Spent the day writing on my book. Finished Grouse - & started on the Turkey -[261] nearly 25 pages today - very good for a man with the b—y ache - Hope the writing will show no symptoms of the malady.

Had my other tent pitched & a good fire made. It has been a raw Novr day except in afternoon, when the sun came out warm. Sent Joe out to look for water for my next march - found none. Will have to change my direction. Many fish caught today - among others an 8 pound cat on a small trout fly, by a teamster - Foote lent him the fly -

Monday, September 20, 1875

Diaroeha very bad. My Dr. book says let it alone - or take a dose of castor oil. I let it alone. Wrote considerably today. Dr. McG[illicuddy]. & party came in late in afternoon. They have had a fine trip. Not out today at all. Dr. Mc. & others at my tent at night - pleasant reunion. He is a really nice intelligent fellow - To bed late ——

Thursday, September 21, 1875

Diaroeha much better owing to the brandy & water drank last night with the Dr. Still however have no confidence in my bowels - Determined to move, after a consultation with Dr. McG. Issued rations for his party to 6th Oct. For all others to 30th, except Coale. <Sept> Ordered his rations to 15th Oct, to be weighed out, & left here for him - Gave orders to move early tomorw - Late at night wrote a letter to Jenney, pitching into him amiably for not coming in time -[262] Orders for Coale - Am sorry to believe I have a thieving Comd. Several articles were stolen last night. Shot a willow grouse this a.m. in camp. It flew a hundred or so yards & fell - a scamp of A Co[mpany] bagged it, & I have not been able to find the man. Am out a grouse. If

261. See *PNA*, pp. 213–15, 218–23.
262. Dodge wrote "to time."

I catch any of the thieves I'll make it lively for them. Dr. McG. goes to junction of N & S Cheyenne - mapping both rivers -

Wednesday, September 22, 1875

Equinox - but no storm. Broke camp 6.45 a.m. Travelled in a S. W. direction for the mountains. Crossed long slopes & some bad breaks, but the road was very good. Struck for the point where Elk Ck comes out of the Hills, tho' no one was certain we would find water there. Was quite sick again, going out every few moments. I am getting very weak, & my comfortable girth has shrunk to the circumference of an aldermans thumb.

Had a shot at an Antelope at about 300 yds. Put my bullet into his chest - he was looking at me - & broke one of his shoulders. He went a little distance stopped & I thought I had him sure, but he saw us & put in his best licks on 3 legs. I sent back for Joe & his dog, but the antelope was too smart, keeping in the cactus where the dog could'nt come. He finally got away, for I was too weak to follow far. When we got to the foot hills I crossed lots of dry arroyos & was beginning to despair when we came upon the true Elk, where I struck it a little rill, but rapidly increasing in volume. I went down about a mile & camped in a beautiful spot. Plenty of delicious water, a boon from Heaven after the alkali of the Belle Fourche - good grass & fine oak timber for fuel - dry at that - We made a good long march, 22 miles, but we were all glad to get off at that, & with so fine a camp.

A Black Tail buck jumped up by the train today, but was so fat that he could not run, & was pulled down by the train dogs - "Curs of low degree".[263] The first time I have ever known of a wild animal getting too fat for its own protection. Foote, who saw the affair, says the deer could not run at all He trotted & hopped - & made scarcely any fight with the dogs. Indeed one caught & pulled him down, but couldn't hold him. The others then came up & they held him till the men arrived -

---

263. From Oliver Goldsmith's "Elegy on the Death of a Mad Dog."

Got to the camping place & sent back to direct the train   While waiting a grouse started   I went after <them> ∧ him & got up a pack - bagged 3 - & left the others on a nice side hill but where in my weakened condition I could not go   When the train got in I took my fishing rod, & in a short time took 36 dace - some of them quite half a pound, but the majority about 6 inches long. Could not go far or work much - & came back as soon as my tent was ready. The day has been excessively hot. Had a pleasant evening. No trouble with bowels, & have fairly reveled in water drinking - satisfying a 7 days thirst -   To bed 9 pm

Thursday, September 23, 1875

Broke camp 7 am   Directed the wagons to follow Custers trail to where it came out of the mountains. Went up the creek, & got into the valley between the mts & foot hills - Very hot day. Marched all day along the foot of the mts occasionally going up a canon, but saw nothing except 4 antelope at a long distance off.

Left Custer, & struck off for Rapid. At 2 pm struck a most lovely spring & went into camp. Call it Camp Warren[264]   May remain here a week, that is the troops may. I go tomorw with Foote into the Hills for a hunt -

March today 17 miles, & not hard except from heat. Had pleasant evening, several officers being around my Camp fire - Gave orders for my start tomorw. Leave Fred, as he is tired of hunting. Went to bed rather late.

Friday, September 24, 1875

Gave all final directions took an escort of 6 men 2 wagons & my ambulance & started. I got off at 9 am, Joe & the wagons half an hour later. Foote & I struck across country. - The ground

---

264. The camp was named after Lieutenant Gouverneur K. Warren, early explorer of the Black Hills, who in 1875 was major of engineers and brevet major general.

is very broken, much cut up by canons We hunted faithfully for four or five miles without seeing any thing. I then saw 2 deer, & followed them off to the eastward Foote being then a few hundred yards to my left. Failing to find them I went on a little way, & stopped & waited for Foote but finally concluded he was still on my left. Crossed a nasty canon, killing a deer on the way. I doubt if I had crossed it so easily but that I came upon a large old Indian trail. Within a short time after crossing this I struck a stream of running water - Knew it must be Camelco[265] & followed it down, & in less than half a mile came to Custer's trail & the point designated for camp tonight. Went down stream to see the ground. Got a long shot at another deer, but the thicket was so dense I could not hit him.

Joe & the wagons were not up, & Foote supposed lost. Came back, had the horses unsaddled & leaving the two orderlies with them went on foot up the Creek Deer & elk sign plenty, but not an animal did I see larger than a squirrel Came back disgusted about 4 pm to find camp pitched. Got my fishing rod, & went to work. Took a fine 2 lb. sucker & 41 dace out of one hole - Took the sucker with fresh venison as bait. Dr. Lane a few days ago took a sucker with a bit of beefsteak. The suckers in Belle Fourche were not good - soft and tasteless. This tonight was splendid, the real *Rapid* sucker. While I was fishing Foote rode up. Not finding the trail by which I crossed he had been unable to cross the big canon, & finally became alarmed lest he might

---

265. On the map prepared for Dodge's official report and reprinted with minor revision in *The Black Hills*, the name of this watercourse, a tributary of Box Elder Creek, was spelled "Kamelque." The name derives from an incident said to have occurred, in which California Joe successfully played on the credulity of H. P. Jenney. Pointing as evidence to the skeleton of a bull elk which he identified as that of a "camelk," he convinced the geologist that the Black Hills actually harbored such a zoological curiosity. The camelk, he explained, had originated from crossbreeding between elk and the camels that had supposedly been imported into the region by the War Department. See Parker, *Gold in the Black Hills*, p. 64; and for an earlier account, King, *Campaigning with Crook*, pp. 154–55.

not get into camp. Went back nearly to our permanent camp, & took the wagon trail. He travelled at least 20 miles more than there was any necessity of, & got no game. His orderly killed a deer, & one of the guard got another. So we have plenty to eat.

To bed about 9 p.m. Diaroeha all gone. Feel first rate —

Saturday, September 25, 1875

Started out a little after 6 am, leaving Old Joe & Sergt Molloy to move camp. Took pack mule with me. Went up the little creek near the mouth of which we camped & which I supposed to be Camelco. About 2 miles from camp Locke one of the orderlies told me he saw a black tailed deer in a thicket of quaking asp. While I was trying to see it, a herd of elk started out, & went at speed to the top of the ridge - so managing the flight that I could not even get a running shot. Some of them stopped on top of the ridge - & one enormous buck stood broadside, but nearly 400 yds off & so covered by timber & hemmed in by trees that I could only see about 6 inches of him - I took the chance, but failed. He went off. I went as fast as possible to the top of the ridge, but though I could then see for a thousand yards all were gone, & I could hear the Buck piping on an adjacent hill - Just then 3 deer attempted to pass me. In 3 shots all were down, & another presenting himself opportunely I knocked him also. The ground was bad thickets rocks & fallen timber so that I only bagged 3 of them. The other was the first one shot & I was so blown getting up the hill that I put the bullet too far back. I shot & killed another, & my wounded one stopped about 150 yds off & the 3rd ran up along side of it. I fired at the one already wounded It fell & rolled down the hill - Yet when I came to look for the dead, I found the first, & one which I did not shoot at, while the one with 2 bullets through it got away. This is the second time on this trip that I have killed a second deer, with a bullet that passed through a first. One of my 3 black tails at Camp Terry was killed so. Followed up the stream or ravine, for it becomes perfectly dry, till finding it bore too much to the South

I took up a right hand branch. Crossed some open park country, and came to some deep brakes which I did not doubt led directly into Box Elder. While hunting a way to get down, I found the old Indian trail & followed it down a tremendous canon, to a beautiful running stream. Followed this up for 4 or 5 miles, expecting constantly to come into Egan's trail, & to my surprise & very great disgust, I at last emerged from the box cañon (from which I could not get before) to find myself on my own road from Crook to Terry & only 5 miles from Camp Crook. I was thoroughly disgusted for it was now 12 m. & I was at least 15 miles from where I had directed the Comd to camp. There was no time or use to worry, so I took Egan's false trail to near his first camp ∧^{near} which I killed a nice buck - Then struck across country for the camp where I took Genl Crook hunting. Then the question was, whether to follow Egan's or Custer's trail. Both were bad but I thought Egans, a little nearer. At least it would put me in rear of & on the trail of my party, while by the other I might miss camp, if delayed until dark. Took Egan's. Just at my old hunting camp saw 2 deer coming to water. Crept down on them through the willows & bagged both. Egan's trail is much better than I thought it was. About a mile & a half from Box Elder, on the divide & in the small pine, came onto 2 bucks and bagged one.

Struck Box Elder at last & the trail of my party. Followed it to camp, saying bad words against Old Joe for persuading me to come here, & giving thanks that I had daylight to travel in, or I would have had to stay out. Got into camp about 5 pm after a round of at least 30 miles to make 12 - during which I have been forced by stress of canon to travel at every point of the compass. I forgot to say that in the box canon, <I> finding no signs of large game, I shot the head off a grouse

<Was> Am satisfied with my day tho I lost the elk & made a great circuit quite unnecessarily - if I could have got out of that miserable canon. Yet 7 deer & a grouse is not a bad days bag.

It was a tiresome but delightful day. Had a pleasant evening with Foote & Old Joe - neither of whom killed anything.

Went to bed about the usual hour ——

Sunday, September 26, 1875

One of my unlucky days Started out about 7 a.m. Sent the Sergt and party back to Box Elder - Took Custer's trail westward. It is as crooked as a rams horn. Saw nothing till we got near Beaver Dam Ck, when I shot at a deer not more than 75 yds off & missed it clear - at least I did not get the deer & saw no blood. Shortly after I had a splendid shot at a deer in a Beaver dam & bagged it. Foote was in my way, as he will push ahead, yet can never kill anything himself. Finally sent him off towards camp, & worked hard for an hour or two without getting a shot, though I saw 2 more deer together —— I then started down the Canon of Beaver Dam which soon ran into Box Elder, & a more infernal canon I never saw, rocks, thickets, beaver dams, mud, fallen trees every obstacle that could be put in the way, & yet not make it impassable.

After three hours of nasty work, & a variety of bad words, I got to camp too tired & worn out even to go fishing, which I had relied on to finish my afternoon. I am more tired out than I was yesterday, though the actual distance travelled is not half so much.

Lovely camp. Had a short nap, which did not suffice. Am sick of this kind of hunting & gave orders to go in tomorw. There is no game to be found, unless one travels miles for every deer he sees, & the travelling is abominable. Hurt my horses back today. Express from Hawley. Coales is in with part of his Compy. Will send him on to Spotted Tail - Letter from Fred in fine spirits ——

Monday, September 27, 1875

Started at 6.25 am going directly down Box Elder by the road - Did not take the trouble to hunt, but killed a fine buck before

I got to the 1st camp. Seperated there & hunted a little, but though I saw lots of deer was too eager to get in to work hard - Got into camp 12.30 - travelled about 15 miles - by the trail - The wagons got in about 3 pm - Found the guards not vigilant & pitched into several captains. Gave orders for Coales to leave in the morning, for Camp Sheridan.[266] Wrote to Chambers[267] begging him to send out my corn at all hazzards. Found Fred & all well. Relieved all the men of Coales Compy except Sergt Davis.[268] Wrote to Father & Mother. Very hot in the valley today after coming off the mountain - Jenney is said to want to stay out till 1st Novr. Dont see it - Got Trouts Com[missar]y file - & made out all the mess bills - 87 1/2 cts per day for each little enough —— I am sorry now that I did not make my hunting camp at my first camp out. There was a great deal of game about there & we would have done better. We went through the game. There was nothing far up in the Hills. Went to bed late for Camp -

Tuesday, September 28, 1875

Very tired & lazy - tho' got Coales off - in fair time, & with instructions to go through to Spotted Tail in 5 days if possible. Did little of anything except sleep & rest. Wrote a little at night to bed early. Very hot day. Dr. Lane went with Coales.

266. Lieutenant Coale, with Company C, Second Cavalry, was to march to Camp Sheridan as quickly as possible, via Rapid Creek to its mouth and crossing from there to White River. Coale took with him a detail from Company K, Third Cavalry, which was to return from Camp Sheridan as escort to a wagon train bringing forage. In case Coale should meet the Jenney party, the detachment of troops escorting Jenney was to be relieved by the men from Company K, and the men so relieved were to assume the duties assigned to the detachment accompanying Coale. Upon their arrival at Camp Sheridan, Lieutenant Coale and his company were relieved from duty with the Black Hills Expedition. California Joe was to accompany the troops to Camp Sheridan and also the wagon train on its return (BHE S.O. 34, September 27).
267. Major Alexander Chambers, Fourth Infantry, was in command of Camp Sheridan.
268. Sergeant Davis, Company C, Second Cavalry, was to remain with the command as master sergeant (BHE S.O. 34, September 27).

Wednesday, September 29, 1875
   Repetition of yesterday. Remained in Camp all day, but spent nearly the whole time ∧ writing. Gave orders about issues tomorw. Wrote until my candles burned out - & went to bed. Storm came up in night - -
   Very hot day, & also quite warm at night.

Thursday, September 30, 1875
   Woke up this a.m. with the wind howling & the rain pattering on my tent. Thought of Coales & his passage of the bad lands today. By 9 ock the rain had ceased, but the wind blew with great violence, & the day has been cold & most uncomfortable. I went to bed about 12 m, and taking my tablets commenced writing - or rather continued - for I had been at it all morning. By 8 at night I had gotten through with all that part of my book devoted to hunting - have arranged it to suit me, & I may say that my book is finished. Of course I shall have to go over it all this winter at Omaha, revise correct punctuate & prepare it for the press -
   I have 340 pages of Mss on hunting, which makes all together about 1100 pages. About dark the wind went down & we have a clear night, but cold, & will be colder, as the geese & cranes are going over us constantly - bound south -
   Came near having a serious fire today, but finally got it out. Orders to start early tomorw. To bed 9 pm

Friday, October 1, 1875
   Broke camp 7 a.m. Followed the trail of Coales Comd down the Rapid which is a beautiful stream though after getting 6 or 8 miles from the Hills it loses its purity & rapidity and becomes murky and discolored, tho' the water is good, and though not a slow stream anywhere so far, it has long reaches of comparatively still water seperated from each other by rapids. The bed of the creek is here filled with grass, & it becomes a fine feeding

ground for ducks & geese. I saw great numbers today - but after shooting some, I would lose so much time getting them that the comd would get ahead & scare all the game - Oh, if I only had a good dog. Mem - never to go on such an expedition without one or more ———

I bagged 17 ducks & 3 grouse. Had several 600 & 1000 yds shot[s] at antelope but got none. When we got into Camp, Foote, Dr. & I went fishing. I got a very good lot - (see table) -[269]

It [has][270] been a most perfect day, just cool enough, yet bright & beautiful. Everyone was delighted. Marched 19 miles. Road excellent - not a particle of work for the Pioneers all day. Nice camp on a spring of fine water near Rapid. Wood water & grass plenty & good. Dr & I filled cartridges at night, and we all had a good time around my camp fire. To bed 9.30 pm

Saturday, October 2, 1875

Broke Camp, 7.00 a.m. Followed Coale's trail which still led down the creek. The crossings were bad. Foote went ahead & did not watch the Pioneers. I went duck hunting & finding none, went out on the prarie after antelope Found & bagged a big buck, & when I returned to trail, found the comd had not yet passed. Said some bad words, & when the Comd did arrive I let them know forcibly that the march would have to be made if it took till dark. It was then 12 m & they had made 5 miles a mile an hour - Made Foot stay with it. Fortunately there was but one more bad crossing, & by a little after 4 pm, all <were confined> had arrived
ʌ at the Cheyenne river - Found Jenney, Dr. McGillicuddy & all waiting for us, the first time J. has been on time. He is however in a refractory mood, & is determined not to go in - I tried to get him to go over to White river with me, where he could get grain, but he will not go. Neither will he tell me where he is

---

269. Dodge's table, not reproduced here, is on p. [89V] of the manuscript.
270. Dodge wrote "was."

going how long he is to be gone or give me any satisfaction whatever. He says he dont know, he must go where the work takes him, & stay as long as he thinks necessary. He places me in a very delicate & difficult situation. I am sent on this expedition to escort him & his party. I suppose I might claim that we have finished the work for which the expedition was organized, viz the Survey of the Black Hills - & that I have therefore nothing to do but return to my legitimate duties. Waiving this, however, I have a much stronger reason for going in. Before the last train was sent in for Supplies, I sent for Mr J. and asked him to detail to me his plans - where he wanted to go, & how long to stay out. This was necessary to enable me to give proper orders, as to where the supply train was to meet us, & absolutely requisite to enable me to make requisition for supplies. He then detailed his projected route - (which by the by he has not stuck to) & told me that he wanted to get back to Ft Laramie by the 15th Oct - I made requisition for supplies, rations &c to 15th Oct - & when those had been delivered to me, I relieved the Infy Cos, which had been escorting my supply trains & sent them with all extra wagons, & surplus of every kind back to their post.[271] Now on this 2d Octr. he tells me that his work is not done, & that he must remain out an indefinite time beyond that fixed & provided for -

Three courses are open to me - 1st. To force him in, by refusing him an escort, or pack mules. This would cause ill feeling, & probably a scandal, & widen the breach between the Interior & War Depts. He would undoubtedly report me, for hindering the completion of his work, & in defense, I would be obliged to show his indecisive vasallating character - & tell the facts of the case.

2d. To send in to Camp Sheridan for supplies. Should I do this I risk the loss of men & animals in storms, which may now be expected. Besides which Mr Jenney will give me no information or dat<g>a, on which to base requisitions. I have no

271. Dodge had made these arrangements at Camp Bradley on September 4.

train to send in & no provision has been made for supplying me from that post -

3rd To leave him to go his own way, & to go in to Ft Laramie at the appointed time whether he comes or not. This will look badly, & as if we had had a quarrel (which is not the case) I appear to be deserting him, which I am not, for he acts as though he wanted me to go & leave him to himself, and this is I believe the true reason of his action. He hopes to <f> make some extraordinary discoveries in the bone fields - He wants to keep these to himself, & on them to base a chance of another expedition. He knows that he cannot hope to have the secret kept if a dozen or more intelligent officers pass over the same ground with him, & his object is now to get rid of us -

He is not an imbecile by any means, & must have some plan. If he has, and wanted me with him, he could give me some data on which I could make requisitions. He will not tell me any thing, avoids the subject When I ask him a question, evades it by a story of numbers of antelope - or how scared the Indians were - &c. He has got 3 wagons, & an escort of 12 men from a Compy to be stationed this winter at Red Cloud.[272] This escort is rationed to 15th. I have finally determined to go on, as per programme - leaving him to himself as he evidently wishes. I shall direct the Sergt in chg of his escort, to be at his post, Camp Sheridan, on 15th. He ∧ Jenney can take care of himself, & in this country at this time and season he is in no danger, though he may lose some stock, which will be bad for me — This is really the only course that seems to be open to me. I am truly sorry that this so harmonious & successful expedition, should have had this faux pas at the end of it - but it is not of my seeking or making. I am doing the best[273] I can so far as my judgment goes, & if any

---

272. Upon the dissolution of the Black Hills Expedition, Captain Russell's Company K, Third Cavalry, had been ordered to take post at Camp Robinson.

273. Perhaps in a pause for thought, Dodge followed this word with a comma, which is omitted here.

mishap occurs I shall not be able to blame myself, tho' I may be blamed by others —

If Mr Newton or Dr McG. were the head of the Scientific Expn nothing of this kind would have occurred -

Struck the bad Lands about 12 miles from here on Rapid - The Creek is still rapid, & and there are no beaver dams today the water is not pure enough. The creek is very boggy in some places - Said to be no fish in it here. Didnt try - Dont believe it however. Rapid Ck valley very lovely. Distance today about 16 miles - Jenney & all over to my tent at night. J. went away very happy, - in avoiding explanation & getting rid of me. I go tomorw — To bed late.

Sunday, October 3, 1875

Broke camp 8. a.m. the crossing of creek having to be worked before we could start. Marched up the S. Cheyenne, crossed Spring Ck which comes apparently directly from the south, turns sharp to the east at only 3/4 of a mile <for> & joins the Ch[eyenne] about a mile & a half above Crossing of Spg Ck Crossed the Cheyenne River The bed is here over 400 yds, though the thread of water running in it now is only 20 to 50 feet according to depth and rapidity. The stream does not now carry as much water as the Rapid brings to it. The road is very good except in the sandy bed, & bottom of the river. Went up stream about 2 miles above Crossing, & waited for return of the Sergt Major, whom I had sent early this morning to ascertain the truth of reports made to me by Mr Jenney, that there was plenty of wood & water in a canon about 6 miles from here. The Sergt met me at 11 am with the report that there is neither wood nor water there. This is about on a level with Jenneys reports usually. He is either the most remorseless liar in the world, who lies simply for the sake & love of lying, or he is constitutionally incapable of telling the truth. I am sometimes disposed to believe that his stories are simply colorings of his imagination which he really believes truths - but I cant see how the imagination of the most sanguine youth, can see wood & water in a dry desert of the Bad Lands, & see it so plainly as to report it officially - Had I more confidence in him I might have got into a serious difficulty with my whole Comd, but I had so little confidence that last night when he told me I sent for Sergt McClellan & gave him orders to go out this morning & see if Jenney's reports were true. This I did in Jenneys presence & he must have felt himself a convicted liar at the time - I turned down to the river & went into camp, making only about 7 miles today but getting myself in position for a good march tomorw. When I woke up this am the rain was pattering on the tent. Knowing the horrible nature of the bad lands in wet weather, I was in great tribulation, but nevertheless made all arrangements for pushing on tomorw. The morning was very raw and uncomfortable. The clouds were heavy & threatening & occasionally there were little spits of rain, or rather mist. Soon after I turned into Camp the clouds cleared away, the sun came out, & tonight is as clear as a bell, & there is every assurance of a cool but lovely day tomorw -

Gave orders for a very early start. Had a pleasant evening. Took a nap in afternoon. To bed about 9. pm

Monday, October 4, 1875

Broke camp 6.20 am Followed Joe's trail, got onto the mesa without difficulty. A mile beyond came upon the edge of the bad lands. - Imagine an immense irregular bowl of earth, from 8 to 10 miles in diameter. The sides 150 to 200 feet high, & cut into a million of irregular & fantastic shapes. The general bottom of this bowl is level, but scattered through[ou]t it are hills & mounds of all shapes & sizes, cut into inconceivable designs by water. Castles & towers, domes & pinacles obelisks <pin> monuments

The 5th Avenue palace & the Indian teepe are here side by side, & all the varied forms are fluted & frescoed by water, & painted in various colored earths, making a grand coup d'oeil, that no man can conceive, imagine or realize until he sees it. Bad lands are very varied in the degree of their badness. Where just beginning to be bad they are at their very worst for travelling & as they get more decidedly bad lands they improve. This <is> appears a contradiction - is yet a truth. They are formed by the action of water. They were originally the beds of lakes. A vast quantity of sediment has been brought down the streams and deposited in the bottoms of these lakes. This sediment is composed of mud clay and various alkalies All this deposite was finally lifted from the waters & exposed to the action of rain. The peculiarity of this soil is that it does not all equally resist or yield to the action of <the> water. Some of the ingredients dissolve readily & are carried off. The others seem to get harder & stiffer from their loss. Narrow channels are at first cut in the surface. These get wider & deeper in course of time but the walls remain nearly perpendicular. <While the> The surface is continually torn - the sides worn away until at last all the vast deposite has been washed away & carried off, & the bad lands become no longer bad lands for travelling -

During the earlier stages of this process, while the surface is yet only cut by narrow but deep channels, or while the amount of material to be washed away is yet considerable, these bad lands are many times absolutely impassible for wagons. When the water has worn away the projections which intervened between the <water> channels & the whole area has become practically a desert plain the travelling is not difficult

Where we first struck the rim of the bowl today, the prospect was disheartening in the extreme. The ground far below the mesa, was torn & worn into a thousand fantastic shapes, but the divides or mounds of earth, yet between the water channels, were so large & steep, that not even a horseman could have made his way over them -

This we avoided & keeping along the rim for several miles finally descended by a terrible road, to a comparative plain, where much the larger portion of the peculiar deposite had been washed away. Through this we made our way with some difficulty, for some miles, when to the delight of everyone we struck a great Indian teepe trail, & soon after a wagon road (whose, we do not know) along which we bowled merrily & comfortably - At the southern boundary of the particular bowl into which we had descended, we had to ascend again, by a very steep & difficult road. We made it however, & thence had an easy descent to the White River. The wagons did not get in until 5 pm - a long and trying days march, tho' we have made only about 22 miles.

White River is nearly dry, only standing in pools - those containing only the very worst & most alkaline water. The camp is poor tolerable grass, very little wood, tho' enough, & abominable water. Fortunately we still have enough for ourselves & men, brought from Warren's Spring, but the animals must be disgusted — We are all very thankful that the much dreaded passage of the bad lands has been effected safely & well, and are in no mood to <h>quarrel even with a poor camp.

The bad lands continue about & to the south of us, but in somewhat different form the White River serving as drainage to its bowl, & all the torn lands, pouring at every rain storm, part of their ingredients into its bed -

The river bed is here about 200 feet wide - is shallow & sandy but gives evidence of carrying sometimes a great deal of water -

We stopped all along the route today to examine the bone fields, as these great mounds in the bad lands are called. Found thousands of fossils, but principally turtles of huge size, some in a fair state of preservation Many bones of animals are among them, but generally we found only fragments, too small for us ignorant people, to tell what they were. Fred loaded himself with a half bushel of specimens.

Coale made a dry camp about 5 miles north of this camp, at the foot of the high southern rim. If he had come up the hill he would have found a good spring -

Ten lodges of Indians encamped 8 miles above us last night. Edgar, going to Jenneys camp, got into their[s] by mistake. They treated him well - gave him supper & a bed - a buffalo robe & blanket. They came with him to our camp this a.m., but fortunately we were gone -

Tuesday, October 5, 1875

Raining again when I woke up, but we pulled out at 8 a.m. We went diagonally away from the *river* & in a little while I noticed that all the little gulches in which the fallen rain was running, went *away* from the river. This puzzled me decidedly. After two or three miles seeing no sign of the River on our right, & the streams running to our left increasing in size, I was finally led to the conclusion, that we had not yet seen White River, & that what we supposed that river, was only the wide bed of a sandy creek coming from the bad lands - This suspicion was finally made certainty. About 10 am there was no doubt of it, & I started to go down to the stream on our left to make sure, when I came upon a large Camp of Indians. I did not go down to it, as I could not talk to them & knew they would be begging for everything. A great many came out of their lodges & looked at us, & finally the Chief & a few of his orderlies came galloping up. Fortunately Dr. Jaquette & Lt Lawson were ahead. The Chief went to the Dr. & taking him for the big chief commenced to beg for a beef. I was near enough to call to the Dr. not to tell the Chief who I was. The Chief turned out to be Black Tomahawk a Minneconjou - & had letters of recommendation from Dr Hinman. All right for the Indian, but who will give a letter of recommendation to Hinman? He could not find the big chief, each officer turned him away telling him to go to the Big Chief. I kept away & after following us for some miles, they departed in sorrow, casting longing looks at the beeves They belong to Ft. Sully & are on their road home from the Council - Kept up the White for some 8 miles further, & went into camp in a lovely spot. Wood water & grass all excellent.

Shot 4 ducks just after getting to camp & caught 8 white chubs - small. About 4 30 pm Joe came in to our great delight & a few moments after Lt Lemle, from Spotted Tail,[274] with our grain & an escort. Every body delighted - Chambers sent me a box of cigars - Mrs. C. a tin can of butter - Mrs. Lemle some bread, & apples. There was no mail for us at Spotted Tail - a blunder of mine or of Bradley's. Chambers wrote me a pleasant letter & sent me some papers -

The weather cleared off nicely about 3 pm, but at this time 10 pm it is raining again a little. We are on the real White River now, about <3>40 miles from Spotted Tail - It is a nice stream, bed of about 100 feet - about 500 inches of water - pretty swift. Beautiful bottoms - wide fine grassed, & well timbered -

Wednesday, October 6, 1875

Broke camp 6.20 am Road excelent. Made a long march - about 25 miles & camped in a beautiful place on the White River here a sluggish rather nasty looking stream, with banks covered with willow to the waters edge. The water is 1 to 3 feet deep from bank to bank, & about 30 ft wide Looks more like a canal than any thing else - The banks & bottom are miry, & we had to water our stock with buckets. Excellent camp otherwise Tried fishing & had the best success I've had on the trip. In little over an hour took 3 cats of 3 lbs to 3 1/2 lbs, 3 large White fish, 7 or 8 smaller cats, & a dozen chubs - over 20 lbs fish.

After 8 miles from Camp we were overtaken by Jenney. He is out of rations. He reported to me that he was *"done."* So I ordered his escort back to its compy, & now he will go in with us. So my plan was right tho' somewhat risky -

---

274. Second Lieutenant Henry R. Lemly, of Company E, Third Cavalry, was stationed at Camp Sheridan.

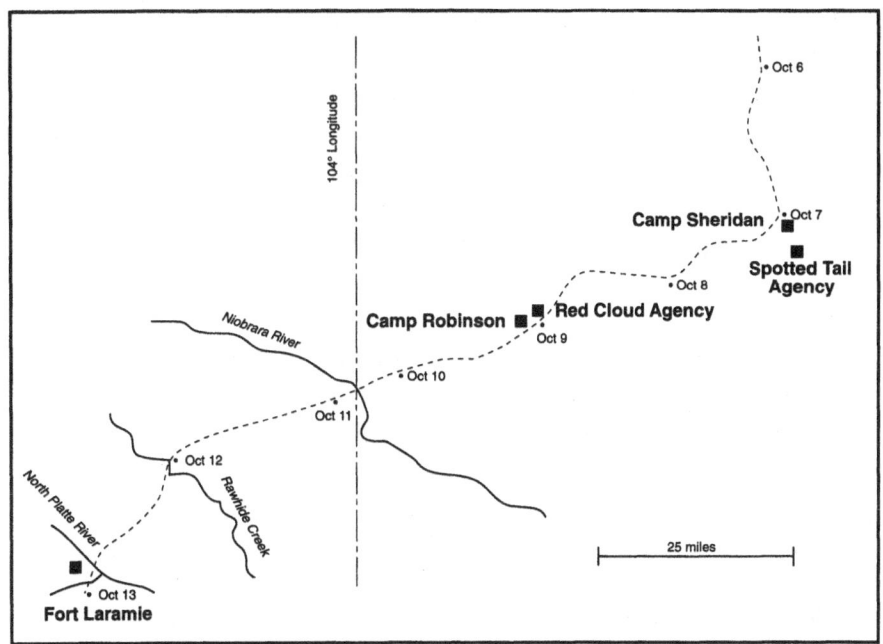

Itinerary, October 6–13

Jenney & several offs over at my camp fire. Everything splendid. We are about 23 miles from Spotted Tail. Met several Indians today. Carried no gun today might have got ducks & grouse

Thursday, October 7, 1875
Broke camp 6.45 am. Marched up the White River <for> by a good road for 14 miles to the old Agency - then up the Beaver 7 miles to Camp Sheridan - Arrived at the latter post 2.15 p.m. Chambers made me go to his house. Fred & I dined with him. He has a nice & pleasant little wife. Visited Capt Mills & wife,[275] & Lt Lemle & wife in evening. Came back to Camp very early. Dont want to be stationed at this post. It is a poor affair, & surrounded as one would expect by hoards of savages. Several

275. Captain Anson Mills, Company E, Third Cavalry.

thousands encamped about here. Went to billiard room at night & found it occupied by a lout of half drunken citizens & soldiers - Came away promptly. Got hay & wood from Chambers, in return gave him 3 wagons to bring his family & goods to Ft Laramie. Country very broken & roads difficult. Dr. Jaquette spent evening with me. Got to bed late - Played 3 games of billiards with Chambers, & beat him tho' could not play well.

Friday, October 8, 1875
Broke camp 6.30 a.m. before Camp Sheridan was awake. The road has been very fine, & all came along well. But how horribly monotonous these plains are after the beauty & variety of the Hills. And then this travelling along a road - no game in the country - Indians all about, & consequently not dangerous. One has no need of a gun either for sport or protection. I get more tired in ten miles of such travelling than in a jaunt of 40 miles w[h]ere game and variety attracts one - Got into Camp about 2.30 pm on a small brook. Took my fishing rod & went after anything I could get. To my very great astonishment the dace were most plentiful & voracious. I got them almost as fast as I could throw in. A teamster volunteered his assistance & after some time he said, "Well I suppose if I told anybody that you caught fish faster than I can string them, they wouldn't believe me, but it's so & I am working hard too" I fished less than 2 hours and took 150 dace - that is more than 1 per minute. Some of them would weigh quite half a pound, & in all the trip, I have seen no such dace fishing - I could have got any number more but quit on 150 - thinking that number enough -

Very good camp - grass not first rate - wood not very plentiful - but still enough of both. To bed 9 p.m. No mail yesterday & rather mad today -

Saturday, October 9, 1875
Broke camp 6.35 am Travelled over a good road crossing many running streams & dry arroyos all tributary to White River, &

arrived at the Agency[276] before 12 m. It happens to be ration day, & hundreds of Indians were collected in & about the agency, in all their finery -. We stopped for some time to see the sight, which was picturesque in the extreme - Arrived at Camp Robinson about 1. pm. I have heard a good deal about the beauty & desirability of this post but dont want any in mine. Capt Jordan Comdg Off very polite. Went into camp half a mile from the post. Miserable camp - water bad filled with dead animals, refuse of Indian camps &c. No wood & no grass. Got wood & grain from the Post but no hay. Was going to lay over here but gave orders to start at usual hour tomorw. Almost all the Officers of the Garrison called on me at night - & had a very pleasant evening with them. River here quite small, only a brook - Country monotonous Nothing to interest one or make the post desirable except the Indian - Dont fancy him -

Sunday, October 10, 1875

Broke camp 6.40 am Road led directly up river crossing frequently. The banks are very high & steep, & the road one of the crookedest & up & down I have ever seen. It is however tho hard on animals a very fair road. Came up 12 miles. Found a place where grass <use> is pretty fair & went into camp. Wagons & all in by 12 m. White River changes its whole character above the post. Instead of the whitish water from which it takes its name, it is as clear here as any water I have ever seen - So clear indeed, that though there are fish, fishing is out of the question, as the finny tribe run under the banks at the approach of a man, & wont be seduced out - Eleven head of our cattle missing this morning, made a row, sent the herders out, with threats to charge all the lost animals to them. Result all the cattle up this evening except one, & that heard from -

Parted with Capt Russell 3d Cav & Compy this morning. He has been with me for the whole expedition & is an excellent officer

---

276. Red Cloud Agency, approximately forty miles south of west from Spotted Tail Agency.

and his Company is a good and reliable one. Am now reduced to 3 Cos -

This creek or river runs through a rather pretty country, high hills on each side, covered with a sparse growth of pine - some of it very good lumber - Both these posts have saw mills. Indians in great numbers for about 5 miles up the river from post - Some in camp this afternoon but none appear to be encamped near here.

Monday, October 11, 1875

Broke Camp 6.40 a.m. Continued up White River by a much better road for five miles - then on to the divide, & by a gradual descent to the Niobrara The days march was only about 16 miles, though we expected at least 21 - & we were in before 12 m. Niobrara a nice stream - 10 ft wide by 6 in. deep, very clear & pure. Not a tree, bush, or even a willow twig on its banks - We brought wood however & as the grass & water are good we have a good camp. Very cold raw & foggy this a.m. but cleared up about 11 am. Bagged 4 grouse on the road over. Went fishing as soon as I got in - or rather after lunch. I have never seen such quantities of fish in any stream - small suckers small cats - dace I took 1 sucker & 105 dace from one single hole not over 10 feet square, & 3 feet deep. Some of the dace very large - a foot long, & all much larger than the average. Got tired & came in after taking 112. Took a nap. Jenney Dr. McG. & Newton over to see <us> me tonight. Had a pleasant evening, gave my paper on Formation of Black Hills to Newton & asked him to revise and correct the geology. He was very clever, & promised to do so, & also to give me any items that might seem to him to require mention -[277] Fred much better - quite himself

277. Dodge's entire discussion of geology in *The Black Hills*, pp. 29–43, was furnished him by Newton. Introducing that text, with its lucid commentary, diagrams, and tables, Dodge praised the "accomplished assistant geologist" for his steady professional labor in the Black Hills, "so patient and so indefatigable that it would hardly be too much to say that there is scarcely a rock in the whole length and breadth of the 'Hills' which does not bear the mark of his hammer" (p. 29).

If I am ever so unfortunate as to be stationed at one of the Agencies, I will work up the Niobrara. I think it a glorious stream for fishing & hunting -

Tuesday, October 12, 1875

Broke camp 6.40 am Left the Niobrara at once & marched south west over a long succession of rolling prarie - in some places very sandy. Reached the Rawhide at 12.50 p.m. distance 23 miles. Wagons got in at 3 pm, which was doing wonderfully considering the road & the distance - Tried fishing but the fish are scarce & small - fished out - too near the settlements. Day lovely, & the night perfect. Had a delightful camp fire reunion, & went to bed about 9 p.m. Country passed today fit for nothing but grazing but will sometime support great herds of cattle. Rawhide an insignificant stream, though it has some timber, which the larger Niobrara has not —

Wednesday, October 13, 1875

Broke camp 6.45 a.m. Marched over long slopes & on the same road on which we went out; our trail last night connecting at the crossing of Rawhide with the trail made by us on the 26th day of May - one hundred & forty days ago.

What a long succession of pleasurable incidents & emotions in that 140 days! - Arrived at the North Platte, 12. m. Crossed, forded by a ford rather deep but with a good bottom, & camped on west bank of Laramie River half a mile below the post. The wind stayed till we had selected & pitched camp, & then commenced in a style to remind one that we have again come onto the plains - <It>I went up to the post about 1 pm. Reported my arrival to Genl Bradley who appeared delighted to see me. Mason[278] & wife arrived while I was in Bradleys house. Was

---

278. Lieutenant Colonel John S. Mason, Fourth Infantry, who was a member of a general court-martial about to be convened.

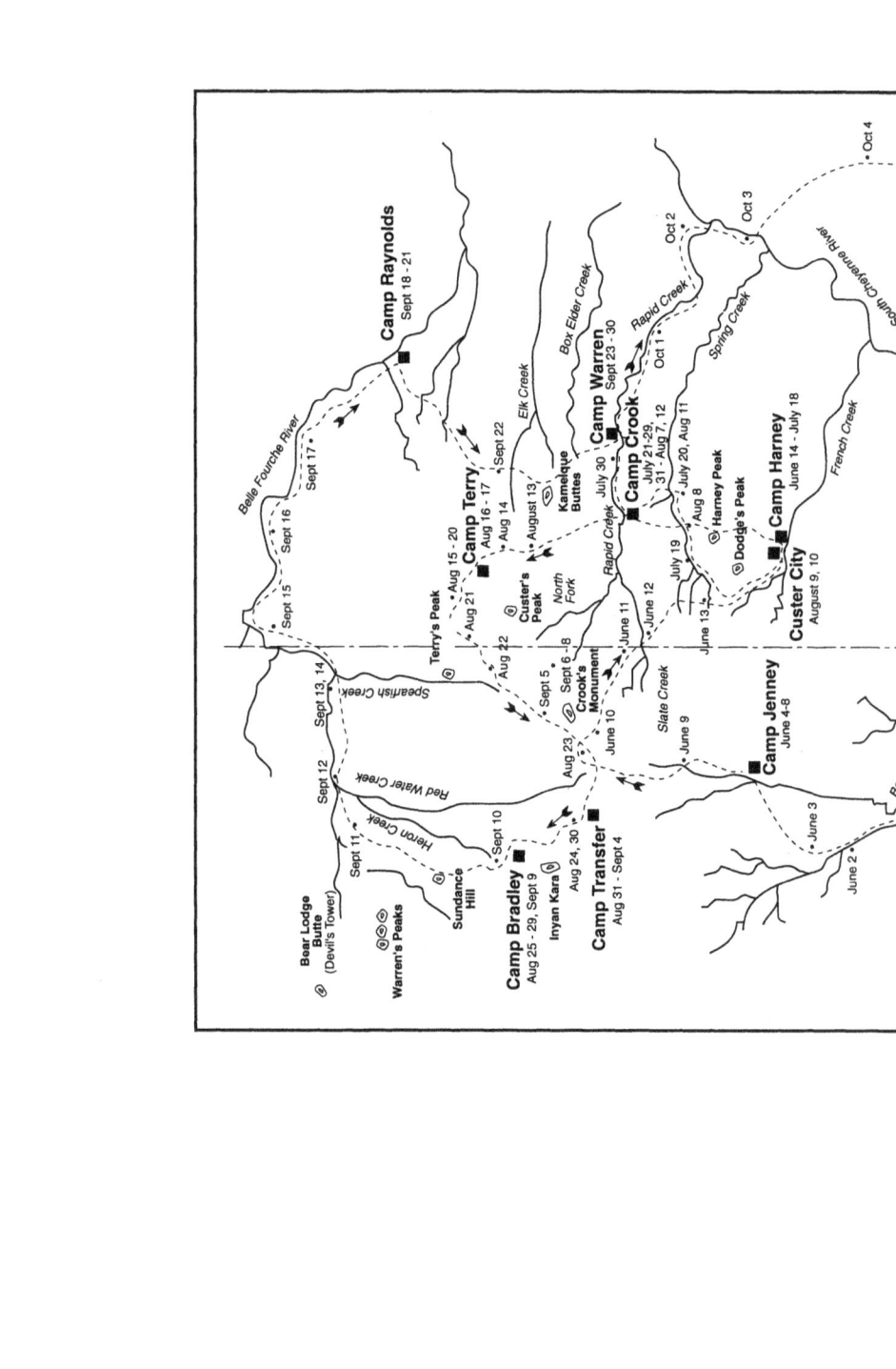

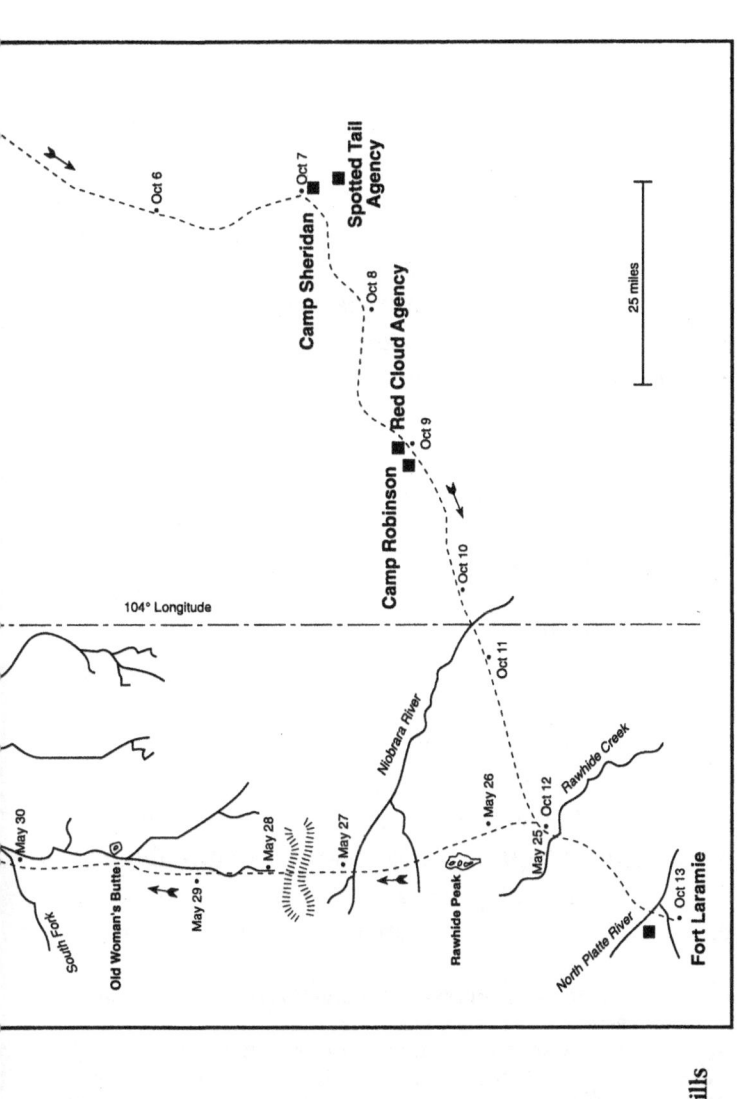

Itinerary, the Black Hills
Expedition, 1875

introduced to Genl Brackett.[279] Saw many of the officers - Burt Munson Devine,[280] &c. Spent an hour in the Billiard room of Comm[issar]y - by which time the dust was blowing so thick that one could not see across the post - Went to telegraph office. Sent two messages to Genl Crook - one announcing my arrival, & the receipt of his telegram directing distribution of Companies, the other about Stanton & the payment of these troops (mine). Return to Camp 3.30 pm Got my mail - letters from everybody except my wife, who never will write - No orders or com[municatio]ns of any special consequence except the telegrams - Blowing like blazes all afternoon and keeping it up now, 10 pm The Black Hills Expedition is Busted ——

Thursday, October 14, 1875

Up about 7 this am After breakfast went up to see Genl Bradley. Stopped Stanton's coming. Trout got everything turned over - papers not made out yet - Hope to be through tomorw. Played billiards. Called on Mrs Burt & Mrs Mix & dined with General Bradley, Mason & wife, a Mrs King, & the Genl's family I suspect Mrs. King is a mother in law. Fred was with me. He is in fine feather. There is to be a hop tomorw night. Foote got telegram that his mother is very ill Starts tomorw to see her. Paid his mess bill. Went to Collins for bill Would not take anything. Said I had more than paid a dozen such bills, by my kindness to his people - Came back to Camp about 8 pm Got tired of the pitch playing lot of topers in the billiard room. A very big Court is in session with plenty of rank[281]

279. Lieutenant Colonel Albert G. Brackett, Second Cavalry, whom Dodge refers to in his brevet rank.
280. Captain John D. Devin, who commanded Company B, Ninth Infantry.
281. A general court-martial of Captain Avery B. Cain, Fourth Infantry, began on this day with Lieutenant Colonel Brackett as president. Captain Cain was charged with habitual drunkenness and with conduct unbecoming an officer and a gentleman. He was found guilty and sentenced by the court to be cashiered; however, in light of his service during the Civil War and his promise to abstain from liquor, President Grant remitted his sentence (General Court-Martial Orders No. 5, January 22, 1876).

Chambers arrived today.[282] Must call on his wife. Wrote out my order breaking up the Comd. Foot cant sign it as he goes early in the morning with Jenney.[283] Had several remarks about my book at table. Couldn't tell whether in earnest or in sarcasm. Rather think it simply in the way of compliment as none of them can know whether I can write or not - I think they will be surprised, though it may be my vanity - To bed early, but read & wrote till 11 pm.

Old Joe desperately drunk in a tent not far off, making night hideous.[284] Dont like to be hard on him, as he is really a valuable man. Want to get off on Saturday & am urging everything to that end. Trout is extra good, & works like a horse, lame as he is ——

Platte & Laramie rivers both very low -

Friday, October 15, 1875

Woke up early & had breakfast by 7 1/2 am Went to packing immediately after. Issued orders breaking up the Comd.[285] Genl Bradley came down to see me, & I availed myself of his offer of a room. Got through packing inspecting & signing papers by 12 m, & came to post. Heavy loafing for an hour or two - Dined with Genl Bradley 4 pm Paid Hubert & Mac,[286] after dinner also 2 dols for washing -

Went to hop, danced only once, with Miss Hyatt, or Wyeth or something -

---

282. Major Chambers was a member of the general court-martial now in session. He was about to be relieved from command at Camp Robinson and assigned to command at Fort Fetterman.

283. Lieutenant Foote had been granted a ten-day leave of absence before reporting to Dodge at Omaha.

284. See Pope, *The Dunciad*, III, 166.

285. In BHE G.O. 6, of this date, Dodge directed the eight companies of the escort to their new stations. He congratulated the members of his late command "on their generally very faithful and efficient performance of duty," and he thanked them "for their cordial cooperation and assistance."

286. The soldiers who had acted as Dodge's cook and personal servant.

Played billiards - got beat discounting King - gave him some good advice at parting.

Went with the Mixes to their house, & took a parting drink late about 12 pm - Took a final nightcap with Genl Bradley - & got to bed a little after 1 a.m. Old Joe called to bid me good by - tolerably sober & contrite - Chambers & Tim Baker drunk as fidlers sows this evening. Broke up everything today & start tomorrow a.m. for Cheyenne. Fred had a glorious time tonight

Saturday, October 16, 1875

Up at 7 1/2. Breakfast at 8. Made a row about the ambulance provided for me, which was abominable & unfit Got another & a good one - Started 9.30 am after bidding goodby to all. Genl Bradley and family all excellent people, & I like them very much. Said adieu to Mrs. Mix & all the others. Overtook Hawley & the Comd[287] about 16 miles from post. Another hand shaking Met & passed Spaulding & wife. Mules very tired but arrived at Phillips 6 pm - 43 miles - a part of the Indians came in with us at Phillips

Sunday, October 17, 1875

Got off 7.30 am later than we wished. Arrived at Fagan's[288] 25 miles 12.30. Mules fed & watered. Started again 2 pm Arrived at Cheyenne 7 pm Road very fine. Total dist today, <43>52 miles. Excellent supper & choice rooms at the R.R. House - Jones' - To bed at 10 p.m. ———

Old Beauvais & the Indian party[289] with us last night & tonight

---

287. Dodge had ordered Captain Hawley to march to Fort D. A. Russell with Companies A, H, and I, Third Cavalry.
288. One of several ranches that were regular stopping places between Portugee Philips's and Cheyenne; others included Schwartz's and Davis's.
289. G. P. Beauvais, of St. Louis, was one of the U.S. commissioners who had recently negotiated unsuccessfully with the Sioux for sale of the Black Hills.

Monday, October 18, 1875

Left Cheyenne 3 p.m. Trout got pass for Fred, & also permission to take all my stuff in Baggage Car. Saw many of the Officers. Paid Major Stanton, Express $1 - also the grocery man for Whiskey $10.00. Telegraphed to Rice to send down Wagon.

Tuesday, October 19, 1875

Arrived safe & sound. Rice met me at Depot. Everything all right - a splendid wind up to a splendid trip —

[*The text that follows is written with the notebook reversed, from the last sheet forward through p. [86V] in the original pagination.*]

The flora of Red Water very *eastern*. Cotton wood ash, box elder & willow, with some dwarf oak. Wild plums quite plenty. Red Water the largest stream so far seen in the Hills.

September 13

The finest agricultural valley yet struck - & superb grazing region - "Spear fish" - Grapes found today - Winter or frost grapes - Stream about size of Red Water - Country all secondary - no appearance of granite - Canons very deep - Topped with limestone everywhere. Fine pine near Crow Peaks & a great deal of oak, but small, crooked & very knotty. Do admirably for posts, but not for lumber —

Jenney's gold mine not in this region — Ash and Elm quite 2 feet in diameter - Oak not so large - saw a rail in swamp. Weather perfect. There has apparently been very little frost here yet.

September 14

Red Water quite one third larger than "Spear fish" at junction. No evidence of high water on either stream The combined streams are a fine almost river - the largest water course yet found in the Hills. No game in this vecinity. Fish abundant - suckers cat-fish, whitefish & dace - All the streams have rock bottoms - No ducks therefore - No game of any kind, except a few grouse on the hills -

September 15

Recommend that a piece of Country along Morton's Creek <1>20 by 1<6>0 miles be reserved for future military purposes. From its Junction with Red Water on N. 20 m[ile]s. south - This will give a beautiful site for Post - with hay bottoms, gardens &c on the north. Limestone & lumber on the south -

September 16

Not yet decided whether we are on Belle Fourche -

September 17

Excitement on Belle F runs high. Bets being made pro and con - <18> Crossed Custers trail which decided the matter even to the satisfaction of the beaten parties -

September 18

Vast fun at the expense of Foster who insisted & bet that twas not Belle Fourche An officer got off the following

> "There was a young topog named Foster,
> Who found La Belle Fourche and then lost her
> Getting mad, bet his pile
> Which Sam took with a smile
> And scooped this young topog named Foster" ——

September 19

8 lb. catfish caught with a *small trout* fly by a teamster - Lat of Camp Raynolds - 44° 29' 39"

September 24

Saw 6 deer today by twos. In every case they were a doe & a fawn - No Bucks seen today. Where are they? - Joe saw 8, <doe> all does & fawns. Foote saw 1 doe & 2 fawns - Sergt Molloy went out this p.m. & saw a great number of deer just coming to water -

---

Red deer not running yet ———[290]

September 30

Rapid a splendid creek. Its debouch from Hills a splendid place for post. Fine hay bottoms - good oak timber - lovely water - pine near & abundant & plenty of building stone -

---

October 2

Lower portion of Rapid somewhat alkaline, but still good water. Splendid bottom, & for 1<2>5 miles above its mouth an abundance of timber - Cottonwood, Ash, elm, box elder & willow.

October 3

Cheyenne a nasty stream - Water alkaline & scarcely fit to drink though the animals appear to like it.

The bed is a wide expanse of sand, from 2 to 500 yds in width - in which runs now a shallow current of water - tolerably swift - but shallow, & from <3>20 to <4>60 feet in width. It has

---

290. On the four pages that follow, pp. [91R], [90V], [90R], and [89V] in the original sequence, Dodge drew three maps and compiled a hunting record. The map on p. [91R], labeled "2d. day-," shows "1st camp," "2 Camp," "Crook," three trails, and Rapid, False, Box Elder, Camelco, and Egan Creeks. The map on p. [90V] includes no place names but locates three "x" marks, probably camps, along two watercourse systems; a trail connecting two of the "x" marks passes near two conspicuous dots that may be springs. The hunting record, on p. [90R], details animals taken on October 1, 2, 4, 6, 8, 12, and 13. The map on p. [89V] consists simply of three lines probably representing watercourses and a dotted line representing a trail; the map is unlabeled.

not so much water above, as it receives from Rapid. The bottom is from 3/4 to a mile wide - well timbered. It has fine grass, but is too sandy to be good for agriculture. Bad land soil terrible in wet weather - sticky as tar - & no bottom to the mud if it rains enough

---

October 5

The false White on which we camped last night is a sandy bed of 200 ft - The White a deep stream difficult to cross because of mud - only about 30 to 40 feet wide. Plenty of fish - <No> White River has but little bottom but that is very rich - Splendid country for stock farms -

October 7

Dont think much of this post. Small & very dirty as all Indian infested posts are. Country broken & rather picturesque Fine pine timber in vecinity -

---

October 9

Camp Robinson worse than Sheridan - miserable Surroundings - poor water - no hunting or fishing - Would prefer the upper post. White River has narrow but rich bottom - Is a fine grazing country. Above the post the water is clear & pure - Crossed it 13 times.

October 11

Niobrara a pretty stream from 600 to 1000 miners inches & quite rapid - plenty of fish - small - suckers cats & dace - the latter however very large of the kind - Many grouse. No timber or wood of any kind, not even a willow break.

October 12

Rawhide not over 50 miners inches - some little timber, but no dry wood - all used - grass poor - too many freight teams.

<G> Soil sandy, fit only for grazing. The bottom land of Rawhide no better than the prarie. Spring about 3 miles from Rawhide towards Niobrara - Wants digging out & fixing - Fish few & very small in Rawhide - Antelope on road today - not many[291]

291. The text written with the notebook in reversed position ends at this point, p. [86V] in the original pagination. Pages [86R] and [85V] are blank. On the inside back cover Dodge has drawn a map, marking main watercourses in ink. The map shows "Inyan" at the bottom of the page, with an "x" mark near it probably indicating a camp. A dotted line passes from near this mark to the top of the page, where at an abrupt turn in the dotted line Dodge has written "12 day from Inyan."

Bibliography

MANUSCRIPT MATERIALS

Black Hills Expedition, 1875. General and Special Orders. National Archives and Records Service, Washington, D.C. Record Group 393, part 1, entry 3749.

Blackmore, William. Papers. History Library, Museum of New Mexico, Santa Fe.

Bourke, John G. Diary. U.S. Military Academy, West Point, N.Y.

Bradley, Luther P. Papers. U.S. Army Military History Institute, Carlisle Barracks, Pa.

Crook, George. Papers. U.S. Army Military History Institute, Carlisle Barracks, Pa.

Dodge, Richard Irving. Papers. Beinecke Library, Yale University, New Haven, Conn.

———. Papers, 1865–1949. Everett R. Graff Collection of Western Americana, Newberry Library, Chicago.

Military Division of the Missouri Papers. U.S. Army Military History Institute, Carlisle Barracks, Pa.

Order of the Indian Wars. Papers. U.S. Army Military History Institute, Carlisle Barracks, Pa.

Palmer, William J. Papers. U.S. Army Military History Institute, Carlisle Barracks, Pa.

Secretary of War. Letters Sent Relating to Military Affairs, 1875. National Archives and Records Service Microcopy M6, rolls 70, 71.

Sherman, William T. Papers. Manuscript Division, Library of Congress, Washington, D.C.

U.S. Army. Adjutant General's Office. Richard Irving Dodge Personnel File. National Archives and Records Service, Washington, D.C. Record Group 94.

———. Department of the Platte. Black Hills Expedition. Order Book. National Archives and Records Service, Washington, D.C. Record Group 393, part 1, entry 3749, item 1.

———. Department of the Platte. General and Special Orders Issued, 1875. National Archives and Records Service, Washington, D.C. Record Group 393, items 3740, 3741.

———. Fort Laramie Post Returns, 1861–76. National Archives and Records Service Microcopy No. 617, reel 596.

———. Second Cavalry Regimental Returns, 1872–79. National Archives and Records Service Microcopy No. M744, reel 19.

———. Third Cavalry Regimental Returns, 1868–75. National Archives and Records Service Microcopy No. M744, reel 30.

———. Twenty-third Infantry Regimental Returns, 1874–82. National Archives and Records Service Microcopy No. 665, reel 237.

U.S. Military Academy. Archives. Richard Irving Dodge Application File. West Point, N.Y.

GOVERNMENT PUBLICATIONS

Official Army Register. Washington, D.C.: Government Printing Office, 1873–76.

U.S. Congress. House. *Report of the Commissioner of Indian Affairs* (1875). Executive Documents No. 1, Part 5, 44th Congress, 1st Session. Serial 1680.

———. House. *Report of the Commissioner of Indian Affairs* (1876). Executive Documents No. 1, Part 5, 44th Congress, 2nd Session. Serial 1749.

———. House. *Report of the Secretary of the Interior* (1875). Executive Documents No. 1, Part 5, 44th Congress, 1st Session. Serial 1680.

———. House. *Report of the Secretary of War* (1875). Executive Documents No. 1, Part 2, 44th Congress, 1st Session. Serial 1674.

———. House. *Report of the Secretary of War* (1876). Executive Documents No. 1, Part 2, 44th Congress, 2nd Session. Serial 1742.

———. House. *Report of the Secretary of War* (1877). Executive Documents No. 1, Part 2, 45th Congress, 1st Session. Serial 1794.

———. House. *Report of the Secretary of War* (1878). Executive Documents No. 1, Part 2, 45th Congress, 3rd Session. Serial 1843.

———. House. *Survey of the Black Hills.* Executive Documents No. 125, 44th Congress, 1st Session (1876). Serial 1689.

———. Senate. *Report of the Expedition to the Black Hills of Dakota, Under Command of Bvt. Maj.-Gen. G. A. Custer.* Executive Documents No. 32, 43rd Congress, 2nd Session (1875). Serial 1629.

———. Senate. *Report on the Mineral Wealth, Climate, and Rain-fall, and Natural Resources of the Black Hills of Dakota.* By Walter P. Jenney, E.M. Executive Documents No. 51, 44th Congress, 1st Session (1876). Serial 1664.

War Department. Adjutant General's Office. General Court-Martial Orders, 1874–76.

NEWSPAPERS AND PERIODICALS

Army and Navy Journal, 1875–76.
Chicago Inter-Ocean, 1875.
Chicago Tribune, 1875.
New York Daily Tribune, 1875.
New York Herald, 1874, 1875.

ARTICLES

Anderson, Grant K. "Samuel D. Hinman and the Opening of the Black Hills." *Nebraska History* 60 (1979): 520–42.

Buecker, Thomas R. "The Journals of James S. McClellan, 1st Sgt., Company H, 3rd Cavalry." *Annals of Wyoming* 57 (Spring 1985): 21–34.

Henry, Guy V. "A Winter March to the Black Hills." *Harper's Weekly* 39 (July 27, 1895): 700.

Mattes, Merrill J. "The Sutler's Store at Fort Laramie." *Annals of Wyoming* 18 (July 1946): 93–132.

McLaird, James D., and Lesta V. Turchen. "Exploring the Black Hills, 1855–1875: Reports of the Government Expeditions." *South Dakota History* 4 (1974): 161–97, 281–319, 403–38.

Parker, Watson. "The Report of Captain John Mix of a Scout to the Black Hills, March–April 1875." *South Dakota History* 7 (Fall 1977): 385–401.

———. "Report of the Reverend Samuel D. Hinman of an Expedition to the Black Hills during August, 1874." *Bits and Pieces* 5 (November 1969): 5–9.
Welty, Raymond L. "Supplying the Frontier Military Posts." *Kansas Historical Quarterly* 7 (May 1938): 154–69.

BOOKS

Allen, Joel Asaph. *History of the American Bison*, Bison Americanus. Washington, D.C.: Government Printing Office, 1877.
Baird, Spencer F. *Catalogue of North American Birds, Chiefly in the Museum of the Smithsonian Institution*. Washington, D.C.: Smithsonian Institution, 1859.
Bourke, John G. *On the Border with Crook*. Lincoln: University of Nebraska Press, 1971.
Bradley, Hugh. *Such Was Saratoga*. New York: Doubleday, Doran, 1940.
Brayer, Herbert O. *William Blackmore: A Case Study in the Economic Development of the West*. 2 vols. Denver: Bradford-Robinson, 1949.
Canary, Martha. *Calamity Jane's Letters to Her Daughter*. San Lorenzo, Calif.: Shameless Hussey Press, 1976.
Cassin, John. *Illustrations of the Birds of California, Texas, Oregon, British, and Russian America*. Philadelphia: J. B. Lippincott, 1856.
The Centennial of the United States Military Academy at West Point, New York, 1802–1902. 2 vols. Washington, D.C.: Government Printing Office, 1904.
City Directories of the United States, 1860–1901: Guide to the Microfilm Collection. Woodbridge, Conn.: Research Publications, 1983.
Collins, John S. *My Experiences in the West*. Chicago: Lakeside Press, 1970.
Crawford, Lewis F. *Ranching Days in Dakota, and Custer's Black Hills Expedition of 1874*. Baltimore: Wirth Brothers, 1950.
Crook, George. *General George Crook: His Autobiography*. Edited by Martin F. Schmitt. Norman: University of Oklahoma Press, 1961.
Cullum, George W. *Biographical Register of the Officers and Graduates of the U. S. Military Academy from 1802 to 1890*. Boston: Houghton Mifflin, 1891.
Custer, George A. *My Life on the Plains; or, Personal Experiences with Indians*. New York: Sheldon, 1874.

———. *My Life on the Plains; or, Personal Experiences with Indians.* Edited with an introduction by Edgar I. Stewart. Norman: University of Oklahoma Press, 1962.
Dodge, Richard Irving. *The Black Hills. A Minute Description of the Routes, Scenery, Soil, Climate, Timber, Gold, Geology, Zoölogy, etc. With an Accurate Map, Four Sectional Drawings, and Ten Plates from Photographs, Taken on the Spot.* New York: J. Miller, 1876.
———. *Our Wild Indians: Thirty Three Years' Personal Experience among the Red Men of the Great West. A Popular Account of Their Social Life, Religion, Habits, Traits, Customs, Exploits, etc. With Thrilling Adventures and Experiences on the Great Plains and in the Mountains of Our Wide Frontier. With an Introduction by General Sherman.* Hartford: A. D. Worthington, 1882.
———. *The Plains of North America and Their Inhabitants.* Edited by Wayne R. Kime. Newark: University of Delaware Press, 1989.
Feldmann, Rodney M. *The Black Hills: Field Guide.* Dubuque, Iowa: Kendall-Hunt, 1980.
Fisher, John S. *A Builder of the West* [William J. Palmer]. Caldwell, Idaho: Caxton Press, 1939.
Foner, Jack D. *The United States Soldier between Two Wars: Army Life and Reforms, 1865–1898.* New York: Humanities Press, 1970.
Frazer, Robert W. *Forts of the West: Military Forts and Presidios Commonly Called Forts West of the Mississippi River to 1898.* Norman: University of Oklahoma Press, 1965.
Goetzmann, William H. *Exploration and Empire: The Explorer and the Scientist in the Winning of the American West.* New York: Columbia University Press, 1966.
Grange, Roger T. *Fort Robinson: Outpost on the Plains.* Lincoln: Nebraska State Historical Society, 1965.
Gray, John S. *Centennial Campaign: The Sioux War of 1876.* Fort Collins, Colo.: Old Army Press, 1976.
Hafen, LeRoy R., and Ann W. Hafen, eds. *Powder River Campaigns and Sawyer's Expedition of 1865.* Glendale, Calif.: Arthur H. Clark, 1961.
Hafen, LeRoy R., and Francis Marion Young. *Fort Laramie and the Pageant of the West, 1834–1890.* Glendale, Calif.: Arthur H. Clark, 1967.

Hamersley, Thomas, comp. *Complete Regular Army Register of the United States: For One Hundred Years (1779 to 1879)*. 2 vols. Washington, D.C.: L. R. Hamersley, 1880.

———. *Records of Living Officers of the U.S. Army*. Philadelphia: L. R. Hamersley, 1884.

Hedren, Paul L. *Fort Laramie in 1876: Chronicle of a Frontier Post at War*. Lincoln: University of Nebraska Press, 1988.

———. *With Crook in the Black Hills: Stanley J. Morrow's 1876 Photographic Legacy*. Boulder, Colo.: Pruett, 1985.

Heitman, Francis B. *Historical Register and Dictionary of the United States Army, from its Organization, September 29, 1789, to March 2, 1903*. 2 vols. Washington, D.C.: Government Printing Office, 1903.

Hill, Edward E. *The Office of Indian Affairs, 1874–1880: Historical Sketches*. New York: Clearwater Publishing, 1974.

Hollon, Eugene. *The Great American Desert: Then and Now*. New York: Oxford University Press, 1966.

Hughes, Richard B. *Pioneer Years in the Black Hills*. Edited by Agnes Wright Spring. Glendale, Calif.: Arthur H. Clark, 1957.

Hutton, Paul Andrew. *Phil Sheridan and His Army*. Lincoln: University of Nebraska Press, 1985.

Hyde, George E. *Red Cloud's Folk: A History of the Oglala Sioux Indians*. Norman: University of Oklahoma Press, 1957.

———. *Spotted Tail's Folk: A History of the Brulé Sioux*. Norman: University of Oklahoma Press, 1961.

Jackson, Donald D. *Custer's Gold: The United States Cavalry Expedition of 1874*. New Haven: Yale University Press, 1966.

Jennewein, J. Leonard. *Calamity Jane of the Western Trails*. Mitchell, S.D.: Dan Grigg, 1965.

King, Charles. *Campaigning with Crook and Stories of Army Life*. New York: Harper and Brothers, 1890.

Knight, Oliver. *Following the Indian Wars: The Story of the Newspaper Correspondents among the Indian Campaigners*. Norman: University of Oklahoma Press, 1960.

Krause, Herbert, and Gary D. Olson. *Prelude to Glory: The Newspaper Account of Custer's 1874 Expedition to the Black Hills*. Sioux Falls, S.D.: Brevet Press, 1974.

Lakeside Annual Directory of the City of Chicago. 1874–1875. Chicago: Williams, Donnelly, 1874.

Ludlow, William. *Report of a Reconnaissance of the Black Hills of Dakota, Made in the Summer of 1874*. Washington, D.C.: Government Printing Office, 1875.

Marcy, Randolph B. *Thirty Years of Army Life on the Border. Comprising Descriptions of the Indian Nomads of the Plains; Explorations of New Territory; A Trip Across the Rocky Mountains in the Winter; Descriptions of the Habits of Different Animals Found in the West, and the Methods of Hunting Them: With Incidents in the Life of Different Frontier Men, &c. &c.* New York: Harper and Brothers, 1866.

Mathews, Mitford M., ed. *Dictionary of Americanisms*. 2 vols. Chicago: University of Chicago Press, 1951.

Mattes, Merrill J. *Indians, Infants, and Infantry: Andrew and Elizabeth Burt on the Frontier*. Denver: Old West Publishing, 1960.

McGillycuddy, Julia B. *McGillycuddy, Agent: A Biography of Dr. Valentine T. McGillycuddy*. Stanford: Stanford University Press, 1941.

Milner, Joe E. *California Joe: Noted Scout and Indian Fighter*. Caldwell, Idaho: Caxton Printers, 1935.

Newton, Henry, and Walter P. Jenney. *Report on the Geology and Resources of the Black Hills of Dakota, with Atlas*. 2 vols. Washington, D.C.: Government Printing Office, 1880.

Parker, Watson. *Gold in the Black Hills*. Norman: University of Oklahoma Press, 1966.

Peattie, Roderick, ed. *The Black Hills*. New York: Vanguard Press, 1952.

Porter, Joseph C. *Paper Medicine Man: John Gregory Bourke and His American West*. Norman: University of Oklahoma Press, 1986.

Prucha, Francis Paul. *American Indian Policy in Crisis: Christian Reformers and the Indian, 1865–1900*. Norman: University of Oklahoma Press, 1976.

Reber, Bruce. *The United States Army and the Indian Wars in the Trans-Mississippi West, 1860–1898*. Special Bibliography 17. Carlisle Barracks, Pa.: U.S. Army Military History Institute, 1978.

Record of Engagements with Hostile Indians within the Military Division of the Missouri, from 1868 to 1882, Lieutenant-General P. H. Sheridan, Commanding. Washington, D.C.: Government Printing Office, 1882.

Report of the Commission Appointed to Treat with the Sioux Indians for the Relinquishment of the Black Hills. Washington, D.C.: Government Printing Office, 1875.

Rickey, Don. *Forty Miles a Day on Beans and Hay: The Enlisted Soldier Fighting the Indian Wars*. Norman: University of Oklahoma Press, 1963.

Roberts, Robert B. *Encyclopedia of Historic Forts: The Military, Pioneer, and Trading Posts of the United States*. New York: Macmillan, 1985.

Schuchert, Charles, and Clara Mae LeVene. *O. C. Marsh, Pioneer in Paleontology*. New Haven: Yale University Press, 1940.

Smith, Sherry L. *Sagebrush Soldier: Private William Earl Smith's View of the Sioux War of 1876*. Norman: University of Oklahoma Press, 1989.

Spring, Agnes Wright. *The Cheyenne and Black Hills Stage and Express Routes*. Glendale, Calif.: Arthur H. Clark, 1949.

Stanton, W. S. *Tables of Distances and Itineraries of Routes Between the Military Posts in, and to Certain Points Contiguous to, the Department of the Platte*. Omaha: Headquarters, Department of the Platte, 1877.

Stokes, George W., with Howard R. Driggs. *Deadwood Gold: A Story of the Black Hills*. Yonkers-on-Hudson: World Book, 1936.

Storm, Colton. *A Catalogue of the Everett D. Graff Collection of Western Americana*. Chicago: University of Chicago Press for the Newberry Library, 1968.

Tallent, Annie T. *The Black Hills; or, The Last Hunting Ground of the Dakotahs*. St. Louis: Nixon-Jones, 1899.

Turchen, Lesta V., and James D. McLaird. *The Black Hills Expedition of 1875*. Mitchell, S.D.: Dakota Wesleyan University Press, 1975.

U.S. Army, Military Division of the Missouri. *Outline Descriptions of the Posts in the Military Division of the Missouri*. Chicago: Headquarters, Military Division of the Missouri, 1876.

U.S. Bureau of Indian Affairs. *Biographical and Historical Index of American Indians and Persons Involved in Indian Affairs*. 8 vols. Boston: G. K. Hall, 1966.

Utley, Robert M. *Frontier Regulars: The United States Army and the Indian, 1866–1891*. New York: Macmillan, 1973.

———. *The Indian Frontier of the American West, 1846–1890*. Albuquerque: University of New Mexico Press, 1961.

———. *The Last Days of the Sioux Nation*. New Haven: Yale University Press, 1963.

Warren, Gouverneur K. *Preliminary Report of Explorations in Nebraska and Dakota in the Years 1855, '56, '57*. Washington, D.C.: Government Printing Office, 1858.

Wood, George B., and Franklin Bache. *The Dispensatory of the United States of America*. 16th ed. Philadelphia: J. B. Lippincott, 1892.

Wooster, Robert. *The Military and United States Indian Policy, 1865–1903*. New Haven: Yale University Press, 1988.

Young, Harry !Sam). *Hard Knocks: A Life Story of the Vanishing West*. Portland: Wells, 1915.

Index

The following abbreviations are used in the index:
BHE   Black Hills Expedition
PNA   *The Plains of North America and Their Inhabitants*
RID   Richard Irving Dodge

Aconite, 159
Adair, John, 41, 43, 188
Afrucus, 40
Allen, A., 167 n
Allen, Joel Asaph, 148 n
Allen, R. L., 154, 157
Allison, William B., 10. See also Indian Commission
Andrews, William H., 71 n, 196, 197
Ants, 142, 173
Arizona Territory, 7 n, 103
Army of the Potomac, 154
Ash (tree), 214, 247, 249
Ashby, W. H., 145
Antelope, 48, 54, 60, 200, 211, 213, 217, 218, 220, 221, 228, 230, 251; RID's chapter for *PNA* on, 184; herd of, 197

Bad lands, 58, 80, 227, 231–34
Baird, Spencer, *Catalogue of North American Birds*, 205
Baker, Tim, 246
Barbettes, 88
Bare Butte Creek, 218
Barn swallow, 176
Bats, 173, 176
Bear, 57, 64, 85, 183, 200, 201, 209; absence of, 68; signs of, 178
Bear Lodge Butte (Devil's Tower), 76, 97, 160, 207

Bear Lodge Creek, 190, 207
Beauvais, G. P., 246
Beaver, 183; captured and released, 63; dams of, 71, 79–80, 171, 183, 191, 204, 211, 213
Beaver Creek, 54, 67, 69, 74, 101–2, 112, 237; bad water of, 57; branches of, 58–59; bridge over, 58–59, 90 n, 94 n; cutoff at, 156–57 n; headwaters of, 72. See also Spaulding's Creek
Beaver Dam Creek, 225
Beecher, Henry Ward, 129
Bees, 141
Belknap, William North, 40
Belle Fourche River, 160, 198, 207, 222; alkaline water of, 220; identification of, 215–16, 217, 248
Benecke, R., 96 n
Benteen, Frederick W., 165, 166, 167, 168; miners' dislike of, 208
Big Horn Expedition (1874), 217 n
Big Horn Mountains, 192, 205
Billiards, 40, 41, 238, 244, 246
Bird, Charles, 96
Birds: new species of, 21; migratory, 209, 210
Bitter Creek, 57
Black Beaver, 120
Blackbird, 204; tame specimen of, 173, 176
Black Hills: abundant water of, 72, 75, 78, 80, 83; bad water in, 59, 73, 102, 206; beauty of, 15, 50, 82, 137; boggy terrain

Black Hills (*continued*)
in, 71, 72, 80, 81, 83, 84; broken terrain in, 71, 74, 82, 92, 101–2, 103–4, 133, 201; climate of, 64, 77, 77, 78, 109, 110, 117, 126, 137; distant view of, 50, 57; excellence of water in, 67, 85, 88, 105, 138, 214; flowers in, 75, 78; future of, 83, 153; general observations on, 101–2; gold deposits in, 3–4, 83, 85, 89, 95n, 104, 144, 174; grasses of, 78, 80, 83, 86, 88, 92, 105, 135, 137, 181, 203; grazing lands in, 58, 83, 89, 105, 137, 138; Indian trails through, 59, 72, 74, 76, 96; legal status of, 4–5, 10, 24, 25, 43–44; little explored, 12; maps of, 23, 206, 208, 216; military post in, 106, 138, 214, 216, 247, 248, 249; name of, 72; not an Indian country, 83, 105, 139; oasis in the plains, 109, 238; photographs of, 85n; scenery in, 72, 76, 80, 81–82, 85, 86, 92, 118, 131, 135, 193; soil of, 78, 82, 83, 109, 137, 206; timber in, 63, 64, 68, 78, 80–81, 82–83, 85, 86, 89, 102, 105, 118, 138, 144, 172, 206, 214, 249; watershed of, 76; wealth of, 11, 89, 105, 106

Black Hills, The (book by RID): discussion of geology in, 240n; journals used in, 20–21, 139; map in, 222n; quoted, 41

Black Hills Expedition (BHE): accomplishments of, 23, 25; cavalry companies of, 54–55; cattle herd of, 44, 53, 69, 73, 78, 122, 150, 190, 191, 207, 236, 239; condition of command, 90n, 107, 138; "delightful pic nic," 138; difficulties of transportation, 12–14, 16–17, 50–51, 52, 67–69, 71, 73, 75, 76, 84, 94n, 149, 177–78, 179–80, 182–83, 206, 121–13, 234; fight with Sioux predicted, 39; infantry companies of, 54–55, 121, 123, 129, 150, 198, 207, 229; itinerary of, 106, 136, 153, 171, 206–7, 221, 229; July 4 celebration of, 117; and lost-mail incident, 114; mail received by, 95, 188, 196; and miners, 8–9; mining activities of, 116, 119, 121; newspaper coverage of, 8, 11–12, 23–24; officers of, 56, 69, 78, 85, 97, 116, 130n, 135, 157, 181, 198, 221; official photographer of, 45, 46, 48, 96n; official report of, 26; ordnance of, 42, 61n, 103, 199; physicians of, 58; progress of, 18, 59–60, 152; purpose of, 6–7, 11, 14, 104, 146, 229; scientific party of, 6, 12, 14, 45, 54, 86, 90, 104–5, 138, 151, 161; security measures of, 10, 50, 61, 95, 96, 97n, 98, 226; size of, 13; staff of, 44; supplies and equipment for, 14, 38–40, 60, 61, 62, 90; supply trains of, 13, 62, 96, 97, 100, 102, 121, 128, 160–61, 206, 229; sutler of, 99, 199; thievery from within, 114, 219

Blackmore, William: and BHE, 43, 196; and *PNA*, 19

Black-tailed deer, 53, 68, 106, 118, 136, 149, 179, 180, 181, 182, 190, 193–94, 201, 203, 208, 222, 223; RID's chapter for *PNA* on, 150, 151; obese specimen of, 220. *See also* Deer

Black Tomahawk, 235

Black Twin, 65

Blackwood's Edinburgh Magazine, 121

Blair, Francis Preston (Frank), 197

Bluebirds, 141, 176

"Bone fields," 17, 207, 234; Jenney's wish to explore, 207, 230

Bordeaux, Louis, 39n, 166n

Bourke, John G., 8n, 93n, 138; aide-de-camp to Gen. Crook, 89n; RID on, 97; on RID, 18; and Egyptian military service, 95; on Jenney, 15; as mapmaker, 56, 107, 208; mess bill of, 44, 97; quoted, 24–25, 48, 60–61n; relieved from duty, 97; topographical engineer of BHE, 42, 44

Box elder (tree), 63, 214, 247, 249

Box Elder Creek, 103, 121, 151, 154, 172, 180, 222n, 224, 225, 249n; branch of, 171; camp on, 174; head of, 159; hunting on, 18, 174

Brackett, Albert G., 244

Bradley, Luther P., 7n, 38, 40–44, 45, 207, 236, 241, 244; affidavits of, 107; assists BHE, 49; and Fort Laramie ferry, 132; hospitality of, 244, 245, 246; letters from 114, 128, 196; letters and reports to, 48, 62, 90, 97, 100, 115, 132; map prepared for, 159

Bradley, Willie, 40

Brady, George K., 39

Brant, Louis P., 188

Bratton, J., 89n, 123, 162n; characterized, 125

INDEX 265

Brown, John, Jr., 98
Brown thrush, 144, 173, 176
Buffalo: RID's chapter for *PNA* on, 19, 99, 114, 115, 148, 208; trade in hides and meat of, 115
Buffalo bird, 174, 176
Buffalo wolf, 172, 196. *See also* Wolf
Bullfrogs, 142, 210
Bullock, William B. ("Colonel"), 42, 71, 92, 114, 118, 131, 144; departure from BHE, 160–61; distant relation of RID, 40
Bunkie (RID's hunting dog), 192
Burt, Andrew S., 48, 99, 119, 124, 130, 135, 152, 153, 169, 189, 205, 244; in Benteen's camp, 166; camp of, 134, 136, 156, 157, 158, 161, 164; conversations with, 97, 158; RID's opinion of, 61, 100–101, 159, 164; errand to Indian Springs, 160 n, 187 n; hunting experiences of, 60; interest in RID's book, 147, 148; and Jenney, 120; and lost-mail incident, 112–16, 117; mining operations of, 17, 100–101; newspaper letters of, 8 n, 100, 112, 129; quoted, 60 n; son of, struck by lightning, 126; and supply train, 62, 94, 99, 196, 197, 198; trail of, 127; wife of, 244
Burt's Spring, 205 n
Butterflies, 142
Buzzards, 176, 210

Cadmus, 134
Cain, Avery B., 244 n
"Calamity Jane," 21–22
"California Joe," 22–23, 71 n, 143, 149, 160, 198, 199, 200, 201, 202, 219, 221, 223, 225, 249; and Camelco Creek, 222 n; conversations with, 121, 139; Custer on, 22, 70; and Custer's trail, 172; discharged from BHE, 45; RID's opinion of, 70, 245; dog of, 217, 218, 221; drunk at Fort Laramie, 45, 245; hired by BHE, 44, 151; permitted to accompany BHE, 70 n, 135; services as guide, 162, 182–83, 184, 186, 187, 190, 202, 211–13, 226 n, 232
Cambridge Observatory, Mass., 55 n
Camelco Creek, 222, 223, 249 n
Campbell, Mr., 154 n
Camp Bradley, 189, 202–203, 204, 205

Camp Collins, 10, 24, 152. *See also* Pollock, Edwin
Camp Crook, 143, 156, 169, 170, 172, 174, 181, 249 n; road to Camp Terry from, 224; vicinity of, 173
Camp Harney, 14, 86, 88, 89, 90, 91, 92, 100 n, 102, 111–12, 114, 117, 134, 136, 144, 157 n, 162, 164, 173; distance from Camp Sheridan of, 107; location of, 109; vicinity of, 118
Camp Jenney, 13, 14, 62, 64, 72, 89, 90 n, 102–3, 112, 117; alkaline water at, 96; description of, 60–61, 63; grasshoppers at, 96; location of, 49 n, 65, 109; new route to, 94
Camp Raynolds, 248 n
Camp Robinson, 4, 42, 44 n, 56 n, 115, 145 n, 157 n; and Camp Sheridan, 250; description of, 239. *See also* Red Cloud Agency
Camp Sheridan, 44 n, 229–30, 236, 237; description of, 237–38; RID's opinion of, 250; errand of Lt. Coale to, 226. *See also* Spotted Tail Agency
Camp Transfer, 195, 199, 206
Camp Warren, 221
Canary, Jane or Martha. *See* "Calamity Jane"
Camp Terry, 181, 182, 190, 197, 204, 223, 224; road to, 199
Carpenter, "Captain," 124, 125, 126
Cassin, John, *Illustrations of the Birds...,* 205
Castle Creek, 79, 80, 112 n, 169
Catbird, 173, 176
Catfish, 215, 216, 219, 236, 240, 250
Cath (cousin of RID), 154, 157
Chambers, 246
Chambers, Alexander, 226, 236, 237, 238, 245; wife of, 236, 237, 245
Chase, Mr. *See* Craig, C. L.
Cheyenne (Wyoming Territory), 3, 7–8, 38, 54, 154 n, 203, 246, 247
Cheyenne Depot, 38
Cheyenne Indians, 25, 122. *See also* Indians, American
Cheyenne River, 12 n, 53, 54, 102, 118, 228, 231; alkaline water of, 249 n; fire in vicinity of, 122. *See also* North Cheyenne River; South Cheyenne River
Chicago Inter-Ocean, 8 n, 57, 117, 199; controversy with *Chicago Tribune*, 130; on gold in Black Hills, 11, 90

Chicago Tribune, 77 n, 113, 123 n; attack on RID, 130; on gold in Black Hills, 11
Chipmunk, 209
Chubs, 46, 80, 236
Chugwater Creek, 39, 40
Cincinnati Gazette, 8 n
Civil War (U.S.), 45 n, 154 n, 188 n, 244 n
Clark, S. H. H., 37
Cleveland, Rev., 166 n
Coal, 102
Coale, John H., 170, 198, 219, 225, 226, 227, 228, 235; with Gen. Crook, 154; hunting experiences of, 151, 155; newspaper letters by, 199 n; surname misspelled by RID, 98 n
Cold Spring, 196, 205
Collins, Gilbert H., 40 n
Collins, John S., 43–44 n, 99 n, 145 n; bookkeeper of, 111, 112, 117; and RID's offer of payment, 244; "spirituous outfit" of, 40, 41
Colorado, 7 n
Columbia School of Mines (New York), 6
Comingo, Abraham, 145 n
Connolly, John R., 188, 197
Cook, Charles E. (orderly), 193
Cooper, Tom, 167 n
Corduroy bridges, 51, 72, 84; defined, 51 n
Cottonwood, 52, 58, 75, 214, 247, 249
Cougar. *See* Mountain lion
Cowbirds, 174, 176, 204
Coyote, 196
Craig, C. L., 167
Craycroft, William T., 166 n
Crazy Horse, 65
Cribbage, 69
Crook, George, 9, 10, 24, 25, 38, 87, 89, 128; and BHE, 6–7, 9, 151–57, 174; at Fort Laramie, 42; hunting party of, 18, 171, 174, 224; instructions to RID, 167–68; letters and reports to, 48, 62, 90, 91, 100, 102–7, 115, 132, 136–39, 161, 168, 169, 198, 206–8, 244; and miners, 9, 24, 152–53, 163, 175; note from, 150; rumors of, 122, 124, 126, 128; and Gen. Sheridan, 167; and Gen. Terry, 165; wife of, 138
Crook Avenue (Custer City), 167
Crow Peak Mountains, 206, 213, 214, 247
Custer, George A., 79, 187, 192; in Black Hills, 3–4, 5, 12, 80, 165, 175 n; and BHE, 6–7; Black Hills map of, 74, 82, 91; on "California Joe," 70; cited, 105; and climate of Black Hills, 78, 80; and gold in Black Hills, 3, 4, 11, 90 n, 95, 104; "Morass" of, 84; *My Life on the Plains*, 22; as pathfinder, 21; trail of, 77, 81, 84, 103, 127, 172, 188, 193, 200, 202, 205 n, 211–12, 217, 221, 222, 224–25, 248
Custer, City, 175; described, 164–65; name of, 166, 167; vicinity of, 168
Custer's Gulch. *See* Camp Harney
Custer's Park, 132
Custer's Peak, 177, 180, 182, 204, 206

Dace, 80, 142, 145, 170, 173, 190, 215, 216, 221, 222, 248, 250; large catches of, 238, 240
Dallas, Alexander J., 38
Dalton, Jane. *See* "Calamity Jane"
Daniels, J. W., 145 n
Davenport, Reuben B., 8 n, 69, 70, 91, 93, 119, 169; cited, 99 n; credulousness and cowardice of, 56; RID's opinion of, 58; and Jenney, 15 n, 54–55, 129; interviews Spotted Tail, 166 n; leaves BHE, 195, 198; lost letters of, 111–14; messenger to, 196; published letters of, 129, 130; sketch of RID by, 129
Davis (quartermaster sergeant), 195, 226
Davis, Jefferson C., 158
Davis's (ranch), 246 n
Deer, 53, 54, 57, 62, 64, 81, 83, 85, 128, 155, 156, 164, 166, 171, 174, 175, 178, 179, 180, 181, 187, 189, 190, 191, 192, 195, 199–200, 201, 202, 203, 213, 216, 222, 224, 225, 226, 249; abundance of, 64; tracks of, 68. *See also* Black-tailed deer; White-tailed deer
De Lany, Hayden, 124, 158
Denver and Rio Grande Railroad, 157
Department of Dakota, 165
Department of the Interior, 16 n, 130; RID's opinion of, 96; and future of Black Hills, 83; and War Department, 229
Department of the Missouri, 26, 118
Department of the Platte, 6, 37 n, 42 n, 95 n, 122. *See also* District of the Black Hills
Department of the West, 82 n
Department of War. *See* War Department
De Rudio, Charles C., 166 n

INDEX   267

Devil's Tower. *See* Bear Lodge Butte (Devil's Tower)
Devin, John D., 244
Dewey, Grace, 40
Dewey, Ione (Mrs. Luther P. Bradley), 40
Dewey, Louise, 40
Dickens, Charles, 93, 94; *Great Expectations*, 119; *Our Mutual Friend*, 100
District of the Black Hills, 7
Divides, 67
Division of the Missouri, 12 n
Dodge, Frederick Paulding (RID's son), 7, 21, 26, 46, 52, 54, 62, 63, 64, 85, 115, 116, 118, 122, 123, 127, 128, 133, 144, 157, 188, 202, 204, 211, 226, 234, 240, 247; described by Bourke, 46 n; fishing experiences of, 148, 150, 151, 170; at Fort Laramie, 244, 246; hunting experiences of, 18, 143, 179, 221; illness of, 89, 192, 194; injuries of, 184, 185, 204; marksmanship of, 99–100; as sick nurse, 159
Dodge, James R. (RID's father): letters from, 128, 154, 159, 188; letters to, 38, 43, 48, 62, 90, 96, 100, 115, 132, 157, 158, 159, 197
Dodge, Julia Rhinelander Paulding (RID's wife), 37, 128, 152, 159; letters from, 41, 43, 48, 154, 157; letters to, 38, 41, 43, 44, 48, 62, 90, 91, 96, 100, 115, 132, 151, 159, 197; photographs of, 154; poor correspondent, 244; at Saratoga, N.Y., 154, 157, 188
Dodge, Mary Helen (Sis Molly), 111, 157
Dodge, Richard Irving (RID): appearance of, 19 n; appointed to command BHE escort, 7; assumes control of scientific party, 17, 162–64; book manuscript (*PNA*) of, 18–20, 92, 94, 98, 99, 101, 107, 114–22, 125, 126, 127, 148, 150, 151, 158, 182, 184, 190–91, 192, 202, 218–19, 227, 245; on cavalrymen, 168; as conversationalist, 19, 129 n; on Custer, 82, 84; described by R. Davenport, 129 n; "The Doomed Buffalo" by, 117 n; dysentery of, 216, 217–18, 219, 220; exploratory rides of, 115, 118, 123, 131–32, 133; on federal Indian policy, 25, 108; fishing experiences of, 18, 46, 57, 61, 80, 81, 134, 145, 147, 151, 170, 215, 216, 217, 221, 222, 236, 238, 240; geological observations of, 51, 68, 72, 78, 102, 139–41, 233, 240; gold purchases of, 116; on guides, 84; and Harney's Peak, 93, 123–24; hunting experiences of, 18, 46, 85, 118, 128, 144–45, 149, 155, 171, 179, 180, 181, 183, 184, 185, 190, 191, 193–94, 195, 196, 199–202, 211, 213–14, 217, 218, 219, 220–26, 228; hunting records kept by, 206 n, 211 n, 228, 249 n; and W. P. Jenney, 15–16, 54–55, 59, 77, 120, 152, 163–64, 219, 229–31; journals of, 21, 27–33; list of Indian leaders, 65; and lost-mail incident, 111–15; mapmaking of, 90, 91, 117, 118, 125, 127, 129–30, 132, 205–6 n, 249 n, 251 n; marksmanship of, 119, 155, 194, 203; and miners, 8–9, 64, 86–87, 104, 105–6, 127, 150, 153, 165; at miners' meeting, 8–9, 153; nicknamed "Richard the First," 17; official report of, 185 n; plays billiards, 40, 41, 238, 244, 246; reading of, 92, 93, 94, 100, 121; remarkable rifle shots by, 181, 194, 223; report of gold by, 90 n; reports to Gen. Crook, 14, 87, 89, 102–7, 136–39, 206–8, 244; rifle of, 99, 116, 119, 183, 200; separates escort from scientific party, 230–31; shotgun of, 190, 211, 213; skill as hunter, 156; speech to Red Dog, 10–11, 25, 146; storytelling by, 100, 121. *See also Black Hills, The*; *Plains of North America and Their Inhabitants, The* (*PNA*)
Dodge, Susan Williams (RID's mother), 38 n, 128, 197
Dodge Avenue (Custer City), 167
Dodge's Peak, 18
Dogs, 220. *See also* "California Joe"
Doves, 46, 176
Ducks, 183, 186, 191, 192, 211, 213, 215, 227, 236, 237, 248. *See also* Mallard; Sheldrake; Teal
Duffell (packer), 45
Dye, William McE., 95 n

Edgar (unidentified), 235
Egan, James, 37, 38, 145, 154, 224; wife of, 37
Egan Creek, 249

Egypt, 95
Elk, 18, 19, 57, 60, 61, 62, 85, 106, 155, 156, 171, 174, 175, 176, 185, 191, 198, 200–201, 203, 204, 208, 209, 222, 224; RID's chapter for *PNA* on, 122, 126, 127, 148; herd of, 223; signs of, 68, 183, 201, 209; skill at hiding, 203
Elk Creek, 178, 179, 180, 220
Elm, 214, 249
Elting, Oscar, 132
Engineer Department. *See* United States Army
English snipe, 204
Erwin ("Old Erwin"), 182

Fagan's (ranch), 246
False White River, 234–35, 249, 250
Fast (Quick) Bear, 5
Ferry boat, 41, 45, 132
Flies, 125, 142, 175, 204
"Floral Valley," 13, 79, 187, 188, 202, 205n, 206n; described, 78
Flowers, 138, 142
Foote, Morris Cooper, 44, 48, 81, 92, 114, 123, 127, 133, 148, 149, 150, 172, 178, 190, 194, 196, 198, 199, 201, 208, 211, 214, 219, 220, 222–23, 225, 228, 244, 245, 249; as acting quartermaster, 185; on RID's rifle, 200; fishing experiences of, 215, 218; hunting experiences of, 183, 221–22, 225; mountain climbing of, 93, 192, 205; visit to miners, 86
Foote's Canyon, 194
Foote's Park, 143
Ford, John W., 111
Forsyth, George Alexander, 77, 79, 192
Fort D. A. Russell, 97, 246
Fort Fetterman, 50
Fort Hartsuff, 122
Fort Laramie, 4, 6, 12, 13, 22, 58, 70, 90n, 105, 111, 112, 116, 117, 119, 121n, 124n, 128, 130, 189, 195, 196, 238; billiard room at, 244; BHE parties sent to, 89, 102, 131n; court-martial at, 244; "hops" at, 43, 245, 246; preparations for BHE at, 40–45; quartermaster at, 42; return of command to, 17, 207, 229, 230; route from BHE to, 49n, 156n, 157n; telegraph operator at, 111
Fort Laramie Treaty of 1868, 3–4
Fort Larned, 86
Fort Pierre, 49n

Fort Randall, 165
Fort Sanders, 37
Fort Sedgwick, 158n
Fort Sully, 145n, 236
Fossils, 52. *See also* "Bone fields"
Foster, Mr. (of New York), 154
Foster, James E. H., 96, 122, 128–29, 135, 152, 159, 160, 170, 182, 190; in command of pack train, 162, 163; limerick about, 248; surveying and mapmaking by, 117, 118, 129, 206, 208; as topographical officer, 153
Foxes, 201, 209
Fred's Peak, 18, 133, 134
Fremont, Nebr., 37, 38
French Creek, 4, 39, 84, 86, 95n, 102, 103, 104, 119, 134, 142, 165, 166, 170; camp on, 175; canyon of, 85, 128, 129; gold discovered on, 90n; grass along, 165; miners of, 167; mining prospects on, 150; vicinity of, 144

Gantt, Thomas Tasker, 154, 157, 196, 197
Garnett, William, 39
Garrison, A., 167
Garter snakes, 210. *See also* Snakes
Geese, 227
Gillespie, G. L., 23n
Goatsucker, 173, 176
Gold, 100, 247; best diggings for, 174; discoveries of, 11, 63, 83, 88, 90, 93, 104, 109, 130; doubts of its abundance, 109; exchange value of, 99n; reported presence of, 23, 55, 136–37; samples shown RID, 87
Goldsmith, Oliver, "Elegy on the Death of a Mad Dog," 220
Gooseberries, 118, 205
Gordon party, 4, 39n; former members of, 99n; stockade of, 85, 87–88, 98, 103
Gramma grass, 203
Grand Island, Nebr., 38
Grant, Ulysses S., 41n, 107n, 108, 244n
Grape, 214, 247
Grasshoppers, 61, 81, 96, 109
Grinnell, George B., 175n
Groundhog, 209
"Ground-hog case," 191
Grouse, 140, 170, 172, 186, 214, 216, 221, 224, 237, 248, 250. *See also* Ruff grouse; Sage grouse; Spike grouse; Willow grouse

INDEX 269

Guides, 82. *See also name of individual*
Guerin, A. 96n
Gypsum, 102

Hall, Christopher T., 64, 71, 92, 149, 162, 164, 168, 169, 195; company of, 71, 97, 98, 166, 207; RID's opinion of, 189; guide to Gen. Crook, 157; trader's impudence toward, 116
Harney, William S., 82n
Harney City, 39, 103
Harney's Peak, 82, 102, 131-32, 134, 141; appearance of, 88, 104, 124, 136, 144; ascent of, 71, 93; effort to locate, 123-24
Harrison, W., 86, 127, 167
Hawks, 138, 141, 176
Hawley, William, 93, 94, 117, 118, 135, 147, 148, 189, 194, 195, 225, 246; in command at Camp Jenney, 69n, 102-3; company of, 170, 180
Hayes, Rutherford B., 41n
Hazelnuts, 118
Henry, Guy V., 4, 152
Heron, 210
Herring, 214
Hickory shad, 214
Hinman, Samuel D., 5, 145-46; letter of recommendation from, 235
Hinsdill, H. M., 7n
Holly, 188
Hops, 204, 205
Horse Creek, 39
Horse thieves, 157
House martin, 144, 173, 176. *See also* Martins
Howard, E. O, 39n, 165, 166, 169
Hubert (cook), 144, 170, 191, 245
Huckleberries, 188
Hurd, Mr. 37

Indian Commission, 10, 126, 246; council meeting of, 24, 198, 236; meeting place of, 145 n; visit to BHE command by, 145-47
Indian Ring, 89, 105, 106, 107 n, 108-9
Indians, American, 250; absence of, 100, 139; near agencies, 238, 239, 240; begging of, 235; in Black Hills, 54, 58, 60, 62, 63-64, 97 n, 106, 175, 235; Black Hills used by, 89, 105; camps of, 63, 79, 102, 235; conversation with,

43; and N. H. Winchell, 96, 98, 151, 228-29; surname misspelled, 90-91, 95 n, 130; secretiveness of, 70, 16, 92, 162, 169; reports by, 11, 24, 55, BHE, 41-42; relations with colleagues, 170, 207, 226, 228-31; preparations for Black Hills, 62, 95; plans of, 77, 97-98, 199; miners hired by, 161-63; opinion of lies told by, 231; loses pack mule, 190, 188-89; letters to, 129, 151, 161, 219, 69-70, 88, 90; letters from, 157, 161, 226 n; inexperience of, 6; jealousy of, 122, 123, 138, 153, 161, 162-63, 198, explorations of, 80, 83, 97-98, 119-20, 15-16, 38-39, 54, 57, 79-90-91, 95-96, 118, 136, 161-63, 191-92, 222 n; Kara, 192, 205; RID's opinions of, Burt, 164, and Custer, 95; climbs Inyan soldiers' assistance to, 120; and A. S. 195, 218, 235, 236-37, 240, 245, 247; 102, 121, 144, 152, 172, 182, 191, 194, Jenney, Horace P., 45, 58, 61, 68, 71, 89, and Lt. Trout, 184
RID's mess, 154; thermometer of, 150; 238; campfire of, 151; removed from 116, 125, 158, 190, 192, 194, 228, 235, Jaquette, George P., 58 n, 69n, 73, 100, little value of, 116
discharged, 147; and RID's rifle, 73; James (RID's servant), 37, 39, 70 n, 128; Jacksnipe. *See English snipe*

Irwin, Corporal: and lost-mail incident, 111-14, 115, 116, 117
Iron, 102
Ireland, rifle team of, 129
Inyan Kara Creek, 190, 193, 205, 207
183; vicinity of, 189, 192
near, 204, Custer and, 76, 192; road to, Inyan Kara, 202, 206, 207, 251; BHE camp Indian Springs, 75, 160 n, 187, 189, 196, 205 n
Indians; Pawnee Indians; Sioux Indians parties of, 51, 52. *See also* Cheyenne 62, 63, 191, 214, 222, 224, 234; war named Mr. Lo, 79, 95; trails of, 49, 50, 108, 109; lodgepoles of, 79, 105; nick- of, 58, hostilities with, 95; insults to, opinion of, 105, 106, 237, 239; grave Washington, D.C., of, 8, 95, 107; RID's 132; and Custer, 5, 78; delegation to

Jenney-Dodge Expedition. *See* Black Hills
  Expedition (BHE)
Joe (RID's servant), 158
Joe's Spring, 199
Jones' (hotel), 246
Jordan, William H., 115, 239
Juniper, 75

Kamelque Creek. *See* Cameleo Creek
Kansas, 7 n
King, Albert, 94, 170, 197, 202, 213; RID
  gives advice to, 246; hunting experiences
  of, 162, 198; joke on, 71; mother-in-law
  of, 244
Kingbird, 176
Kingfisher, 208
Kingsbury, Frederick W., 195, 198

Lane, J. R., 58 n, 69 n, 93, 99 n, 127, 128,
  158, 169, 198, 218, 222, 226; explora-
  tions of, 71, 114; member of RID's mess,
  101; as newspaper correspondent, 8 n,
  113, 199 n; quoted, 155–56 n
Laramie (Wyoming Territory), 37
Laramie River, 241, 245
Larks, 176
Laura (RID's domestic servant), 158
Lawson, Joseph, 131, 197, 235
Lehane, James, 184
Lemly, Henry R., 236, 237
Lewis and Clark Expedition, 175
Lewis and Clark's woodpecker, 173, 175,
  176, 205. *See also* Woodpeckers
Lightning, 126
Limerick, 248
Little Big Man, 65
Little Eagle, 145 n
Little Hawk, 65
Little Missouri River, 80
Lo, Mr. *See* Indians, American
Long, Andrew Kennedy, 39
Long Branch, N.J., 188
Longitude, 104° West, 16–17, 59, 69, 97 n
Loup River, 122
Ludlow, William, Black Hills map of, 12,
  13, 74, 91
Lynx, 203, 209

Mac (RID's servant), 245
McClellan, George B., 154 n

McClellan, James S., 217–18 n, 231–32
McGillycuddy, Valentine T., 59, 115, 117 n,
  152, 159, 160, 182, 184, 198, 219, 228,
  240; anecdote of Joe Merivale, 12–13 n;
  anger at Jenney, 170; RID's opinion of,
  56, 116, 219, 231; effort to make him
  drunk, 71; explorations of, 97, 98, 128,
  129, 138, 153, 162, 163, 183, 220; and
  Indian grave, 58; map of Black Hills by,
  56 n; newspaper letters of, 199 n
MacKenzie, Ranald S., 193 n
MacMillan, Thomas C., 8 n, 93 n, 130, 199;
  and RID's book, 116, 117; RID's opinion
  of, 57; and lost-mail incident, 113–14;
  115; quoted, 98 n
Mallard, 72, 172, 176, 190, 192, 213. *See
  also* Ducks
Mallory, T. H., 169
Mama. *See* Dodge, Julia Rhinelander
  Paulding (RID's wife)
Man-Who-Kills-The-Hawk, The, 145 n
Maps, 48–49, 156, 204
Marcy, R. B., 147 n; *Thirty Years of Army
  Life*, 120–21
Marryat, Frederick, *Mister Midshipman
  Easy*, 92
Marsh, Othniel C., 107
Martins, 141, 175. *See also* House martin
Mary (aunt), 197
Mason, John S., 241, 244
Maulux, John, 167 n
Medicine Bow Mountains, 80
Medicine Bow Station, 50 n
Merivale, Joe, 12–13, 23, 64, 75, 84, 113,
  145; as courier, 91, 112; errand to Red
  Cloud Agency, 115, 116; guide to BHE,
  46, 48, 53, 82; guide to Indian commis-
  sioners, 147
Mice, 141, 208
Middle Park (Colo.), 80
Mills, Anson, 238
Mills, J. L., 166 n
Milner, Moses E. *See* "California Joe"
Miners, 86–87, 116, 164; arrival of, 100,
  114, 122, 124 n, 127, 129, and BHE, 8,
  52–53, 64, 89, 127, 129, 131, 132, 138;
  camps of, 125, 175; departure of, 119,
  122, 158, 169; expelled from Black Hills,
  150, 152–53, 167, 168; gratitude to Gen.
  Crook, 10, 208; meetings of, 9–10, 87,

INDEX 271

153, 164, 167–69, 207; operations of, 119, 127; optimism of, 104–5, 130; presence in Black Hills of, 3–4, 5, 134; on Rapid Creek, 174; work habits of, 134–35, 144
Minnesota Academy of Science, 5
Missouri River, 49n, 160, 165
Mister Midshipman Easy. See Marryat, Frederick
Mix, John, 4, 39n, 87, 152, 246; affidavits by, 107; anger between RID and, 156, 158; company of, 150; letters to, 62, 96; trail to Black Hills of, 4, 48, 156, 157n; wife of, 40, 41, 43, 244, 246
Molloy (headquarters sergeant), 147n, 188, 223, 249
Montana Territory, 53
Morton, Charles, 148, 152, 157, 159, 160, 172, 181, 183–84, 198; assists in finding road, 181, 182–83; caught in a canyon, 159–60; as engineer officer, 97; explorations of, 71, 153; mapmaking of, 128, 149, 206, 208; wife of, 188, 197
Morton's Canyon, 186
Morton's Creek, 216, 248
Moore, James M., 38
Mosquitoes, 142
Mountain buffalo, 148. *See also* Buffalo
Mountain ivy
Mountain lion, 60, 178, 209
Mountain sheep, 105, 156, 174, 175
Munson, Samuel, 62, 116, 150, 151, 152, 153, 198, 199, 244; company of, 99, 147; RID's opinion of, 135; and Jenney, 120, and lost-mail incident, 113, 115
Newberry, J. S., 6n
Newspaper correspondents, 3 n, 24, 169, 199, identified, 8n; on "Calamity Jane," 22; on Jenney, 15; at miners' meeting, 167n
Newton, Henry, 24, 128, 160, 161; contributes to RID's *The Black Hills*, 240; RID's opinion of, 231, 240; opinion of Jenney, 161; quoted, 49 n
New York Herald, 8n, 54, 70, 91, 129, 196; flag of, 56; interview with Spotted Tail in, 166n; missing letters to, 117; quoted, 95n
New York partridge. *See* Ruff grouse
New York Tribune, 8n, 112n

Night hawk, 176
Nick (uncle), 197
Nickerson, Azor H., 42, 95n
Niobrara River, 48, 49, 50, 112, 240, 250, 251; fishing and hunting along, 241
No Flesh, 145n
North Carolina, 38, 174, 176, 214; flora of, 188, "old field" in, 204
North Cheyenne River, 220. *See also* Cheyenne River
Northern Boundary Survey (1873–74), 56n
North Platte River, 41, 45, 128, 241, 245
Noyes, Henry E., 64
Oak, 214, 220, 247, 249
O'Connor, Mr. (of Washington, D.C.), 154n
Office of Indian Affairs, 16, 24, 95n, 107n; RID's opinion of, 21, 107–8; motives of, 5, 6
Old Joe. *See* "California Joe"
Old Woman Creek, 50, 51, 52, 53
Omaha, Nebr., 67, 95n, 208, 227
Omaha Barracks, 7, 37n, 43, 192n
Omaha National Bank, 158
Ord, E. O. C., 6n
Owls, 56, 176

Palmer, William J., 157
Paulding, Grace (Gracie), 188
Paulding, Maria (RID's mother-in-law), 38, 188
Pawnee Indians, 37, 122n
Petrified wood, 61–62
Phillips, "Portugee," 39, 40, 246
Pine, 57, 68, 76, 79, 92, 102, bark of, 118; dense forest of, 72, 75, 83, struck by lightning, 196
Pine Ridge Agency, 56n
Plains of North America and Their Inhabitants, The (PNA) (book by RID): Black Hills journals used in, 20, chapters on birds, fish, and other animals, 191, 218; chapters on game animals, 19, 20, 99, 114, 115, 117, 120, 122, 126, 127, 148, 150, 258, 182, 184, 190–91, 192; fishing and hunting accounts in, 20; officers' remarks about, 245; on plains streams, 63n; title of, 20n. *See also* Dodge, Richard Irving (RID)
Platte River. *See* North Platte River
Plover, 172, 204

272 INDEX

Plum trees, 68
Poirrier (Pourier), Baptiste, 49
Pollock, Edwin, 151 n, 152, 162, 190, 195; appearance of, 196-97; camp of, 195; character of, 10, 153; RID's assistance to, 189, 199, 207; RID's directions to, 153, 168
Pope, Alexander: *The Dunciad*, 245; *Essay on Man*, 79 n
Potatoes, 44, 45, 46, 48, 197
Potter, Joseph Haydn, 120
Porcupine Creek, 207
Powder River country, 59
Powder River Expedition (1876), 193 n, 217 n
Powell, J. W., 56 n
Prospect Peak, 81-82, 88

Quaking aspen, 68, 75, 76, 155, 185, 188, 223
Quartz, 85, 88, 110, 115, 137

Rail (bird), 247
"Rain Crow," 176
Rapid Creek, 84, 98, 103, 106, 121, 136, 143, 144, 153, 160, 172, 173, 186, 201, 221, 226 n, 249, 250; announcement of gold deposits in, 130-31; in canyon of, 118; clarity of water in, 148; downstream waters of, 207, 227, 231; grass along, 165; headwaters of, 204; hunting in vicinity of, 198, 199-202; suckers in, vicinity of, 144
Rattlesnakes, 54, 144, 173, 210, 215
Ravens, 176
Rawhide Butte, 48
Rawhide Creek, 46, 48, 241, 250-51
Raynolds, William F., 49, 50
Red Cloud, 39, 43 n
Red Cloud Agency, 4, 5 n, 8, 89, 107, 115, 145 n, 230; Indian Commission meeting near, 195, 186; on ration day, 239
Red deer. *See* White-tailed deer
Red Dog, 10-11, 25, 145-46
Red-headed woodpecker, 144, 173, 176. *See also* Woodpeckers
Red Water Creek, 74, 103, 180, 187, 188-89, 205, 213, 214, 217, 248, "eastern" flora on, 247; headwaters of, 160; Indian signs on, 191; possible military post on, 214
Reynolds, Joseph J., 37
Rice, William F., 157, 247

Richfield Springs, N.Y., 188
Robe-Raiser, 139
Robins, 138, 141, 144, 152, 169, 173, 176
Rockbird, 176
Rocky Mountain suckers, 61. *See also* Suckers
Root, William H., 144, 152, 169
Ruff grouse, 106, 162, 174, 176, 178, 180, 202. *See also* Grouse
Ruggles, George D., 40
Russell, Gerald, 124, 130, 162, 164, 183, 197, 198; company of, 122, 158, 230 n, 240; RID's opinion of, 239

Sage grouse, 190, 204, 210, 216, 218, 219. *See also* Grouse
Sage hen. *See* Sage grouse
St. Louis, Mo., 96 n, 124 n, 154 n, 246
St. Patrick, 144
St. Paul, Minn., 128
Sanders, James, 53 n, 128, 167 n
Sandhill cranes, 172, 174, 176, 186, 203, 204, 227
Sandpipers, 173, 176, 205
San Francisco Alta California, 8 n
Sapsuckers, 141, 176
Saratoga, N.Y., 154, 157
Saurians, 210
Saville, J. J., 39 n, 107 n
Sawyer, James A., 53
Schwartz's (ranch), 246 n
Secretary of War, U.S., 4, 41
Shakespeare, William: *Hamlet*, 58; *Julius Caesar*, 108; *Othello*, 59
Shankland, Samuel, 167 n
Sheep, 110. *See also* Mountain sheep
Sheldrake, 150, 174, 176. *See also* Ducks
Sheridan, Philip H., 15 n, 42 n, 77
Sherman, William T., 4, 124 n
Shiner (fish), 57
Shooting matches, 155-56 n, 158
Shovelbills, 204, 210
Side Hill Spring, 201
Sidney, Nebr., 38
Sidney Barracks, 198 n
Sioux City, Iowa, 3, 53, 137
Sioux Indians, 95 n, 122 n; and Black Hills, 3-4, 11, 24, 39, 50, 246; delegation to Washington, D.C., 8, 39; depredations by, 9 n; regard for John S. Collins, 43 n; war anticipated with, 25
Sis Molly. *See* Dodge, Mary Helen (Sis Molly)

INDEX 273

Skunks, 142
Smith, Edward P., 11 n, 95n, 107–8
Smith, William Sooy, 154n, 155, 156
Snakes, 142, 170, 173. *See also* Rattlesnakes; Water snakes; Garter snakes
Snipe, 176. *See also* English snipe
Snowbird, 125, 141, 176, 193
South Cheyenne River, 52, 103, 220, 231. *See also* Cheyenne River
Sparrows, 138, 141, 174, 176
Spaulding, Edward J., 40, 42, 43, 45, 54, 64, 71, 75, 94, 114–15, 118, 119, 123, 127, 131, 132, 133, 144, 149, 155, 156, 174, 246; company of, 71, 103, 158; designation for "honest miner" of, 144; gun of, 85; hunting experiences of, 60, 68, 83, 148, 151; journey to Beaver Creek of, 90–91, 93–94, 112; and lost-mail incident, 112, 114–15, 117; seeker of shortcuts, 67, 81; shooting match with RID, 155–56n; and wagon train, 160–61
Spaulding's Creek, 74, 101, 102, 103, 105, 160n, 205n, 206; canyon of, 75, 78
Spearfish Creek, 213, 214, 247
Spearfish Valley, 247
Spike grouse, 78, 106, 128, 141, 211, 213. *See also* Grouse
Spotted Tail, 39, 43 n, 165, 166n
Spotted Tail Agency, 8, 10–11, 107 n, 145 n
Spring Creek, 83, 84, 103, 121, 123, 133, 142, 149, 160, 170, 231; camp on, 129; climate of, 135; compared to Rapid and French Creeks, 135, 173–74; crossings of, 169; grass along, 165; mining, 123 n
130n, 150
Spruce, 79
"Squaw men," 139
Squirrels, 100, 141, 209, 222
Stanton, Thaddeus H., 44, 45, 150, 152, 154, 155, 156, 157, 244, 247
Stanton, W. S., 39
Stockade. *See* Gordon party
Stonewall (proposed city name), 166
Strawberries, 68, 78, 116
Suckers, 142, 145, 149, 170, 173, 213, 215, 222, 240, 248, 250; eastern variety of, 148; red variety of, 215
Sundance Hills, 211
Surrey County, N.C., 121 n
Sutorius, Alexander, 44

Teal, 192, 204, 210, 213. *See also* Ducks
Telegraph, 111, 120 n
Terry, Alfred H., 165
Terry's Peak, 177, 180, 182, 183, 204, 206
Texas and Southwest Railroad, 6 n
Thompson, A., 167 n
Thompson, John Charles, 157
Thorn apple, 118
Tiger lilies, 142
Tilton, Theodore, 129
Timber wolf, 172, 176. *See also* Wolf
Toads, 142
Tooty. *See* Dodge, Julia Rhinelander Paulding (RID's wife)
Trainor (miner), 127
Transfer Valley, 205 n
Trask, A. D., 167
Trout, John F., 41, 42, 52, 53, 62, 69 n, 80, 89, 90–91, 93–94, 97, 103, 116, 119, 122, 127, 131, 145, 147, 148, 154, 170, 171, 181, 183, 191, 226, 247; compass of, 128; RID's high estimate of, 72, 107, 134, 185, 197; exaggerates own accomplishments, 73; fishing experiences of, 147; good spirits of, 186, 187, 188, 202, 204, 207; hard work of, 44, 45 n, 198, 245; hunting experiences of, 128, and lost-mail incident, 112; injury of, 21, 184–85, 204, 207–8; quartermaster of BHE, 44; stays with BHE, 191, 207–8; retirement from army, 185 n; as roadmaker, 177, 179, 180; skill crossing bogs, 81; unreasonableness of, 98
Tula grass, 213
Turkey, RID's chapter for *PNA* on, 219
Turtle, 170, 210
Tuttle, Horace P., 55–56, 59; attack of jimjams, 97; effort to establish longitude, 57; refuses to accompany Jenney party, 160, 161

Union Pacific Railroad, 9 n, 37, 50, 141
United States, rifle team of, 129
United States Army; and miners, 4, 8; Topographical Engineers, 49, 208
United States Congress, 168
United States Geological Survey, 6 n

United States government: BHE authorized by, 6–7; efforts to renegotiate Black Hills treaty, 8, 10, 24, 25, 95, 145–46; and future of Black Hills, 83, 105; and Indian agents' salaries, 141; short of cash, 114; and U.S. citizens in Black Hills, 3–4. *See also* Department of Dakota; Department of the Interior; Department of the Missouri; Department of the Platte; Department of the West; District of the Black Hills; Division of the Missouri; Indian Commission; Office of Indian Affairs; Secretary of War; United States Army; United States Congress; United States Geological Survey; War Department
Van Mall, J. H., 71n
Venus (planet), 97
Virginia (state), 40
Ward, Seth E., 40n
War Department, 6, 165, 170, 222n
Warren, Gouverneur K., 49n, 82n, 221; in Black Hills, 72, 74
Warren's Spring, 234
Washington, D.C., 39, 43, 95, 108, 109
Water snakes, 173, 210
Welch (soldier), 126
Wells, Elijah R., 152
Wessells, Henry W., 83, 89, 90, 100, 132, 183, 197; company of, 71, 103; RID's opinion of, 72; slow progress of, 121, 128
Wheaton, Charles, 37, 38
Whisky, 38, 76, 247; used to "cut" bad water, 67
Whist, 69

White birch, 68
Whitefish, 215, 216, 217, 236, 248
White River, 207, 226n, 228, 234, 235, 236, 237, 238, 250; change in character of, 239, 240. *See also* False White River
White River country 59
White-tailed deer, 18, 85, 118, 136, 141, 145, 179, 182, 206, 208; abundant in valleys, 106; RID's chapter for PNA on, 182; not running yet, 249. *See also* Deer
Whitman, Royal E., 196, 197, 198
Willard, H. ("Deacon"), 99, 199n
Wild cattle, RID's chapter for PNA on, 19, 117
Wild cherry, 118
Wild plum, 247
Wild roses, 142
Willow, 247
Willow grouse, 216, 217, 218, 219–20. *See also* Grouse
Wilson, George, 154n
Winchell, Newton H., 5, 96
Wolf, 142, 171–72, 196, 209; serenade from, 202. *See also* Buffalo wolf; Timber wolf
Woodchuck Creek, 81
Woodchucks, 141
Woodpeckers, 141, 151, 173. *See also* Lewis and Clark's woodpecker
Wooley, J. D., 38
Wyoming Territory border with Dakota Territory 7n, 16–17, 55 n, 59

Yellowbird, 208
Yellowhammer, 176
Yellowstone Expedition (1873), 148
Yellowstone region, 49n, 192n
Young, Harry, 23